ALBIE SACHS

The Jail Diary of Albie Sachs

PALADIN
GRAFTON BOOKS

A Division of the Collins Publishing Group

LONDON GLASGOW
TORONTO SYDNEY AUCKLAND

Paladin
Grafton Books
A Division of the Collins Publishing Group
8 Grafton Street, London W1X 3LA

Published in Paladin Books 1990

First published in Great Britain by
The Harvill Press Ltd 1966

Copyright © The Harvill Press Ltd 1966
Foreword © Albie Sachs 1990

A CIP catalogue record for this book is
available from the British Library

ISBN 0-586-09057-6

Printed and bound in Great Britain by
Collins, Glasgow

Set in Caledonia

ACKNOWLEDGEMENT
*Mr E. S. Sachs wishes to express his sincere
gratitude to Mrs Barbara Cheeseman
and Mrs Barbara Fox for the speed and
accuracy with which they typed the manuscript.*

Albie Sachs was born in 1935 and brought up and educated in Cape Town. He joined the Anti-Apartheid Student Movement at Cape Town University and was arrested for the first time while taking part in the Passive Resistance Campaign. After graduating he spent several months in England. He was called to the Cape Town Bar in 1957. After leaving South Africa he taught law at the University of Southampton before going to work as a professor of law in Mozambique.

By the same author

The Soft Vengeance of a Freedom Fighter

For Dot, who helped me in more
ways than I can tell

Preface to the Paladin edition

I can barely remember the actual writing of my *Jail Diary*. It was just after my release from 168 days of solitary confinement, and I was so elated to be out amongst people again that I recall I wrote it all by hand, rapidly, in secret, and relied on friends to have it typed. The police were everywhere; we had to be careful, the typists as well as myself. This was the time when Nelson Mandela and others, including two very close friends of mine, were on trial for their lives. Our movement was being crushed. It was a bitter period, and writing was more than a release for me. It was the only joyous activity I could manage, an intimate form of clandestine resistance.

I arranged for the manuscript to be smuggled out of the country and sent to Ruth First in London. I called the book *168 Days*. Ruth got a message to me saying that she liked the book very much, but suggested that my father rather than she be responsible for finding a publisher. Only later did I discover that Ruth had herself written a fine book on her own detention in solitary confinement, and given it the title *117 Days*.

Some months later, and this is a part that I remember well, I received a visit from William Collins, the London publisher. Being called upon by the person responsible for publishing Collins dictionaries was a great honour, like being visited by Mr E. Britannica. Yet, as soon as he began to give me the good news that his firm would be publishing the book, I jumped up, grabbed him by the arm and yanked him out of my office. He was startled. 'I'm sorry, Mr Collins,' I said, deeply embarrassed, 'but I am sure my office is bugged. . . .'

Standing in the corridor, I explained that not only were all my writings banned in South Africa, but that I was prohibited from preparing anything for publication. I was eager for him to go ahead with bringing the book out as soon as possible, I explained, and willing to take the consequences, but did not wish to give advance warning to the police.

In fact, I was detained a second time by the security police; publication was delayed; I went into exile in England, and the only punishment I received was a lashing from a conservative reviewer in the *Sacramento Bee* who wrote that the book made him feel sorry for my jailers.

I forgot about the book. Years in exile passed. I had a busy life, wrote other things, participated in campaigns up and down Britain and in Europe for the release of all political prisoners in South Africa. Then, just as I was about to leave London to work in the newly independent state of Mozambique, I received a phone call from David Edgar asking if I would mind if he transformed the book into a play for the Royal Shakespeare Company. We met, chatted for a while, and I went off to Maputo and forgot about the book again.

Ten years later, the day after the bomb which nearly took my life went off, four Albie Sachses got in touch with David Edgar to find out how I was getting on. The play had been put on at various theatres and broadcast on radio and television by the BBC, and when I eventually emerged from hospital, the four were waiting to put on a special benefit performance on my behalf. It turned out to be a memorable evening, one I hoped never to forget, and, also, one I wished never to repeat.

Over the years I had been amused to hear that not only had the book been prescribed as a set-work in British schools and as recommended reading in university literature courses, but that at a certain stage it had been required reading for members of the South African security forces. Now, at last, after twenty-five years, it can be read openly by anyone in South Africa. The ANC has been unbanned, Nelson Mandela has been released, and we have new opportunities to struggle for the non-racial, democratic South Africa that has always been at the centre of our longings.

I am proud of our generation. We believed, we fought, and we took many blows. We have thousands and thousands of stories to tell, and each will do it in his or her own way. The freedom struggle needs intimacy and softness as much as it requires firmness – of that I am convinced. This was my little contribution towards recording what it was like in those days of suffering and hope.

Albie Sachs, London, February 1990

Contents

PART ONE

Maitland

Diary of Love

1 Introduction

SO THIS IS WHAT PRISON IS LIKE. THE QUIET IS COMPLETE and I am alone in my cell, the shock of the slammed door still echoing in my head. So this is what it's like. The floor is hard, fresh creamy paint shines on the walls and the windows are high—higher than my eyes can reach even if, as now, I stand on tiptoe. In the corner, partly partitioned off, is a toilet moulded in concrete with two wooden strips for the seat. The water in the pan is clean. A metal loop juts through a hole in the wall. That must be the chain. I put my finger through the loop and pull. It is the chain, which like a snake's tongue sticks out from the wall before sliding back into the hole. Water is disgorged and the room echoes with the surf of the refilling toilet. I pull the loop again. It flushes instantly: an excellent lavatory: my only source of music. I flush it once more. A wonderful mechanical contrivance. I reach yet again for the loop . . . no, don't be silly, I tell my arm, and I turn round to survey the rest of my domain. The walls are quite clean and antiseptic. On the floor is a mat woven of dried grass, yellow and long, with a pile of dirty grey blankets at one end. I lie full length on the mat. It is not too hard and a little longer than I. I sit up and decide to count the blankets. Should I stand while I count or should I sit on the mat? Standing and bending is tiring and I'm very tired. If the cat sat on the mat why shouldn't I? It's awkward sitting on the floor. There are six blankets. That's quite a lot really.

The cell is completely bare; no bed, no mattress, no bunk, no chair, no table. Hell, that's terrible. Not even a bunk. I gaze round and round. The world, even this tiny alien world, looks

18

peculiar from the floor. There is something else wrong with this room. It is not just the angle from which I see it that makes it look so strange. I have it now; it's not a room at all, it's an empty concrete cube with me, a human being, inside. Gravity keeps me to the floor, otherwise I would float around like a spaceman. That's what is wrong. There is no world outside. There is no outside that I am aware of. *I cannot see out of my cell.* The windows are too high. The walls are the outer limit of my environment. I jump up rapidly and then tell myself wryly, there's no hurry, no hurry. Ninety days is a long time. And then another ninety days, and another, and another . . . no hurry. I slowly work out the dimensions of my new abode. Heel, toe—my shoe is exactly a foot long—heel, toe, heel, toe. First this way, twelve feet, then that way, ten and a half feet. I'm walking around quickly now, feeling the walls, sliding my palms across the shiny surface, pressing and prodding for weak spots. I stretch up to the metal grid over the window and tug. Then, bending down, I scratch with my finger at the floor, first in one corner, then another. I walk to the toilet, and fancy my body gliding down its bowl and out. I must get out. I'll dig a tunnel. I'll hit the guards over the head and grab the keys. My friends will come and blast a hole in the wall. They'll catch the police by surprise, and I'll duck in the opposite corner so the blast won't hit me, and then I'll leap through the hole. . . .

Don't be silly you know you can't escape, I tell myself. Better unpack your stuff and start making yourself at home. I become conscious of a rational brain operating, speaking silently inside my skull. I unzip the small canvas bag containing my belongings, which I unpack and spread out on the floor: sand-shoes, a towel, pyjamas, a bag of toiletry, a change of clothing, and a jersey: my belongings, almost my companions. I take off my suit and hang the jacket and trousers on large metal nuts protruding from the frame of the window grid. The trouser legs dangle like two men suspended from the same noose, but the cell looks less arid now. I hang the towel from another nut. It is a beach towel, its bright checks as colourful and stimulating as a scene through a window, something on which my eyes can rest during their frantic journey round the walls. I take off my white shirt and place it over the trousers. My coming-in shirt, it will be my going-out shirt, whenever that might be, and to wherever that might be. Now, let's see, if I pile up the blankets like this then I don't have to sit right on the floor. That's better. The room looks a little more cheerful now. I wish they hadn't taken away my watch—I wonder what the time is? There's no sunlight in the place at all, though it's not too dark.

Why did it seem so quiet at first? A train rattles past and I hear the faint din of heavy motor traffic some distance away. It is a voiceless world though. The police have disappeared through a series of gates which, like so many valves, open and close and lead to the charge office in the front portion of the building. Above the noise of the traffic I hear a different sound coming from a long way off—the chimes of a church clock striking. It is the three-quarter hour. Oh wonderful, if I listen carefully I can keep track of the time. They can stick my bloody watch. Stripped of access to timepieces, shut off from the sun and deprived of the work periods of a normal life, I will listen for the chimes ringing out over the rooftops, just as the medieval citizenry kept an ear open for their giant communal town clocks.

I walk round the cell again, thrilled by the great new sound; stopping at the toilet, I pull the snake's tongue out of the wall and feel excitement as the water bubbles into the bowl before surging out down its depths.

I clap my hands to see if there is any echo. There can't be anything wrong with clapping my hands, they can't punish me for that. After a short wait I purse my lips and blow air through them in a faint tentative whistle. Nothing happens. No one comes to tell me to be quiet. I whistle louder and louder still, and I stride up to the massive, handleless steel door, and whistle at it furiously, sharp, stentorian notes from Beethoven's Fifth. This is music, the 'V for Victory' theme from the war. You policemen out there, I'm not scared if you hear me, you don't even know what I'm whistling. Now I'm sitting down again, staring once more at the walls, trying to integrate the parts of the cell, to see it as a whole. What a dismal place, how cruel of

15

men to shut other men up in such a tomb, not even a bed, or a bunk. If they treat me, a White man and an advocate, like this, how terrible it must be for the Africans. The walls are so smooth and monotonous, there is nothing on which to focus. God, how lousy it is. I feel so peculiar. I thought I would be able to take it better than I am doing. I never realised it would be this bad. I must stick it out. I wonder who else is locked up in these cells. Hell, surely I'm not going to break down.

I have an idea. I am going to break the smoothness of the walls. I will imprint something of myself and at the same time secure my memory on that sterile surface. The toilet bag contains the necessary instrument. They've kept my razor but left me a tube of shaving cream. The tube's back edge is sharp and firm, and it scratches well into the paintwork. I choose a spot on the wall near the door, so that when they come in they won't be able to see it. Slowly I mark out a map: a sketch of the police station in which I am lodged, based on intensive visual observation on my part as I was moved from one section to another. Most important is to mark the entrance, the main road, the position of the centre of the town, and the mountain. Now working inwards I scratch the charge office, the passage, the gates, the yard, and finally my cell. This should help me locate myself; I will be somewhere not just in a concrete cube; and who knows, it may turn out to be useful for me to have a sketch of the building in which I am shut. It is Tuesday, 1st October. I scratch the figures 1, stroke 10, stroke 1963. The marks are faint but clear enough for me to find again, although a visitor would not notice them. Then a special stroke for the first day. I will keep track of the days. Oh why didn't the previous inhabitants scratch something on the walls and impart something of themselves to this desert spot. In another corner I scratch my initials. They won't be able to prove that it was I who drew the map, for my initials are far away. Any successors of mine in the cell will know I've been there, for whoever lives in a cell soon trains his eyes to pick up any traces of previous occupancy. I'm not the first to have been in the cell and many will follow me. The chain of political prisoners extends far back in time and will go on well into the future.

16

I am back on the mat. I feel very sleepy, but decide not to close my eyes for fear that to sleep now in the afternoon will make it more difficult for me to sleep tonight. I long for tonight, for darkness and for sleep. Just as one gets instant coffee and instant vegetables, so sleep is instant time: a whole night compressed into a closing of eyes and an opening of eyes. Night will also be a marker, denoting the passage of time. After tonight I will have been in solitary confinement for a whole day. I wonder, though, how well I will sleep. I never sleep well the first night in a strange place, even in the best of circumstances. It will be dreadful if I can't sleep. Anyhow, no use worrying about that now. The thing to do is to stay awake so that I'll be utterly exhausted when night comes. Let's see, what can I do next?

I stand up and clear my throat. I cough a few times a little more boldly. Then I hear my voice, humming at first and slowly sounding out snatches of song. This is my voice; I am singing. It's true that things are harder than I thought they would be. I didn't imagine that isolation could be so complete and so punishing. Yet if there is anyone out there also a prisoner, listen this is me singing, I've come to join you, and I'm going to be here a long, long time, because I'm not going to break down, whatever happens. I'm not going to give in. I must see it through.

2 Diary of Love

IT IS THE FIRST DAY. MY CELL IS ON ITS OWN IN THE CORNER
of the yard next to the gates. Who are in the cells across the
yard? There must be other Ninety-Day prisoners here. So
many people have been detained in the past few months that the
police stations in Cape Town must each have a few detainees. I
cannot remember hearing of anyone having been lodged here in
Maitland police station, though. If there are any other detainees
here, I must let them know there is a new arrival. I whistle the
Beethoven again, then sing out the opening phrase, and wait;
I do the same with the Marseillaise. There is no response. I
sing an African song, 'We will follow Lutuli[1]', still no response.
Very carefully, I sing the melody of 'The Red Flag', no answer.
I sing 'Let's Twist Again', silence. Perhaps the others are too
far away to hear me. Perhaps it is 'not done' to sing. Perhaps
they will find their own way to get through to me. Perhaps I
am the only prisoner here.

It is the second day. I have learnt a little. The guards carry
three plates of food. They speak about the 'others', meaning
other prisoners. Where the others are and who they are, I do
not know. It is exercise time. I am escorted to a tiny yard, and
great care is taken to prevent me from looking into the adjoin-
ing main yard which is larger. On the way back to my cell I see
a woman who must be the station commander's wife. She must
be the matron, which means that there is at least one woman
prisoner here. After my door is locked, I hear one of the guards

[1] Albert Lutuli, a leader of the Africans in South Africa and winner of the
Nobel Peace Prize.

yelling out a name. Something in the tone of voice makes me feel that he is addressing a prisoner. The name sounds like 'Zollie'. It must be the Zollie Malindi I know. For years he was a leading African National Congress man; I have defended him on a number of occasions. Now we are both in prison, he an African garageman, I a White lawyer, separated by a concrete yard.

It is the third day. They are less strict at exercise time to-day. While I am in the big yard, they open a cell door and a young woman walks out: a girl of medium height with a dark head and neat clothes. She is about my age and has a good figure. As she is led to one of the small yards I see her face, grave and expressionless. She does not speak as she walks, and as she disappears I retain a memory of heavy eyebrows, large deep brown lips, and long, pinned up tresses of black hair. She looks very brave. I wonder how she can stand it. As I run around the yard I wonder about her. There can be no doubt that she also is a Ninety-Day detainee. From her appearance and clothing, I would say she is not a working-class girl. She does not belong to the Coloured People's Congress, and she is not a Trade Unionist, otherwise I would certainly have come across her before. That means that she must belong to the Alexander Group[1]. I hope I have a chance to see her again at the end of exercise time. When they lock me up, however, she is still in the small yard. Perhaps tomorrow I will see her for longer.

It is the fourth day. She sees me as she comes out of her cell, but makes no acknowledgement of my presence. I say loudly to the guards, 'Let the lady have the main yard this time.' She must hear me. Why does she not speak to them, so that I can hear her voice? I run to the small yard. The connecting door is closed, and I do not see her again. Later, after I have been locked up, I hear Zollie's name being called out once more. When my fruit comes at lunchtime I will ask that some of it be given to the other prisoners.

[1] A group of radical black intellectuals, the most prominent of whom was Neville Alexander, arrested for allegedly discussing the possibilities of armed struggle in South Africa.

19

It is the fifth day. I was right about the name I heard. Today as my cell door is opened I see Zollie, and it is the Zollie I know. He has grown a beard and his body looks flabby. Otherwise he is as I remember him, still carrying his tall bulk on a large relaxed frame. The guards shout at him with a certain amount of affection, much as they would shout at a dog of which they are fond. As he emerges from his cell, which is alongside the dark girl's cell across the yard, he sees me. He does not pause, yet we greet each other. The guards can see nothing—neither of us says anything, or makes any special gesture or facial movement. Yet between him and me there flows recognition. As he walks to his exercise place, I chat to my guard loudly enough for my voice to carry across the yard.

It is in the early afternoon and I am lying in a stupor on my mat when suddenly I become aware of familiar music. The notes are very, very distant, as though floating in from another planet. I can barely follow the melody. It is a faint whistling that I hear, as silvery and tenuous as a wind-blown spider thread. This is not the jolly music of a policeman. The melody, rich, sad and faraway, is repeated. I can make it out! It is the 'Going Home' theme from the 'New World' Symphony. I jump up and listen attentively. Someone is whistling out so that all the prisoners can hear. I cannot tell the direction from which the sound comes, but I must respond as loudly as I can. I wait for the long thin plaintive notes to stop, and then I start whistling at my door. The notes soar out high and loud.

Faintly, distantly, the response comes. Line by line we whistle: salute, answer, salute, answer. First it is my turn, then the whistler's. Once more we leapfrog through the melody, then each whistles the main verse and then the refrain. There are not many people today in South Africa who know the 'Red Flag'. Propaganda for socialism has been virtually outlawed for twelve years. In any event, the African liberation struggle has so dominated radical politics during this time that the freedom songs we learn are almost all African in origin. In South Africa the People's flag is green, gold and black, the flag of the African emancipation movement. Communists, socialists, Ghandhiists, nationalists and liberals—all rally to this one standard.

I am feeling quite emotional now; I start to sing, not using the words until I come to the refrain:

Though cowards flinch, and traitors sneer,
We'll keep the la la la la here.

There is no response.

I return to my mat, and wonder who the whistler is. Almost certainly it is the dark girl. Zollie probably would not know the 'New World' Symphony, and he definitely would know the 'Samlandela Lutuli' song. Also, having been politically active for many years, he probably would know the 'Red Flag', and finally I would expect him to sing rather than to whistle. The dark girl, on the other hand, if she does belong to the Alexander Group, could well know the 'New World' and the 'Red Flag', but not the 'Lutuli' song. What do I know about this crowd other than that they are left-orientated, intellectual, influenced by certain old-guard Trotskyites, very militant in policy and, in my opinion, rather theoretical, paperborne and cut off from the mainstream of African politics? According to newspaper reports, the police have caught their leaders and uncovered plans for revolutionary struggle. The police announced the smashing of what they termed a Chinese terrorist group. Of course none of those due to be tried are Chinese—apart from one Afrikaner, they are all young Coloured men and women, mostly teachers and artisans, all from the area in and around Cape Town. Their leading personality is Dr Neville Alexander, aged about twenty-six, a teacher with a brilliant academic record, whom I vaguely remember having seen at the University of Cape Town before he left to study in Europe.

If, oh dark girl, you belong to the Alexander Group, and if you are the whistler, well, so much the more valuable our present bonds. Outside prison our differences are sharp, but we stand for the same things; inside, let us meet and hold fast to each other. How marvellous it is to be able to speak to someone again, even if we are compelled to use this indistinct tenuous language of whistling. Tomorrow we will, I hope, see each other. Then we can greet each other face to face.

Oh, lovely, lovely dark girl, with your black eyebrows and

pinned up hair, with your sad, brave countenance and silent movements, may we meet tomorrow.

It is the sixth day. The guards are unaware of my excitement as they let me out for exercise. Soon I should know for sure who whistled to me yesterday. I shave with special care, and diligently comb my tumbled hair. I see my face in the mirror, it is quiet and inanimate, and the guards will notice nothing from the little yard in which I wash myself. I hear her cell door being opened and the matron talking to her. In the far distance a policeman is shouting at Zollie. The dark girl and Zollie are probably in the big yard now.

'I left my towel in my cell,' I tell the sergeant who is guarding me. 'Can I run across and get it?'

'Okay,' he answers. He opens the door to the large yard and follows me as I walk quickly to my cell. I notice that the dark girl is moving along a strip of sunlight. She is smoking and her movements are as quiet and solemn as ever. Zollie must be in the other small yard. I go straight into my cell without turning to look at the dark girl. When I come out of the cell we should see each other face to face. I take the towel, smooth my hair, and walk to the door. The sergeant is watching.

'Sometimes I'm very stupid,' I say to him, 'thanks for letting me fetch it.'

As I reach the doorway, I see her straight ahead of me. She is walking in my direction. The fingers holding the cigarette are pointed forward, and thin trails of smoke rise into the air. Her head is up, and her eyes look ahead of her. A neat yellow blouse enfolds her bust, and I notice her hips and legs, clad in un-creased green slacks, moving gently as she walks towards me. In a moment I shall raise my head, and our eyes will meet. I flap the towel a little so that it will engage the sergeant's atten-tion, and step into the yard. My head comes up in a natural movement, and for the first time I look straight at her face. I focus on her eyes. Now, now—my mind urges her—look at me now. She continues to move forward. Her face is quite impas-sive. Her eyes move to the wall and up my body, across my face and back to the wall. There is no recognition. Her body, her face, her eyes tell me nothing. She looks past me as though I am a

22

policeman, or a door, or part of the wall. Confused, baffled, I move away.

The moment of greeting has passed, and I dare not stare at her while the sergeant is watching. I am now back in the little yard, running round and round, puzzled at the dark girl's lack of recognition. The sergeant stands in the doorway between the yards. The door is ajar.

I purse my lips and puff air softly through them as I run: 'Ta ra tata, ta re te ta—here we go round the mulb'ry bush.' I begin to whistle, not strongly, but loudly enough for anyone in the next yard, who listens carefully, to hear.

'Here-we-go-round-the-mul-b'ry-bush.'

My whistling keeps time with the pushing and jogging of my elbows and knees. Then I stop whistling and listen for a response. From the far yard I hear raucous police sounds, somewhat muffled by the distance. The matron says something to the sergeant guarding me. A train clatters by. There is no whistling. I try again. This time I whistle the opening notes of the 'Going Home' theme. The tempo is fast and staccato, coinciding with my paces. I whistle very softly, as though to myself, but still she should be able to hear. Again I wait for some sort of answer. There is nothing as quiet as concrete. All I can hear is the padding of my own feet. Why does she not make some sign?

Exercise time is over and I am lying on my mat. The guards are gone and all is silent. Before I go to sleep I must try to communicate with the whistler. I stand facing the door and whistle out to the rest of the prison. Has the whistler been taken away, I wonder. The notes soar out louder and louder from my lips. I feel desperate now. I do not wish to be alone again. When the last bars are complete, I sit down and listen. It comes, there it comes, from somewhere not too close but not too distant, the faint answering tune. It is exactly as yesterday, thin, liquid and beautiful. Oh whistler, whoever you are, thank you for your support. If you have the chance please, please, declare yourself one day so that I may know who you are.

It is the seventh day. When the guards bring me lunch, I see they have a parcel of food. It is apparently intended for another prisoner. Printed in large letters on the brown paper wrapping are the words: FOR MISS DOROTHY ADAMS.

It is the eighth day. During the middle of the afternoon I hear song coming from across the yard. A deep bass voice sounds through the concrete. It is an African singing. The music is sad, patient and hymnal, and as the verses are repeated over and over again their monotony is broken by subtle shifts of rhythm and pitch. The music, echoed and muffled by the walls, swells and subsides. Rhythmically on and on it pounds; there is something strong and elemental about it, like waves or perhaps like death. I sing back but there is no reply.

It is the ninth day. In the morning as I return to my cell after exercise time I hear water splashing. The sound comes from the washroom across the yard. I look there and notice that the swing-door which is usually open has now been closed. The door covers only the middle half of the doorway—above and below it are large gaps. Beneath the door I see the lower half of two dark legs. They are bare and female and water runs down them. One heel lifts from the ground, the toes press hard on the floor, and I see a pair of hands moving along the naked calves.

Long after my door is slammed and locked, I continue to hear water splashing.

In the afternoon, I am busy doing physical jerks when I become aware of the whistler summoning me. We have agreed to call each other with the 'Going Home' theme. At this moment I am in the middle of my press-ups—fifteen, sixteen, seventeen. The whistler repeats the melody—twenty, twenty-one, twenty-two, twenty-three, twenty-four, twenty-five. I lie prostrate on the mat, panting heavily. This whistling is destroying my regime. The first law of prison is: thou shalt not forget thy fellow-prisoner: we never let each other down. Whatever I am doing, I will cease if the whistler reaches out to me. Similarly the whistler always responds when I whistle, whatever he or she might be doing at the time.

I find, however, that I am subjecting myself to the uncertainties of another's will. The routine which I am carefully trying to build up is being undermined. Sometimes, I am trying

24

to sleep when the whistler calls me. Sometimes I am in the middle of the activities with which I attempt to sustain myself. The worst is when I am in the middle of my physical jerks period. I hate these lonely gymnastics, and once I stop I find it extremely hard to start again. Yet I must keep doing them. I can think of only one solution to my problem—the whistling must be done at a fixed time each day so that each of us can regulate our respective regimes. Oh whistler, wherever you are, it is not simply because I am out of breath that I do not answer you. I am merely waiting till after supper, you must have faith in me, I will never let you down. Every evening we can whistle to each other. Look at the advantages of having a definite time: we can plan for the whistling, and look forward to it all day. We will never disturb each other, but will rendez-vous like lovers who separate each day but meet again the next. At night the traffic is quieter, so we will be able to hear each other more easily. I know it is cruel of me not to answer you now, but this is the only way I can let you know that we must have a set period for communication. Please wait for me, I'm still here, you must have confidence.

In the evening I wait impatiently for the 7.45 chimes to sound. At last they come; I jump up from the mat, stand before the door, and whistle. My whistling is particularly strong, particularly loving. I draw out the rich long notes and phrase the melody with special tenderness. The reply comes back. Never before have I so felt the nobility of this music. We are as lovers re-united. I cannot now remember all the tunes I thought of during the day, but there are still enough to enable me to contribute towards a long and full concert. The Miriam Makeba and the Ella and Louis long-playing records—why did it take me so long to remember them—should keep us going for two nights at least.

For an hour we whistle to each other. Sometimes a tune has to be repeated many times before the listener recognises it. Though my ear is quicker now I still find it very difficult to hear whoever is whistling to me. Perhaps this is why my joy is so great when I do manage to make out a melody.

The nine o'clock chimes ring out. It is time to prepare for

sleep. 'Goodnight Irene,' I whistle. Back comes the response. 'Goodnight Irene,' I whistle again, and a third time. There is more whistling from the depths of the prison. But I do not answer. Whistling period is over for today. Tomorrow at exactly a quarter to eight I will call you again.

Goodnight whistler till we meet again.

Somewhere in this prison I have a friend, someone who will speak with me each evening. It is a pity that I do not know who it is, yet, despite her failure to show even a flicker of recognition during exercise time, I still feel it must be the dark girl.

Whoever you are, oh whistler, thank you for reaching me. I love you for your loyalty, for your concern. You give me strength and remind me of beauty. Human beings are greater than walls. May we both have courage enough to see this through.

Our story deserves a happy ending.

3 Interrogation

SOUNDS OF A CLINKING KEY-RING, OF VOICES, AND FOOT-steps approach my door. There is a metallic rattling as the padlock is undone. I get up off my mat and stand facing the door which swings open. Two men in civilian suits walk up to me and I recognise them as the two lieutenants who had led the search of my office and flat. Lieutenant Potgieter is short with thin, sandy hair and a pleasant, boyish face. His speech is quiet and brisk, but never without a sneering quality; he moves around continually, darting sharp observations at me and watching my face closely for signs of reaction. Lieutenant Wagenaar is tall and burly. Though his body is springy, his long sallow face stands taut on a thick rigid neck. Bustling and aggressive he makes no attempt to hide his hostility. His manner is direct and accusatory, yet I feel somehow that he is the more human and less cruel of the two. I am both pleased and alarmed at seeing them now. When they arrested me they were harsh and brutal. Seven pairs of security branch hands pried into my drawers and fingered their way through my papers. It was particularly hurtful when they untied and examined my briefs, for I felt as though they were violating a privacy between me and my clients. 'These briefs are privileged,' I had protested. 'We'll decide what's privileged or not,' the tall sallow lieutenant had said. 'Oh, so you're the judge as well as police and prosecutor,' I had commented. Later the tall lieutenant had sat in my chair behind my desk. 'I see you're not only police, prosecutor and judge, you are the advocate too,' I had told him. 'The only thing you haven't been yet is the accused,' I added sarcastically. But he had been too absorbed in reading some love letters of mine to show either amusement or offence at my observation. Later he made remarks from time to time to let me know that he was very aware that he was an Afrikaner and I a Jew.

Today both lieutenants carry briefcases and look business-like as, positioned one on either side of me, they begin question-ing me in the yard. The uniformed policeman in charge of the keys stands patiently by. I feel untidy and unprepared for interrogation, for after being so long on the floor it takes a little while for me to adjust to the world of people standing up. Perhaps I shall learn why I have been arrested. Not knowing the reason for my deetntion and the uncertainty of my fate is most unsettling. At times I have felt an urge to call for the interrogators simply for the sake of relieving the tension. In the seven years of my practice as an advocate I never could understand why even hardened criminals made full and detailed confessions to the police, thus providing the information needed for their conviction. Now I realise that isolation produces an almost irresistible urge to communicate. Any fate is better than continued uncertainty. Fortunately the gap between the inter-rogators and myself is so great, and they are so ambitious in their demands, that as soon as I see them my will to resist is strength-ened.

'Well, how are you managing?' the short one asks.

'Not too badly in the circumstances,' I reply.

'Good, well we hope you don't have to stay here too long. It's entirely up to you, you know that. As soon as you answer our questions satisfactorily then things will be easier for you. You know the law. We can keep you for ninety days and then another ninety days and then another ninety days and so on until you answer the questions we want to put to you. Now are you prepared to talk to us?'

'No. I'm not prepared to answer questions.'

'You realise that it is our duty to keep you here until you change your mind. We've got lots of time. You can be sure that you will never be released until you decide to be less obstinate. You'll have to make up your own mind, for we won't allow a soul from outside to see you.'

He pauses; I say nothing.

28

'Oh by the way,' he continues, 'we've got Esme and she's talking, plenty.' His tone is mocking, derisive, sharp. 'She's told us all about you.'

I still say nothing.

'Why aren't you prepared to say anything?' the tall one says aggressively. I swing round to face him. 'Have you got something to hide?' he adds; his voice is harsh.

'I'm prepared to answer any question put to me in Court. Take me to Court and I'll be happy to face any charge you want to bring. If the prosecutor wants to know something in open Court I'll tell him, but I'm not prepared to say anything to you gentlemen here behind closed doors which you can afterwards use as you please.'

'You're an advocate, you should know better,' the tall one continues sarcastically. 'The Ninety-Day law has nothing to do with the Courts: that comes afterwards. The Attorney-General will decide whether or not to prosecute you, that's got nothing to do with us. Our job is to get information from you, and we know you have got that information. If you say you haven't got it, then all you have to do is to explain. But until we are satisfied that you have told us everything you know, the law says we cannot release you.'

'That's not correct. The law says you *may* detain me for ninety days, not that you *must* detain me.'

'Our job is to carry out the law. We don't decide on policy, Parliament does that. We must do what Parliament tells us to do.'

'Well, all I can say is that it is quite uncivilised to lock up a human being all on his own like this with nothing to do but stare at the wall all day.'

'We haven't come here to discuss politics. Our job is to get information from you and you can be sure that we won't let you go until we do.'

'This has got nothing to do with politics. Any prisoner, whatever he may or may not have done, is entitled to civilised conditions.'

'In Ghana or Russia they wouldn't even give you this. They would keep you in worse conditions.'

'Do you like the comparison? I'm speaking about South Africa. It doesn't say much for our police force that they can't get the information they want without using methods which are as bad as torture.'

'Our job is to protect the people of this country, people of *all* races, I might tell you. What methods should we use?'

'The usual police methods used throughout the world—patient investigation, informers and so on.'

'We haven't come here to discuss our duties with you. The law is clear, you'll never leave here until you decide to co-operate with us. It's entirely up to you.'

'Why do you only think of yourself?' the short one intervenes in the argument. 'Think of your wife and children.'

I turn about once more to face him again.

'You people should think of my family, not me.'

'Come let's go. We'll come back one day when you're less stubborn. Any time you want us, just ask the duty sergeant and he'll call us straight away.'

Don't go away, I want to say, stay here and talk to me, even if you are rude. I remain silent. The tall one looks angry as he leaves, the short one is sneering. The door is slammed and I am alone again. I pace backwards and forwards in the cell. My mind is active and I feel that I must get rid of my excitement by walking. For nearly half an hour I walk, going over the interview again and again, sifting out pieces of fact and searching for phrases of significance. All in all, I feel a slight buoyancy. Something in the interview augurs well for me. What is it now? Oh yes, poor Esme. 'We've got her and she's talking plenty.' With her husband Dennis on trial for his life for supporting the underground, she was hoping for some peace for herself and their kids. Obviously they have no mercy, these people. They've harassed her so much, now they'll even detain her in solitary confinement to get information they can use against her husband. Of course she is talking. She can surely have very little to tell them and with so much to contend with she could never stand up to the full rigours of ninety days. With luck they will release her soon and then maybe she will find some peace. There's nothing she can say which could be bad for me. That means the

30

police haven't anything substantial to threaten me with. They're taking a chance with me, fishing in the dark, waiting for me to volunteer information. That bit where they told me to think about my wife and children was a joke. Surely they should know I'm not married. They must have used the phrase out of force of habit. As for my mother here in Cape Town, and my father in exile in London, and my brother also in London waiting for a hole-in-the-heart operation, I'm sure they support me in my stand and would be horrified if I acted dishonourably and thought only of getting myself out of detention. They are liars, these policemen, and nothing they say can be trusted. They use routine tricks to break down prisoners. Yet the more they lie, the better for me, for if they had something which they thought was really solid there would be no need for them to lie. Still, although they haven't any understanding of what makes us tick, they're not the clumsy oafs so many people think them to be. I'll have to be on my guard. I wonder when they'll come again?

The door is opened at unexpected times on two occasions, but not for interrogation. Once it is a police major carrying out an inspection, the other time it is the chief magistrate making his weekly tour. It takes time to get used to being so completely in the power of others. The police refuse to give me a copy of the regulations governing my detention, nor will they let me have any reading matter other than the Bible. When I ask the magistrate whether I cannot be allowed into the yard for more than the twenty minutes a day which I am getting, he tells me that he finds my request strange considering that other prisoners have asked for less time out of their cells.

As the door opens now I see that two other special branch men have come. One is a sergeant whom I had often cross-examined in Court; he has always struck me as being an unimaginative, ponderous but methodical police worker. With him, and clearly the leader of the two, is 'the Englishman'. Perhaps I will find out today what on earth 'the Englishman' is doing with this crowd. I saw him for the first time when my office was being searched. The name and rank of each of the searchers was mentioned to me—save that of this man with the pipe and the calm, distinguished air. The others all spoke Afrikaans, but he spoke English with a cultivated British accent. He did not seem of the group, but rather with them, as though he had come as a consultant. He is of medium height with neatly combed, dark hair and a clean round face. He looks first at me and then around the cell. There is something amused, ironical and wise about his gaze, as though he has seen this all before and expects often to see it again. He takes his pipe out of his mouth and, looking down at the fruit on the floor, says:

'I see they give you plenty of fruit.' His voice is well-modulated, casual, friendly and very English.

'I'm afraid I didn't catch your name the other day,' I reply.

'Freeman,' he answers, 'Phil Freeman.' He shakes my hand. 'You know Sergeant Louw, of course.'

'Yes, I've seen him on many a case.'

He puts his hand in his pocket and takes out a snapshot of a young man posing on Table Mountain. I recognise it as one of the items they took from my office.

'Who's this chap here?' he asks, showing it to me.

'I'm afraid I'm not prepared to answer any questions.'

He puts the picture back in his pocket and smiles pleasantly at me.

'Any complaints about the way they treat you?' he asks in a rather bored voice. The sergeant stands quietly near the door.

'Well, they're not beating me up or anything like that. But, now that you ask, I'd like to say that I think it is extremely cruel to subject a human being to prolonged isolation like this, with nothing to do all day. Also the facilities are rather primitive. I have to live on the floor all day.'

He shrugs. His manner is companionable, almost sympathetic. I wonder how many cells like this he has entered before —in Malaya, Kenya, Cyprus—perhaps the facilities there were far worse.

'Yes, well that's up to them,' he says. 'They say they'll keep you here until you answer their questions.'

'I think it is quite uncivilised to hold people like this, indefinitely without trial.'

82

His composure breaks: 'In your countries in Eastern Europe they wouldn't even hold you. They'd just shoot you without a trial or anything.' He is shouting now. The transformation is startling, and I notice in his eyes a hard fanatical look. He walks around me, taut with rage, 'Yes, they'd just shoot you on the spot.'

I do not say anything but wait for the anger to die down. So that explains why he is working for the South African special branch. He must be one of those who have dedicated themselves to fighting communism, and will work with any persons as long as they are anti-communist. Perhaps too he enjoys playing with the personalities and emotions of people trapped in cells. As each British Colony gets independence there will be less scope for him to indulge in this game.

'All I can say is this,' I start tentatively, the crack has closed up, he has composed himself. I continue 'This is my country, this is the country I know. I know a bit about the law here and how people are treated. I don't wish to argue about general conditions and so on, but I don't see how anyone can say that this Ninety-Day law is civilised.' He lets me talk on. I feel an urge to convince him that I am reasonable and sincere even if I cannot get him to agree with me. 'I don't know if you will agree with me, but I haven't any doubt at all that one day there must be changes in this country. How long it will take I don't know. But if it ever happens that, in this country or any other, I am ever in a position to influence policy in any way, I would do everything I could to oppose treating people like this. I would never support anything like this Ninety-Day law, anywhere, at any time.'

'Of course there must be change,' he replied with resumed casualness. 'The only question is how it is to come about—by evolution or revolution?'

He smiles as he notices my amazement, which I am unable to conceal. Our special branch men never talk like that. To concede that there must be change—why that's rank heresy, if not actual subversion.

'Anyhow,' he adds, 'there's not much point in going into that now.' He looks around the room with his ironical gaze and starts moving towards the door. 'I hope you manage to make yourself comfortable here.'

'Would you like some fruit?' I want to say stay and talk to me. Look how reasonable I am. I am prepared to share my fruit with you, but look what you are like to me.

'No,' he says abruptly. He seems a little annoyed by my offer, but recovers quickly. 'You should try the old army dodge,' he advises, 'you know, get hold of a tin and leave the peel in it and make some booze for yourself.'

He and the sergeant, who is still silent, walk out of the cell and the uniformed policeman with the keys slams and locks my door. It is quiet again and I walk around, thinking and puzzled. Well, this has been an odd interrogation. He only asked one question all the time, and did not even push that one. I suppose he came to size me up. Perhaps he will advise the others on how to deal with me. It's odd the way he refers to his colleagues as 'them', as though he has more in common with me than the people he works with. I know I shouldn't really talk to him at all about anything, but they already know my political views well enough, or so they should after having had me in their files for the past twelve years. They know that I have left-wing views, that I have been associated for many years with the Congress Movement headed by the African National Congress led by Chief Lutuli and Nelson Mandela.[1] They must have tape recordings of the speech I made, before the African National Congress was banned, in which I called on the audience to work for the day when Nobel Peace Prize-winner Albert Lutuli was made Prime Minister of South Africa; and of the speech I made at the University before I was banned in the course of which I warned the White students that if it came to a showdown between Black and White in this country, in the long run the Blacks would win.

They certainly don't need to send him to find out about my views on the situation in South Africa, still I must be careful not to let my tongue run away with me. I'm glad he lost his temper while I kept mine. I wonder why he asked me only about the photograph? Bill would be tickled pink if he knew that the

[1] A very brave and respected African leader who was sentenced to life imprisonment at the Rivonia Trial.

picture I took of him the day we climbed the mountain was being puzzled over by our security men. He should be back in the States by now. I hope to hell he puts up a bit of a show on my behalf when he hears of my detention—if not a stone through the consulate window in Detroit, and this really isn't his style, then at least a poster demonstration. He'd probably think I'm crazy not to tell them who he is, and that we never discussed anything sinister. But the point is either I answer questions or I don't. There's nothing to be gained by answering some questions and refusing to answer others. Once I start answering they'll keep me until they've broken me completely. I must convince them that they are wasting their time in holding me, that I'll never co-operate with them however long they keep me. All I can hope for is that the people outside, especially those overseas, make sufficient fuss about me and the others to compel our jailers to start thinking that they have more to lose by holding us than by letting us go. In any event I don't even know why they have arrested me, or whether they plan to charge me. I would be a complete fool if I started to answer their questions and unwittingly gave them material to use against me or others. I must fight it out day by day. I don't think they'll torture me, I'm too well known and they know I would complain at the first opportunity. Although this aloneness is a greater hell than I ever thought possible to endure, you can't die of it. I would rather suffer here for years than spend the rest of my life knowing that I had bought my freedom at the expense of another's liberty. No, there is only one course open to me. I must refuse to answer any questions whatsoever and I must let them know that, however long and hard they try to interrogate me and whatever smooth characters they send along to trap me, they are wasting their time. Even if I have to kill myself first, I will not answer their questions.

As the days pass the two lieutenants come to see me again and again. I never know when they will come next, and each time the door is opened I wonder if it is for interrogation. Sometimes they catch me half-asleep and undressed, and I get up off the floor feeling animal-like and naked. Their power is immense: they can keep me here as long as they like, sealed off from the world and deprived of all normal association and activity. I notice that a pattern is developing in the interrogation: they ask me something about my facilities so as to get me talking to them. Then they ask if I am prepared to answer questions, and I say no. With each interrogation they get a little harsher. Their main theme is that I will never be released from solitary confinement until I talk. They drop pieces of information about me to suggest that they know every single little thing I have done in the past few years. They always stress that they are not in a hurry, and that I am being stubborn. 'I know how you feel,' the tall lieutenant tells me. 'You want to talk to us, but there is something inside of you that holds you back.'

My feelings towards their visits are ambivalent. These men shatter what little peace I manage to gain for myself. Though the lieutenants constantly goad and prick me, only occasionally do I manage to pierce their aura of confidence and command. When I do catch them off guard and provoke some natural human response, such as anger or laughter, I feel a great elation. Though I hate their intrusions into my life yet, once they come, I do not want them to leave. They constitute the only possible source of information about why I am being held and for how long. They are the only people to whom I am allowed to talk. It is only with them that I can assert myself, that I can hear my voice arguing for me, that I can articulate some of my thoughts. I am often amazed at my braveness and self-composure. It is as though once they appear my body automatically becomes alert and responds as a well-trained boxer's does in the ring.

More than a week has passed. This time when the cell door is swung open I notice someone new has come to see me. I am sleepy and have barely enough time to put on the gown and slippers which I now possess before the interrogators walk in. First comes the short lieutenant, then the new man, and lastly the tall lieutenant. They are smiling, friendly.

'This is Captain Rossouw,' the short lieutenant tells me. 'He is in charge of your investigation.'

The captain puts out his hand affably. 'Pleased to meet you,' he says. 'Well, we shouldn't be long. There are just a few questions I want to ask you and then we'll be off.' He is a large man, as tall as I am, but broad, very broad. Now probably in his middle fifties, he must have been a rugby player in his youth. His head is big and not handsome. A centre parting divides his hair and on his top lip runs a thin dark moustache. At each end of this moustache are small warts which look as though they are beads strung on the corners of his mouth. His suit is large and clean, and when he smiles the edges of his mouth turn up and his face takes on an open, boyish look.

'Well, go ahead,' I say. I am polite and curious to hear him speak. His English is good but accented and rather deliberate, as though he is anxious to find just the right idiom.

'Are you prepared to answer the questions then?'

'What are the questions?'

'First you must tell us whether you will answer them.'

'How can I say if I don't even know what the questions are that you are going to ask?'

'Oh no, if we tell you what the questions are that will give you a chance to think over your answers.'

'Well, the lieutenants here will tell you what my attitude is.'

'I want you to tell us all you know about subversive organisations in this country.'

'What subversive organisations?'

'The Congress of Democrats, the Communist Party, The African National Congress, and, for that matter, the Pan-African Congress.'

'I'm not prepared to answer any questions.'

'Is there absolutely nothing you would like to say to me?'

'Well, there's plenty I'd like to say to you, but I don't think it would do me much good if I did so.'

The short lieutenant chuckles and the atmosphere in the cell eases. The captain does not understand me and gives the lieutenant a puzzled look.

'I mean there are a lot of rude things I'd like to say to you, or anyone who would listen to me, about my conditions and so on. Apart from that, I'm not prepared to answer any questions.'

'How old are you?' the captain asks, and turns grinning towards the lieutenants, adding, 'You know we were all in the police force before you were even born. I remember your father well. We had a lot of dealings with him when he was secretary of the Garment Workers' Union.'

'Well, I'm sure he never answered your questions.'

'There's no point in wasting time, neither my time nor your time,' he says harshly.

'I'm only too happy to waste my time.'

'I'll be seeing lots more of you. I think we'll get to know each other very well, I've still got many years to go before I retire. In the meantime you can think about the statement you are going to make to us. To begin with you can tell us all you know about the sabotage school you attended at Mamre.'

He nods to the lieutenants and they start to leave. As he is about to step outside I remember something.

'Oh captain,' I call. 'There's just one thing I'd like to say.'

He turns round and beams his friendly smile at me. The three of them take up their positions again in the cell as though the interrogation had never stopped. They are all smiling, affable, waiting for me to carry on.

'Please, next time before you come, can't you give me a few minutes warning so that I can put my pants on and receive you properly?'

His smile vanishes. 'I've got better things to do than worry about your bloody pants,' he snaps. The lieutenants seem amused. As long as they are mere spectators they can enjoy watching the captain at work. They seem pleased at his annoyance, as though they had warned him I was not an easy nut to crack and he had told them it was only a matter of the right approach. As he walks out of the cell he is still angry. The lieutenants follow him, chatting amiably to each other. The door slams and I stand smiling, elated at having caused the captain to lose his temper. They cannot say I have been provocative or insulting, for my request was a perfectly reasonable one. It serves him right if he was so vain as to think that I had succumbed to what he regards as his charm and that I was about to give him some important information.

They definitely seemed to be on a fishing expedition. I wonder why they seem to place such emphasis on the Congress

38

of Democrats. I suppose they think it went underground after it was banned last year. Surely they haven't detained me simply over that camp at Mamre. Why does he call it 'the sabotage school'? There were certainly no signs of sabotage training the morning I was there, that was nine months ago. The police themselves found us there, and for months now they must have known all about the camp, so that if it was the camp they were worried about, they could have detained me ages ago. Well, if they want to bring a charge of sabotage against me, I will wait till I get to Court before giving my explanation. Whatever the organisers of the camp might have done when I was not there, they certainly did not make me a party to any unlawful activity. Is it possible that the judge won't believe me? Anyhow, I'll cross that bridge when I come to it. I've got enough on my hands getting through the present without worrying about the future. If they are going to charge me, I must hold out till I get to Court. If they are not going to charge me, I must hold out long enough for the people outside to campaign that I be charged or released. In either event a long hard period lies ahead of me. I will have to draw on all my resources to survive. Yet the alternative is worse even than the suffering I will have to bear. It is rather flattering to have so many high-ups coming to interrogate me and I think I have done pretty well so far. I must, I must keep it up. Look after the days, and the weeks will look after themselves. I sit on the mat and wait for exercise time. I must keep as fit as possible. There will be many, many more interrogations to get through. For this I will need all my patience and all my strength.

4 In the Mirror

THE IMMEDIATE ANIMAL SHOCK OF BEING SHUT IN HAS subsided a little and I start to reflect on my position. A process of self-observation and analysis has begun and with the passage of the days has reached the stage when self-exploration has become a settled part of my daily programme. So complete is my isolation, and so bare my circumstances, that the only object which acts as a source of stimulation is myself. I have become intensely self-aware, physically, emotionally, intellectually, and the eye with which I look at myself is merciless. Every blemish is exposed, and what virtues I find I dissect and separate, so that my personality is taken apart after the fashion of a plastic skeleton dislocated for the purposes of demonstration. Looking at the various disassembled parts, I often wonder how they can ever be integrated into one nature.

Some of the discoveries are amusing. My nose for example is askew, veering, like my views, quite markedly to the left. When did that happen? Perhaps at my birth. Funny that in all my twenty-eight years I have never noticed it before. Then I notice that the bulging part of the right side of my lower lip is more developed than that on the left—I begin to feel sorry for the under-developed left side. Then I laugh at myself for being such an indefatigable supporter of the underdog. Thereafter I reflect on my capacity to laugh at myself—is it a positive balancing force in my character, or merely a defensive mechanism for avoiding passionate and spontaneous involvement? Great things and little, big thoughts and small, all pop around in my brain without much direction or control.

I look at my long thin arms and legs, examining each inch

individually, first from this angle then from that. My tallness—
six foot one and a bit—means nothing in this world where I am
the only inhabitant. I am no longer skinny—'Ghandi' my friends
used to call me on the beach when I wrapped a towel round my
midriff—since I am the measure of my world and my own
prototype. My thinness in fact provides me with that most
treasured of objects—something to do—for I have determined
to try to put on weight, and each day I set aside time for letting
my fingers slip down my rib-cage to feel how much flesh lies over
the bones.

It is strange constantly to examine my body without seeing
my face. There is no mirror in the cell, and the only reflecting
object, the metal clasp on my bag, produces a blurred and distorted image which is most demoralising. The few moments I
spend before the spotted shaving mirror during exercise time
each morning helps in some measure to remind me of my specific
appearance and identity, but time in the yard is far too valuable
to be used up in self-contemplation, and I certainly am not going
to give the police the satisfaction of seeing me preoccupied with
my own image. Thus all I have time to absorb is an impression
of wild, wavy black hair, a long, thin, sad-looking face with high
cheek-bones, strong black eyebrows, a large pink nose, sensitive
lips and a pasty, pimple-prone skin. This image, I feel is me, the
Albie who would respond if someone called my name. My
body could be anybody's body, but the face is mine. When the
guard is not looking, I try to smile, and turn my head to see my
profile, but the view to which I have become used is that of a
serious, curious-eyed face slowly taking shape as wrappings of
lather are peeled off by the razor. My hands, I notice, are pale
and elegant. An interesting, mobile face I conclude each day,
but neither beautiful, as some women have declared to my
astonishment, nor ugly, as others have implied; sad and sleepy
when in repose, yet cheerful and boyish when smiling. A pity I
can not smile more often and let my face cheer me up.

They tell me that I will never be allowed any more visits. In
the first few days two colleagues of mine were allowed to see me
to settle my office affairs. Their warmth, their dignity and their
concern were momentary reminders of another milieu, of a

professional world in which I and they, and all the members, were people of worth and in which everybody mattered. Then suddenly some time later my mother was allowed to visit me. We stood in the yard while a cold wind blew, though she shivered she was happy to help me get the extra few minutes in fresh air, anxious to communicate yet awkward and worried. I felt in a way as though I were visiting her and persuading her not to worry. Then she left, without complaint or self-pity, and if she cried it was not while she was in the police station. Speaking to someone who loved me helped soften some of the hurt of my isolation, but it was nevertheless a strenuous and emotionally confusing occasion. Finally another colleague came, one who is reputed to have the Minister's ear, somehow his visit depressed me and, after he had gone, I nearly wept. I sensed vividly that he was torn between professional regard for me and the needs of his own position, and I felt that his first loyalty was to the Minister and not to me. He too viewed me as a person, but as a person in a limbo into which he dared not enter. I felt desolate and abandoned after his visit. Since then the prison has sealed the gaps through which the outsiders came, and it has swallowed me entirely. My only companionship lies in myself, I am back in the mirror.

Looking at my physical self I always find an entertaining pastime. My measurements and assessments are objective, the conclusions I arrive at not of the slightest importance. The probing of my moral and emotional self, which occupies much more of my time, is a more disturbing process. To look at my body is one thing, to think about my thinking quite another. With a minimum of outside stimulation available to sustain a reasonable level of emotional and psychological activity, it is extremely difficult to think and to feel in a coherent and satis-factory way. Memory and fantasy become increasingly import-ant as aids to mental and emotional activity, but as time goes by memory of the outside world is replaced by recollections of my days inside, as though my life has begun in prison. Meanwhile my fantasies become more and more wish projections based on immediate longings rather than genuine flights of imagination into the world of non-prison. I love my fantasies far more than my memories, for they lift me temporarily out of my harsh circumstances, and transport me to realms in which I am active and have an appreciative audience. Thus some tone and joy are supplied to my flaccid and suffering emotions. Above all I welcome my fantasies as a source of relief from the moral and philosophical problems which bite at my brain like a road-drill penetrating cement.

5 Reflections

ABOUT ONE THING I HAVE NEVER AT ANY STAGE HAD ANY doubts and that was that I have been locked up not for being bad, but for being good. I have done lots of bad things in my life: hurt people, been vain, shown inability to reciprocate generously offered love, and so on. The list is long but it is not for any of these faults that I am being punished. I am being held for daring to demand a better life for my fellow men, for being prepared to work and make sacrifices to that end, and for associating with others of similar persuasions.

As a child I imbibed the normal social attitudes towards prison, regarding it as a place for bad people, but my observations and experiences of later years have so transformed my outlook that I almost begin to feel, at a reflex level, that no bad people are to be found in prison at all. Statistics show that almost one African in ten, man, woman and child, sees the inside of a South African prison each year: mostly for administrative offences, such as failure to produce certain documents on demand. In addition a whole host of excellent people, more particularly the finest leaders of the African, Indian and Coloured communities, have spent weeks, months and years in jail in recent times because they prefer the path of sacrifice to that of submission. Had I not myself, when still a seventeen-year-old student, courted prison by leading a batch of four young Whites into post office seats marked Non-Whites Only, during the Defiance of Unjust Laws Campaign of 1952? Luckily, after being arrested and charged, we were found not guilty but the four of us were quite willing to follow to prison the eight and a half thousand non-Whites who had voluntarily taken punishment during that campaign. That had been at the end of my second year at the University of Cape Town and of my first year of politics.

I grew up in a political home, a home of books, of ideas and of stimulating people. From an early age I learnt that to help your fellow man is the finest end in life, and that people of different colours, nationalities and creeds can live and work quite happily together. For proof I had only to see the camaraderie displayed by divers visitors to my home—men and women of all the many races of South Africa, as well as European and American servicemen from passing Allied convoys. I also absorbed during those years a respect for working men. My views were always very much to the left, yet right through my school days and until the end of my first year at University, I kept clear of active politics and avoided political discussions. Prison, quite naturally, was something which remained remote from my own life. Then I discovered a crowd of young men and women, mostly students, who belonged to a political and cultural organisation known as the Modern Youth Society. I joined the Modern Youth Society, as we called it, and from then onwards prison was placed on my personal agenda, low down, it is true, but there as something bound to face me eventually 'as the struggle sharpened.'

Those were happy and exciting days. The Modern Youth Society was young and energetic, and it was the only actively multi-racial organisation in the whole of South Africa at the time.

Our life was a preparation for storming Heaven. It is true that most of our time was spent in endless woolly discussions and frantic searches for houses in which to hold parties. Yet we felt seriously about the fate of mankind. We were all of the left. We sold left newspapers, we supported meetings of what became known as the Liberatory Movement in South Africa. We also read philosophy, climbed mountains and went into trances at musical evenings. Our arguments were conducted in decisive style, though they decided nothing; our words were passionate, though passion was absent from our personal lives. We all implicitly looked forward to a three-decker future: first stage preparation, second stage ordeal, third stage victory. Of ultimate victory there was never any doubt, and even though we would joke about what we would sing as we walked to the gallows, there was an assumption that each of us would see liberation. Man could and would be splendid and we were lucky to be born in the age of social emancipation. The immediate task was also clear: to equip ourselves for the great battles to come. The ultimate outcome was equally clear, to free mankind. The only vague period was the middle one. The inevitability of sacrifice was recognised, but its content was never carefully considered. How could we consider it realistically? In days when open politics are allowed, when energies can fully be expended in safe, legal work, it is not possible to contemplate with any accuracy or emotional insight the rigours of political activity in a period of extreme tension and shut-down: when all radical opposition is outlawed and when police are granted the widest power. Similarly, though we would talk of the ruling class never giving up without a struggle, and though in debates we had no illusions about the sharpness such struggle was bound to evoke in South Africa, sacrifice was an intellectual concept relating to the future rather than an ever-present reality. We gave wholeheartedly of our time and enthusiams, but neither our liberty nor our lives were jeopardised.

Then gradually the future crept up on us. Some of our number were swept up in the Treason Trial,[1] which dragged on from 1956 until the case collapsed in 1960. Then came the State of Emergency,[2] after the Sharpeville shootings in 1960, during which more ex-members of our crowd were detained in prison, on this occasion without trial. Yet even during this time there was scope for large-scale fully legal political activity, and those held during the Treason Trial and the Emergency emerged from their ordeal in triumph. For years political prosecution ended in fiasco, until about 1962, when a new stage in South African political life was reached. That was the year in which the

[1] Began in 1956 when 156 people of all races were arrested; the Trial lasted four and a half years at the end of which all the accused were acquitted.
[2] Under the Public Safety Act passed in 1953, a state of emergency was declared after the Sharpeville Massacre.

Government finally gave notice that it would ban and make illegal every manifestation of militant non-White opposition to apartheid. That was also the year in which the non-White opposition, with a small sprinkling of White supporters, went over to a new form of struggle—sabotage.

From then onwards the casualties began to mount. Our own small crowd had by now dispersed, the Modern Youth Society having faded away as we grew older, graduated to the professions in our personal lives, and to senior political organisations, headed by the African National Congress, in our political lives.

Though our membership turnover was quite large, the core of our group was never more than about a dozen. The casualty rate amongst this dozen has been high. The first of our ex-members to receive severe knocks from the authorities were three African scholars, from Nyasaland, Northern Rhodesia and South West Africa respectively, who became active in independence movements on returning to their homelands. The student from Nyasaland, now independent Malawi, even achieved the distinction of being titled 'General' by the White press during the time he gave leadership to Nyasan peasant resistance. After being captured he was sentenced to three years' imprisonment. The Northern Rhodesian became one of the lieutenants of Dr Kaunda, present Premier of independent Zambia, and shared many months in confinement with his leader. The South West African was banished to a semi-desert outpost, but still managed to provide some leadership for one of the leading African independence movements in his country. For those of us who continued to live in South Africa, the blows came a bit later. Of our small number, a few dropped out of politics altogether, a few drifted into the category of sympathisers, and most of the remainder were restricted, banned and confined in one way or another by Ministerial decree. The first to be sentenced to imprisonment was Bennie, a land surveyor, who received three years for placing a bomb in a desk in a Court-room normally used for trying Africans for breaches of the laws controlling their movements. The next victim was George, a bricklayer become city councillor, who received one year for incitement, and four years, two suspended, for attempting to explode a bomb outside Cape Town's main prison. Later came Bennie's wife Mary, who served six months for helping the African underground. Arrested shortly before I was detained were Dennis, an engineer, and H., a doctor, both caught in Johannesburg in a police swoop on what Government spokesmen called the headquarters of an underground insurrectionist movement, headed, until his arrest earlier, by Nelson Mandela. They will be placed on trial for their lives. The death sentence is a real possibility. Then there is myself, arrested for I-don't-know-what, to be held for I-don't-know-how-long.

6 A Day in My Life

I WAKE UP. AS IS THE CASE EACH MORNING I AM A LITTLE bewildered to find myself lying on a mat on the floor in this bare cell. It is as though my unconscious is adapting more slowly and at night the hidden sluggish world inside me asserts itself. It is a stabilizer that refuses to kow-tow to the shifts and accidents of daily life. Sleep is a refuge, for my anguish is during the day, and exhausted by constant attempts during wakefulness at self-activation, my mind rests at night. I have few dreams. My emotions, stretched and bereft after vainly seeking engagement for so long, relax when the light goes out. It is night that is normal. Sleep has no geography. I could be at home. That is why each awakening is a shock.

The light is dim. I can see my trousers hanging oddly from the nut below the window; on the opposite wall is the towel, its checks colourless. It must be about 6 a.m., two hours to break-fast. I turn on my side, close my eyes and doze.

I open my eyes again. It is lighter now. The checks in the towel are red and yellow; a half-full bag of oranges leans in the corner. I listen for the chimes. Waiting is not so difficult when I am half asleep. I close my eyes; my mind is at ease, only my hearing is on guard. A train passes, lorries drone by, changing into low gear as they approach the traffic lights nearby. There it sounds—one round of ding-dongs. I wait for another round; it does not come. It must be the quarter hour, quarter past seven. Three-quarters of an hour to breakfast. That's not too long. I try to sleep again. All my life I've had trouble getting up in the morning. Now I'm grateful for my slothfulness. My mind is thick and lazy. I feel the first stirrings of emotion. The sensation is unpleasant. There is only one word for what it's like in the morning—lousy. At this hour I am defenceless: each day I realise anew my predicament. I feel empty and very unhappy but fortunately can still find refuge in semi-sleep.

A key is being turned in the lock and I hear voices. I must have slept again. I throw the blankets off and hurriedly get to my feet. They must not find me lying down. The padlock outside is open, now the door itself is being unlocked. My sand-shoes are on, and as the steel door swings open, I tie the girdle of my gown. It is cold in the cell. I'm glad it's not winter. As usual there are three policemen. A sergeant holds two bunches of keys—large keys for the gates and the cell doors, and smaller keys for the special padlocks attached to the cells of the Ninety-Day prisoners. Unlocking always takes a long time. Sometimes I am glad, because it gives me time to get dressed or to hide things, but usually I find it disturbing, and I pace around the cell excitedly as the men outside struggle with the locks. Today the duty sergeant is accompanied by a White constable. Their pale blue uniforms are neat and impressive. Standing behind them, in light khaki trousers and open necked shirt, is a Coloured constable, holding three tin plates of food. He steps forward and places one plate on the floor of my cell. They are about to withdraw. Nothing has been said.

'Good morning.' I speak the words quietly; my tone is friendly. The sergeant is new to me and I find the continual changes of shift unsettling. It took a long time to build up some kind of human contact with the other sergeants, and now I have to start all over again. The Coloured constable never says a word to me. I am a White prisoner and, though I have no rights at all, the rule is strict—he may not address me, for it would be regarded as an impertinence for him to speak to a White prisoner. The White police treat him with jovial mockery. His job is to fetch and carry and to see that the cells are cleaned out. They never leave him alone with me during exercise time, not even for a second. I feel that if they did he might give me some information about the other prisoners and so wait for my opportunity. The White constable is usually very hearty with me, for he seems to be used to having some sort of relationship with his prisoners. Generally he will shout at them, sometimes he will joke, but to keep completely quiet is unnatural for him and a strain. This morning, with the new sergeant in charge, he keeps quiet, for it is up to the sergeant to speak first. The sergeant says nothing but answers my greeting with a nod and slams the door. The lock is turned, the padlock fastened and locked, and the footsteps and voices move away across the yard. I hear another door being unlocked, and then slammed to, followed by the same sounds a third time. The footsteps and voices come closer again. The yard gate is opened and closed, then the gate leading to the charge office is opened and closed, finally the footsteps and voices disappear altogether.

I bend down to pick up the plate and place it alongside the mat. Then I roll up the blankets and sit on them as I eat. Today it is porridge. I cannot complain about the food—three meals a day, plus food from outside. You are on 'higher rations' the visiting magistrate told me. I have seen the 'lower rations' which the ordinary non-White awaiting trial prisoners received —a slice of bread with a touch of margarine, that was a whole meal. Our food is prepared by the station commander's wife, who is referred to as 'matron'. She and her family stay next door to the police station, which to her must be like an extension of her house; her prison duties, for which she is paid by the Government, are merely an extension of her housekeeping. Imagine voluntarily attaching yourself for life to a prison! Yet she prepares fairly tasty and always well-balanced meals for us Ninety-Day prisoners. The station commander, usually so dour and undemonstrative, blushed with pleasure the other day when I asked him to congratulate his wife on her excellent food.

'Ach, it's just *boerekos*[1],' he said.

Since then he has been less aloof, and the constable seems less worried about being seen exchanging a word with me. The porridge is cold, but not lumpy, and there is a fair amount of sugar and milk with it. I have a better breakfast, I reflect, than I used to have outside, what with my rush then not to be too late each morning. No rushing here.

[1]*Boerekos*=farmer's food.

After breakfast I sit for a while. I am waiting for a fair interval to elapse before I start my next activity, which is timed to fit midway between breakfast and exercise time. My next activity will consist of unmaking the bed, that is, shaking out the blankets, folding them, and placing them in a pile on which I will sit for most of the day. Later in the day I will make the bed again—a separate activity. I sit and try to be stupid. I am training myself to be as inert as possible until exercise time. By then a quarter of the day will have passed, the first significant fraction. The less I do in this quarter, the more I will have saved for later.

Footsteps and voices approach, keys jangle. The keys are louder than the voices, perhaps that is why jail is called 'clink'. The first gate is opened and closed, then the second. The voices, footsteps and keys retreat across the yard. Cell doors are opened. The voices scream out commands and the shuffling of many feet can be heard. Men and women arrested the previous day and night are being lined up and counted. The police voices are almost hysterical. The prisoners are stupid f—ing bastards. They are so bloody slow: they don't even know their own f—ing names. The word 'baas' is heard frequently. No, baas. Yes, baas. Sorry, baas. The previous night the prisoners had more spirit; some were drunk, and yelled back at the police; they banged against the doors and raged for hours in their cells. I never see them, only hear them being dragged in, swearing and being sworn at, and hear their furious and piteous yelling through the night. In the morning, before going off to Court, they are meek and demoralised, but the police still bellow at them. The Law celebrates its triumph with a crescendo of abuse. The captives huddle together ready to run, like sheep out of their pen, into the van waiting outside. The gates are opened, and feet, some bare, some with shoes, race past my cell. The gates are closed; footsteps, voices and keys recede, and in the distance, the van's engine can be heard revving. The episode is over; I have seen nothing, but heard it all. My attention retreats from the yard and creeps back into my cell.

My eyes travel along the walls and across the floor. I survey my domain, lingering a little on each of my possessions—the

52

trousers, the towel, the oranges, the bag with my clothes, my mat, my blankets, myself. I look at my limbs: my knees are up, with my arms lying folded over them. Nightfall seems an infinite distance away. Some days are good, that is they are only fairly bad; some days are bad, that is they are unbearably awful. But good or bad, on each day I suffer from this early morning misery. For what I know will be only the first of many times today, I tell myself: You can't die from it. I try hard not to think. My mind ranges over the programme for the day. I load my activities in favour of the end of the day, so that there is always something to look forward to. Keep the best for last. That long, agonising spell after lunch looms ahead like a trek through a desert. It must now be halfway to blanket-shaking time.

Everything is divided into significant fractions, for these are the dimensions of my world. The day is split up by mealtimes; morning, afternoon and evening further split up by activities. A day is a significant period, as is a week, as is ten days. After ten days, the next target is two weeks, then twenty days, then three weeks, then four weeks, then thirty days, and a whole month. Thirty days is already one third of the way to ninety days. Then more weeks till forty-five days, which will be halfway through, then sixty days, then ninety days. Ninety days will be halfway to the next ninety days. That will be six months, and two thirds of the way to the next ninety days, and so on. After each period the fraction of time completed becomes greater and more significant. Right now I am just over halfway to the first activity after breakfast in the first quarter of the day, the day being the ninth day of the first ninety days, that is one day short of ten days. The date outside, which I will confirm later when I add a day to the calendar scratched on the wall, is 9th October—it is convenient to be arrested on the first of the month. The chimes ring the three-quarter hour. At nine o'clock I will fold the blankets. The bag of oranges leans in the corner near the vivid check towel. On the other wall, suspended from the nut below the window, are my trousers, I think again of two hanged men. Soon it will be exercise time, and I will be out of my cell. Though exercise time is the highlight of the day, I feel sad when I think about it, for it will soon be over, and for the rest of the day it will be behind me.

The chimes ring: four peals, a pause, and then the clock strikes one—I count—two, three, four, five, six, seven, eight, nine, then silence. Even when I am eating, or half asleep, or when the guards have just told me the time, I automatically count each stroke of the hour. It is as though a portion of my mind is permanently tuned in to receive the clock.

I stand up and separate the blankets. I first vigorously shake out each one, and then fold it. It took me a few days to find the best method of folding. The aim is to fold as many times as possible so as to make the final pile rise high off the ground. I shake the blanket, holding it by two corners, then by the next two, then by the next two, then by the next two, until I have shaken it holding each side. Then I turn the blanket over and repeat the process. Shake, shake, shake, shake, I fold and refold and refold until it can be folded no more. Then I do the same with the next blanket, and the next, until all the blankets are done. It is quite tiring. Next I shake the mat, beating the top part with my hand and kicking the lower half, I wish I could beat the fleas out of it. I replace the mat, and pile the folded blankets where it meets the wall. I sit on the pile, breathing heavily. Waiting for exercise time is never too much of a strain. The worst part of it is the thought that exercise time will soon be finished and done. When the first quarter hour chimes, I will get my things ready. I can spend a good few minutes on that, if I am careful. There is the water-jug to be emptied and wiped with toilet paper. I must get my sand-shoes out, and my towel and soap. My shirt and shorts must be taken out of the bag, unfolded, shaken and folded again. My breathing is softer now. I always think more clearly after having done something, especially after having moved around physically. It is hard to follow through a line of thought. What was I thinking about just now? I cannot remember. Hell, I can't even think properly. Unhappiness explodes within me. I want to lie down, to curl up and close my eyes. But I know I must not do that. I must lie down only when my body is sleepy—early in the morning or after eating, or after exercise. Soon it will be exercise time. Until

54

then I will sit and suffer. I stretch my legs and examine them. A conversation comes to mind: 'Mummy, why has Albie got so much hair on his legs?' She had been embarrassed by the question, I remember. I smile. I look at my feet and flex my ankles. Another conversation is recalled. 'At least my *feet* are better looking than yours,' I had said. That had been to someone else, a little while before. I smile again. My thoughts fade. I sit.

A little while later I am still sitting, still feeling wretched. The clock chimes. I get up and walk over to the toilet. I take the toilet paper off the water-jug, and empty the jug into the lavatory. With a few new sheets of toilet paper I begin to clean the jug. It is made of plastic, I am not allowed to have glass or metal objects. I also have a plastic orange squeezer. Anything of plastic will be permitted; if keys could be made of plastic I feel they would let my mother send in plastic keys. Every day when I start to clean the jug I tell myself this joke, and every day it amuses me. The jug's surface has been stamped in diamond shapes, and I give each diamond a polish. I want my jug to be clean and shiny. Only on this basis can I justify to myself the work-effort I expend on the jug each morning. My need for activity is desperate, but there must be some element of usefulness in what I do. If the work is completely senseless, I feel even more demoralised at its completion than if I had done nothing at all. I put the jug on the floor near the door, and start to get my clothing ready for exercise time. The procedure is similar. Each item—the sand-shoes, the shorts, the vest—is dealt with separately and meticulously. From the tiniest bit of work, the sort of thing one normally does casually and without thinking, I construct a methodical and conscious labour. Even going to the toilet becomes an occasion, with its own elaborate, time-consuming ritual. I urinate frequently and defecate on average about three times a day. There is no need for my bladder and bowels to exercise discipline during the day, for there is no activity they can interrupt. I enjoy my trips to the toilet. I relieve my body whenever prompted. This is the only un-programmed activity of the day. It has an element of spontaneity and uncertainty which gives me special pleasure. I regard it as a bonus activity. My sand-shoes are laid out, side by side, the laces at the ready and exactly balanced. Next to them are my shorts and vest, both neatly folded. I take down my towel from the wall, fold it carefully, and place cloth and soap on top of it. Then I sit on my blanket-chair and wait. I hope they come late. The later they come, the later it will be when exercise is over. 'There are some people as just sits and thinks,' I repeat to myself, 'and some as just sits.' That's me, I just sits. The anticipation of being out in the yard and having people around enables me to push back a new wave of misery. I just sits and sits. Thinking is for later; I must save up what themes I have.

A clink of keys, then footsteps and voices. The guards are coming. The first gate is opened and closed, then the second. The voices are outside my cell door, and the padlock is being undone. I stand up and wait for the door to be pushed open. I pace back and forth as the keys are tried one after the other. Now a key is inserted in the door lock, metal turns inside metal, and the door is swung open. 'Time for practice,' the sergeant says to me in English. The Afrikaans word for 'exercise' is the same as the word for 'practice'. I step outside, restraining myself from running. I look up at the sky; it is blue and cloudless. A strip of bright sunshine covers one of the high walls and part of the yard. I now know that it is a fine day and feel very pleased. The sergeant and the constable who brought my porridge are accompanied by another White constable. Exercise time to them is a nuisance, for there is nowhere for them to sit and nothing to do. Seeing the sky and the sunlight, being able to walk as much as twenty yards in one direction, and being in the presence of other humans, makes me buoyant. The police see a smiling figure walk with towel and soap to the tap in one of the tiny yards. I hear the gates open and close again as the matron, the Coloured constable and a Coloured youth join the guards. The matron is a middle-aged Afrikaner woman with a severe rough-skinned face. She uses no make-up, but her dress is colourful and neat. Her voice is shrill but what she says, on the few occasions that she does speak, is not unkindly. Her job now is to supervise the exercise of the woman detainee who is in the cell across the yard. My washing tap is in one of the tiny

56

yards, where a White constable is waiting for me. I strip and wash myself thoroughly. Often I am brought a pail of warm water, but not today. The Coloured youth brings me my shaving kit, a metal mirror, and my comb. I dry myself and put on clean clothing. I change my clothing a couple of times a day; it is something to do. The vest in which I slept last night is splotched with blood. I see a flea crawling on it. I drop my towel and lunge with my right hand, catching the flea between my thumb and forefinger. Then I manœuvre it between my nails, crush it and wash it away. By now I am adept at flea-catching. Other insects I love, but fleas I destroy viciously. They prey on me day and night, and I hate them. My under-wear is so bloody that I have asked the station commander to explain to my mother that I am not being beaten up, it is only the fleas. The other day I killed thirteen fleas, which is my record daily total so far. I enjoy shaving, it is so civilised. Half the fun is seeing my various faces in the spotted mirror—first myself curious to see myself, then a smile, then a look at my beard, then the face with lather, then the new clean face emerging. I hardly ever cut myself these days, even when the water is cold and the lather thin. I comb my hair. Then, fresh from the wash and shave, elated at moving around and doing things, I rush back to my cell and put on my sand-shoes. I hear water splashing in the other tiny yard. Someone else must be washing. My sand-shoes are on and I start running. Every morning I utilise my exercise time to the full. I will have about twenty minutes more out of the cell, and if I am very lucky, I may even have twenty-five minutes. I go to the small yard in which I washed. There is no sun there and it is so small, about twelve foot square, that I get dizzy if I run fast. Still, all I have to give the other two prisoners is the use of the big yard, which is about four times the size of each of the two tiny yards, and the gesture of giving is an even greater source of pleasure than being in the sun. 'Let the lady have the big yard,' I say to the sergeant, loudly so that she can hear me.

Round and round I run in the little yard. I feel the air against my face, and every now and then I look up at the sky. The walls are high so that it is almost as though I were running round in the base of a broad chimney. I am sweating now, panting and happy. The guards are used to my running; they think it is a big joke and tell me to enter for the mile. Two of the White constables are standing in the doorway between my yard and the bigger yard so as to keep both yards under surveillance. They are chatting quietly. I look at them as each circuit brings me past the door and wonder if these were the men who screamed so violently at the prisoners this morning. The one calls out to the sergeant that he heard a funny joke on the bus the other day. He looks at me and says: 'You don't mind a joke, do you, Mr Sachs?'

'No, of course not,' I reply.

'Well,' he says, addressing both yards, 'there were these two skollies[1] on the bus and the one says to the other "Have you heard, old pal, about the woman whose son swallowed a six-pence? Well, she was very worried and was going to take her son to the doctor when her husband said 'Don't take him to the doctor. Take him to a lawyer, he'll get the money out of him quicker' ".'

The constables roar with laughter, and although I have heard the joke before, I also laugh as loudly as my running will permit.

'You don't mind, Mr Sachs?' The joke-teller seems genuinely worried that I might feel offended.

'No, of course not,' I reassure him, 'I enjoy a good joke.'

He carries on talking to his mate, and I strain to listen. They are discussing repairs being done to someone's motor car. I am passionately curious, not about the subject matter as such, but simply to hear them converse. Language flows from the one to the other, occasionally they laugh. A conversation is a wonderful thing. Two human beings are communicating. They are so relaxed and intimate. Each listens to the other and backs him up with an appropriate smile or frown or shake of the head or ejaculation. I wish they would talk a little louder so that I could hear it all. Being able to run in the open air, and hearing people talk, what more could I want?

The joke-teller suddenly yells out a command to the Coloured

[1] ruffian.

58

constable. He does so two or three times every exercise period, as though it is part of a routine, a re-emphasising of relationships, a reassurance that all is well with the world. 'Hurry up, you lazy bugger, we haven't got all morning.' He then turns to me and says: 'Hell, that boy is lazy. He doesn't do a thing himself, but gets the other one to do all the work.' 'The other one' is the Coloured youth who in his turn gets shouted at from time to time by the Coloured constable. Poor youth, he is right at the bottom. In ten years' time, perhaps, he may have risen in the hierarchy so that he himself can yell at someone. For the present, however, he must sweep out the cells as quickly as possible, for all abuse, from the station commander downwards, always ends up on him. I decide now to run in the opposite direction, so as to give both my legs an equal amount of strain. Also, when running in an anti-clockwise direction I can see a little more through the doorway. Round and round I go. I am sweating freely. My calves ache and I must push myself to keep going; as soon as I stop they will end the exercise time. The rhythmic padding of my feet provides a soothing monotonous background to their chatter; the longer I keep it up, the longer they will talk. Sometimes when I run my thoughts flow freely. It is as though my mind is jogged out of its stupor. I recall *The Loneliness of the Long Distance Runner*—I am running through misty forests and a jazz trumpet tootles in the background. Round and round I go. The sergeant comes to have a look. He is grinning. 'I wonder how far I've run by now,' I puff to him. He does not reply. 'It's funny, but the highlight of my day is running round and round like a madman in this little yard.' He is still quiet. I wait a little. 'You know, when I used to see my clients in the cells, I never thought that I'd be there myself one day.' He grunts. Well, that is something, he has made some sound in response to my words. Just as the security police work at getting me to talk to them, so I work at getting the ordinary police to talk to me. Today he grunts, tomorrow he will say good morning, and next week he will be speaking about what colour he is painting his kitchen. I never discuss anything important with the guards, nor do I ever try to extract from them news of the world. To do so would be to jeopardise the little

59

amount of conversation I from time to time do manage to evoke.
He looks at his watch: 'All right, that's enough,' he tells me.
The momentum of running carries me on. I slow down and
stop, I am out of breath. I pick up my towel, shaving kit,
mirror and comb, and move back towards my cell. An idea occurs
to me. I must do it calmly, I tell myself. If I am natural about it,
they won't notice. I hand over the shaving kit and mirror, and
with towel over my hand, re-enter my cell. I feel confident that
it will work. The Coloured youth has just finished sweeping my
floor. I wish they would leave me a broom and a rag so that I
could clean out the cell myself, but they would not allow that—
it is not White man's work. In any event they do not want me
to have anything at all to do. Whenever I ask for work—I'll
even build walls to keep myself in—they refuse. The sergeant
comes to lock the door and, seeing the Coloured youth walking
out with the broom, says to me: 'You should have seen this boy
with the dog yesterday.' I remember the wild yelping I heard
yesterday afternoon which I assumed came from the police
Alsatian. The dog also has his exercise time. 'Show him your
arm,' the sergeant orders the youth. The youth rolls up his
sleeve and I see red wounds all the way from his wrist to his
elbow. He seems proud of his injuries, as though they represent
an achievement, like war wounds. 'How did that happen?' I ask.
'The dog was really excited yesterday and bit right through the
covering the boy had over his arm,' the sergeant explains.
Apparently 'the boy' acts as a live dummy, I presume that the
dog has to get used to the smell of a Coloured man. The sergeant,
obviously a dog lover, adds that the dog is really very intelligent
and is very popular with the men.

The door is slammed to, but I hardly feel the shock I am too
excited by the success of my plan. The keys are turned in the
locks, the footsteps and voices go through the usual pattern of
crossing the yard and passing through the gates, and all is silent
again. I have succeeded. I am tired after the running but
happy, very happy. For hidden under the towel in my right
hand is something I have stolen from right under the eyes of
the guards. More important, the theft opens up a whole new
vein of activity. I drop my towel and, in the safety of my locked

cube, I examine the booty. It is my comb. Long and black, with half the teeth close together and the other half farther apart, it is thick with dirt which, collected in days of combing, lies embedded between the teeth simply waiting, I feel, to be picked out. There is at least twenty minutes of concentrated and fairly useful work to be got out of this comb later today. Furthermore, every three or four days I will have more cleaning to do. Finally, I can now comb my hair more often. I put the comb down next to the soap and towel at the side of the lavatory. I will not hide it, so that if they do find it, I can say I forgot that I was not allowed to have it in my cell. This afternoon I will look for something with which to clean it. Meanwhile I must get through the two hours to lunch time. The first part is easy—sleeping. I lay out two blankets on the mat. Then I strip to my underpants put on my gown and lie between the blankets.

A flea is crawling up my right thigh. I have been sleeping, for how long I do not know. Slowly I pull myself up into a sitting position. I remove the top blanket, carefully open my gown, and dart my hand at the tiny bit of black which tickles so annoyingly. My thumb and forefinger are pressed together. Have I caught him? Cautiously I reduce the pressure of the forefinger, so that the nails of the two fingers are apart. I see nothing there, and open the fingers a bit more. The flea jumps out on to the blanket and vanishes into dark wool. Just you wait, you bastard, I think . . . 'You bastard!' I shout out the words. I can swear as much as I like. There is no one to hear. There is no politeness here, no social order. 'You. . . .' No, even here I cannot really swear hard; I am too well trained. I wonder how long I slept? I will have to wait for the chimes. I lie down again, half asleep, but my hearing alert.

The clock is chiming—one peal, silence, a second peal, silence. It is the half hour. Half past eleven? That would be wonderful. Or is it only half past ten? I will have to wait another half hour to know. I must try to sleep again. I pull the blanket over me, and lie curled in my favourite sleeping position. But I cannot sleep; misery lies on the mat with me. I have lost track of time, I must wait nearly thirty minutes until certainty is restored. It is as though I am treading water until a lifebelt is

thrown to me. You can't die from it, I console myself. Time
will wash by at exactly the same speed, whether I am wretched
and conscious of my loneliness, or happily absorbed and oblivious of my circumstances. The universe is majestic and harsh;
in its immensity I am a small creature in a cage. If I am very
patient and if I am lucky, after a lot of time has passed I will no
longer be in this cage. The three-quarter hour chimes. For the
next fifteen minutes it is the same. My eyes are closed, the bare
cell is shut out from my sight, but inside of me I am aware of
where I am. The chimes ring out again, and the clock strikes.
One, two, three, four, five, six, seven, eight, nine, ten, eleven.
Silence. It is only eleven o'clock. I will sit for another quarter
of an hour and then attend to my calendar. The thought that I
still have the comb to clean buoys me up considerably. It is the
same sense of pleasurable anticipation I remember having had
during my life outside. Yet my depression persists. I feel so
damned useless. It is really ridiculous making such a fuss over
all the tiny things I do during the day. In fact I am not occupied
for more than a total of about three and a half hours a day, even
if I include eating and exercise time as activity. About half of
this short time is spent on stupid activities expanded well beyond their worth. The rest of the day I sleep, or lie, or sit. Like
an idiot I stare at the wall, a healthy human being condemned to
inactivity and isolation. For how long it will go on I do not know.
Certainly it will be a long time, perhaps I will never come out.
I will fight it out till tonight. Another day will have passed, but
so what? The days mean nothing. The Police have the power to
keep me as long as they like. They feel no shame or conscience
at doing this to a human being. They want to break me. Worst
of all, now that I have so much time for thinking, I cannot
control my thoughts. I cannot remember anything. I cannot
develop any theme. I cannot sustain a single train of thought.
I wish I could write it all down. In the meantime I can
watch myself and make mental notes with the hope that, if and
when I am freed, I will be able to recall what it was like. Now
I can hardly remember what it was like not to be locked up
like this; what it was like in the world outside. The quarter
hour chimes. I get up off the floor, fetch my toothpaste-tube,

and scratch up one more day on the wall. I feel a certain triumph as I do so. Nine scratches: nine days passed. Each day is a little victory for me, a defeat for them. I must have patience. They cannot keep me for ever. In any event, there can be no question of giving in. Although I am a captive the battle is not over. I am in the front line. I cannot do much to advance the things that count, but I can help prevent them from capturing more people. We Ninety-Day prisoners are like the thin layer of precious hard metal that protects the mass of soft metal underneath. We will not make any breakthrough ourselves, we cannot even try, but we must stop them from penetrating deeper into our ranks.

I am sitting on the mat, my legs stretched out in front of me, my back resting against the blankets. I must work on this idea of writing about my detention one day to someone who will understand my feelings. Generally speaking my thoughts are not very original, and my experiences not very exciting. Now the experience itself might be worthy of being written up, even if the way I do it is not very good. I must try somehow to make some notes to remind me of it all. What can I use? I have a paper bag filled with pieces of paper and cardboard which I am keeping in case I need them. But with what will I write? Suddenly, I become aware of the obvious thing—the tube of tomato-flavoured cheese I have been allowed to keep. It has been there since the second day, yet I think of it only now. Those psychologists' monkeys, who fitted two sticks together to be able to reach bananas, learnt to use the tools of their cage environment more quickly than I have done. I will try cheese-writing in the late afternoon during the period when I usually play draughts. It was with great excitement that I realised on my second day that the check towel could be used as a draught board. I could not remember how many squares there should be on the board, but guessed at eight by eight. Later I remembered the pieces used in chess, and by counting them found that my guess had been correct. Unfortunately I had given up chess at a very early age, but I could remember draughts, and during the first couple of days of my detention I spent some very pleasant half-hours matching pieces of toilet paper against pieces of orange peel. To heighten the interest, I made a third team out of pea pods and played matches on a league basis. My enthusiasm soon palled, however, for the left hand always knew what the right hand was doing. After the game I would hide the pieces amongst my clothing, and hang the towel on the wall. The guards would never know. Today I am relieved at having found something to replace playing draughts, for with each day of playing my frustration has increased. It looks as though the toilet paper can retire as league winner.

I sit and sit. The half-hour chimes: thirty minutes to lunch. It is time for my morning Bible reading. As it is my only reading matter, it will have to last me a long time. Next to exercise time, reading is the most fruitful activity of the day. I ration myself to quarter of an hour in the morning and quarter of an hour before supper. In this way my progress will be slow and my interest maintained for a long time. The Bible lies with my clothes. I stand up and bend to get it out of the bag. I could have rolled over and pulled it out by merely stretching my arm, but the act of getting up is more dignified and gives the activity I am about to begin the status it deserves. I am back on the mat and, leaning on my right elbow, start to read. It is the Book of Judges:

And he said unto her 'Give me, I pray thee, a little water to drink, for I am thirsty.' And she opened a bottle of milk (did they have bottles of milk then?) *and gave him drink, and covered him. . . . Then Jael, Heber's wife took a nail of the tent and took a hammer in her hand, and went softly unto him, and smote the nail in his temples, and fastened it into the ground; for he was fast asleep and weary. So he died. . . . So God subdued on that day Jabin the King of Canaan before the children of Israel. And the land of the children of Israel prospered. . . .* My right elbow is tiring, so I turn over to rest on my left side, and read on. I come to the story of Samson.

But the Philistines took him, and put out his eyes, and brought him down to Gaza, and bound him with fetters of brass; and he did grind in the prison house. . . . And Samson said, 'Let me die with the Philistines.' And he bowed himself with all his might; and the house fell upon the lords, and upon all the people that were therein.

So the dead which he slew at his death were more than they which he slew in his life. The only good Philistine is a dead Philistine. Yet Samson had a nobility in death which he never had during the years of his freedom. I wonder how it is that so many people find the Bible to be a source of comfort. Perhaps they are consoled by attributing all the slaughter and pain of human history to a plan of God to test humanity. I doubt if I shall ever understand how people can be consoled by submission to such a God. I close the Bible and replace it in my bag. Now I must wait till lunch, which cannot be far off. Reading leaves an afterglow of peace which should last until the guards come. The clock is striking. I have missed the chimes and the last hour strikes, but it must be noon. It is nearly halfway through my day. I have been in for nearly nine and a half days. In the distance is the clink of keys. Footsteps and voices approach, gates are opened and closed, and keys inserted in the locks of my cell. I stand as the door is opened, for they must not find me lying on the floor. 'Hullo, Mr Sachs, how are you feeling?' the joke-telling constable asks. He is accompanied by the other constable, who puts on the floor one of the three plates he is carrying. The first constable hands me a cup of coffee. 'Well,' I reply, 'I'd rather be outside than inside.' That is my invariable answer to such enquiries. 'Here's your fruit and milk,' he says to me, handing me a package. 'Hell, you're lucky man to get such nice fruit,' he adds. Whenever the constables bring me something from outside—the regulations permit food and clothing to be sent in—they tell me how lucky I am. I give my standard answer: 'Well, if you think I am so lucky I'm prepared to swop places with you any day.' The first constable smiles. I notice the second one looks impatient. 'Tell me, constable,' I continue, 'do you think you could give some of the fruit to the other prisoners?' The second constable looks angry now, and mutters that he does not see why they should, and that he would not do a damned thing for me. 'Okay, man,' replies constable number one 'you're all in the same boat, hey.' He takes the fruit, the door is locked, and I ponder over the simile of all of us being in a boat. Yes prison is like a landboat which remains stationary while the world around it, presumably, moves; we prisoners are

65

cabined and confined in this concrete boat which never moves and which is so far from shore. By the time the keys, footsteps, and voices have done their rounds and disappeared from hearing, I am halfway through my lunch. Meat-balls and fresh salad, a slice of buttered bread, an apple, some dried fruit and half a pint of milk, the meal is healthy and substantial. I put a few more pieces of dried fruit in my mouth. The fuller I am, the longer I should be able to sleep. Perhaps I will gain a little weight. The tin plate with the apple core in it is placed near the door. It must be about twenty past twelve; six hours till supper time. The longest stretch of the day is beginning, the special hell that all my devices are powerless to combat. It will begin, but not be rounded off, with a sleep. I am conscious of all the food in my belly and, like a sated animal, I will lie and sleep while my digestive muscles and juices pulp the mixture. I lay out two blankets and place myself between them. I am tired and soon will be asleep. . . .

I wake up to feel a faint tickling sensation on my right side: another damned flea. Half asleep, I roll over to lie on my left side, lift the blanket, sit up carefully, raise my shirt and lunge. I can feel the flea between my nails and, with a muddled and sleepy satisfaction, crack it to death. I place the bloody black speck on a piece of paper, wipe my nails, and fall asleep again. I wake and sleep, and wake again and sleep again, how many times I do not know. Perhaps an hour has passed, perhaps two hours, perhaps only half an hour. I must lie until at least half past two. I listen for the chimes. Eventually they come—the four ding-dongs to mark the hour, and one stroke, followed by silence. It is only one o'clock. I close my eyes again, shutting out thought, trying to sleep before my emotions can start up.

As the afternoon progresses it takes longer and longer for me to fall asleep, and the periods of actual sleep get shorter and shorter. I hear the one-thirty chimes. Only another hour to two-thirty. I am halfway to two-thirty, which will be nearly halfway through the afternoon. I do not feel as miserable as usual this afternoon. There is something pleasant to come later. What is it again? Oh yes, there is the comb to clean and later on the cheese-writing. This should be a good afternoon. I will do

66

my singing and also my physical jerks a bit earlier than usual. Still I must lie until at least half past two. That will help to break up time, to give light and shade to the day. Lying, sitting, standing—each has its appointed time during the day. Now it is lying time. This is a very hard period. My theory is that the normal body posture for most of the day is an upright one; one's ordinary emotions during the day are associated with and conditioned by the bloodflow and the muscle and bone relationships of an upright body. To lie down when not asleep is demoralising: I feel as though my emotions drain into the centre of my body, where they reside unhappily; they are like the humours which the early doctors described as being situated in various parts of the abdomen. Yet it is almost impossible to sit or stand for long periods when there is nothing to do. Later I will be on my feet, and will try in some measure to get through a normal amount of bodily activity for a day. Now I will lie and lie. Even the thought of the comb and the cheese is insufficient to oust a spirit of wretchedness growing within me. Sometimes this anguish lasts right through the day. Today I am lucky; it should not persist for more than a few hours.

This is what it is like to suffer.
I have been very lucky in my life so far. Serious suffering never came my way for long. I regarded it as a state of mind into which some people allowed themselves to fall. Work, reading, the right company and the right attitude were all that were needed to help a person through a spell of suffering. Now I realise that suffering can be very real. At present a series of intrinsically trifling activities may control my unhappiness or, rather, enable me to live with it, but they cannot remove unhappiness from my life. Similarly, happiness is not just a state of mind; it has its base in the circumstances of life, and has to be constantly worked for. I am overcome by a feeling of amazement, almost horror, at the monks of old who voluntarily subjected themselves to a lifetime of silence and isolation. In future I shall no longer think of them as quaint or crazy personages. I shudder at their self-imposed martyrdom and wonder at the depth of religious passion which drove them to such extremes of psychological mutilation. There is no glory

in their conduct: such abasement might extirpate self-pity and vanity, but it also drives out love. Self-denial is admirable when coupled with giving and love, but when it is coupled merely with personal suffering it is absurd. The pain I feel now is not ennobling, it is destructive; it is a special pain, it has no identifiable source. It does not stem from grief at a loss, or frustration at an impediment. It is unlocalised in my body. Where does it hurt? Not in my head, or my chest, or my legs, but all over, in the whole of me. The more I thresh and struggle the worse it gets. Basically I think it is an animal pain, a bodily thing due to my unnatural state of inactivity. My mind and emotions rebel at having nothing with which to engage themselves. The greatest deprivation and source of suffering is the lack of human association. I wonder how the other Ninety-Day prisoners are managing. I visualise various persons I know, some of them close personal friends; I imagine them in their respective cells in different parts of the country. I see them in my mind but they are inert and emotionless, frozen as if in waxwork postures. It is two o'clock now, I hear the chimes. My last train of thought was quite absorbing, I did not count time as it passed. That is the nearest I can come to happiness—not to be aware of time. What was it that so occupied me? I cannot remember now. Oh what can I do to shore up my enfeebled memory? I feel angry and defeated at being unable to recapture the line of thought in which I was so happily absorbed only a few minutes ago. Soon it will be singing time. I will go through the alphabet again: 'Always,' 'Because,' 'Charmaine,' Daisy,' E—what begins with E? Where was I? 'Because,' 'Charmaine' . . . oh yes, what begins with E? It is hopeless to try to think when lying down, only when I am up and moving around can I think properly. Let me see if I can squeeze out a few more minutes of sleep. I try but it is hopeless. I must lie until half past. I lie on my right side then on my left. I lie on my back, I lie with my knees up and body hunched, and I lie stretched out full length. I lie and I lie. At last it comes—the two-thirty chimes, I have waited so long for this moment, but now I feel weak and lazy. I do not want to get up. I push the blanket off, stand up, and run my fingers through my hair. E, what begins with E? 'Embraceable You.' I must remember that. I put on my slippers, shake and fold the blankets. I feel a flea crawling near my ankle; I bend to catch it, but it disappears before my hand can get there. Remembering the dead fleas, I pick up the piece of paper on which they lie and drop them in the lavatory. I pull the snake's tongue out of the wall and hear the music of the toilet. I might as well try to evacuate some of my lunch. Fruit, exercise and water—as long as I had lots of those I would not become constipated. So one of the guards told me. He can understand constipation, but not the pain of having no reading matter or writing materials. My stomach works well. I find I enjoy my animal satisfactions. The toilet roars out its gurgling salute. It is like an organ peal or a trumpet blast announcing the entrance of the next performer on the stage.

Often I feel as though I am a mere thought in somebody else's skull, but now as I step forth to the centre of my cell I feel tall and human: I am going to perform. I shall sing, not merely to pass the time, not just because I enjoy singing, but so that the other prisoners can hear me. I am conscious of an audience, those two lonely people who should be able to hear sound coming from my part of the prison, and who might realise that it is directed towards them. Perhaps they will even be able to make out the songs. I start off with 'Always'. That is my theme song, I have changed the words so as to reflect my present situation. Whatever songs I continue with—through the alphabet, round the world, a country at a time, African songs, Afrikaans songs, songs from the Spanish Civil War, songs from a particular show—I invariably start with 'Always'. It is decorous and gentle. I waltz slowly round my cell and sing in a baritone which to me sounds sweet and sad:

> *I'll be living here, always*
> *Year after year, always*
> *In this little cell*
> *That I know so well*
> *I'll be living swell,*
> *Always, always.*

> *I'll be staying in, always*
> *Keeping up my chin, always*
> *Not for but an hour*
> *Not for but a week*
> *Not for ninety days*
> *But always.*

Next I whistle it, then hum it through, and finally sing out the words again, a little louder this time; all the while whirling my body round in a wild waltz. I next sing 'Because'. It is mostly 'de-da' for I do not know the words. Song by song I work my way through the alphabet. I dance to each song, sometimes shuffling, sometimes a waltz, then a tango or a samba and, as often as possible, the twist. After all, it took me so long to master it and I must keep up with the times. My singing becomes louder and more passionate but I keep it rhythmical and controlled. This is my relief: the equivalent of the screaming and banging on the door by the ordinary overnight prisoners: it is also the way in which I assert myself and penetrate the walls. I can hear myself, my body is moving and I am absorbed. Sometimes during my alphabetical progression, I get stuck over a letter. Often when trying to find a title containing a key word beginning with a particular letter, I think of other titles which I can use lower down in the alphabet. Then by the time I come to those letters, I have forgotten the titles I thought of earlier. It is hard to concentrate and almost impossible to remember anything. Eventually I get through the alphabet. Occasionally I cheat, for example, for X I sing 'Deep in the Heart of Texas,' but I do manage something for each letter. It must be about quarter past three. I enjoyed that. One last concert item and I will start preparing for the next activity. This item consists of carrying the bag of oranges on my back and singing, or rather grunting out, 'The Volga Boat Song'. I cannot explain it, but I feel a need to carry something on my shoulders. Perhaps it is simply a form of work, a desire to exercise my neck and back muscles. Perhaps it helps me to be conscious of my whole body, to be more aware that I am standing up. Perhaps it is psychological, I wish to carry my cross. Whatever the reason, I feel

70

that some need has been satisfied by the time I cease staggering round the cell and replace the oranges in the corner. Carrying the oranges has reminded me of something important: I forgot at lunchtime to ask one of the guards to cut open some oranges for me. They do not permit me at any time to have a knife in my possession. After exercise I like to drink orange juice before lying down, it helps me to feel that I am keeping healthy. With luck the guards will come round on inspection in the course of the afternoon. The rules say that they must come round every hour but they never adhere to the rules. If they do come this afternoon I must, I must remember to ask for the oranges to be cut open. I sit down on my blankets and start thinking about my next activity. My excitement grows as I contemplate cleaning the comb. There is no need to rush, I tell myself. Special activities must be savoured; the anticipation is half the fun. It is nearly half past three, the back of the afternoon has been broken. It is already halfway to supper. At a quarter to four I will start on my comb; at half past four I will do physical jerks, at quarter past five I will try out the cheese-writing, and at a quarter to six I will read the Bible again.

What a crowded afternoon it is turning out to be. If only every day could be like today. I sit and I sit. The three-quarter hour chimes. I sit a little longer, temporarily denying myself the pleasure now due. Then I stand up, walk over to where the comb is lying and pick it up. Thick and slightly oily dirt lies between the teeth. I must find something with which to pick it out. I empty the paper bag which contains the things I am keeping in case I need them. My hoard lies on the floor: pieces of transparent and opaque paper, paper of different colours, a label, a crushed and folded milk carton, a short piece of cotton, a fishbone, and a piece of silver paper. This tiny heap of waste constitutes the sum of possessions which I have acquired since my imprisonment. I am loath to throw away even the smallest scrap of paper. I am glad now that keeping the fishbone has been justified for it will make an ideal comb-picker. I wonder what use I will ever find for the silver paper. After refilling the paper bag with all the possessions save the fishbone, I assemble the materials I will need for the coming opera-

71

tion. A piece of paper, formerly the wrapping of an apple, I place on the floor next to the mat, at its side is the fishbone and nearby is a piece of toilet paper which I will use for the final cleaning touches. I pile my blankets up as high as I can, place the apple-wrapper on my lap, and with a feeling of delight, plunge the fishbone into the first gap between the teeth of the comb—a thick piece of dirt comes out. My pleasure is intense. Little blobs of dirt fall on to the paper as the fishbone picks its way towards the centre of the comb. I pass the halfway mark where the more widely-spaced teeth begin. Here there is less dirt and I soon reach the end. I turn the comb over and work my way back to the beginning. My satisfaction increases as the pile of balls of dirt grows bigger. When I have finished picking out the dirt, I start wiping with the toilet paper. This takes longer and requires more concentration: the paper must be pulled through the gaps between the teeth, first this way, then that. Toilet paper breaks easily so it must be gently handled. Finally the job is done. I look with pride at the clean comb and flush the apple-wrapper and contents down the lavatory. Then, as if in celebration, I comb my hair vigorously again and again until it is smooth and it crackles. I am still busy combing when I hear the approach of keys, voices and footsteps. In an instant the comb is hidden inside a blanket. Don't be silly, I tell myself. It is better to leave it lying around casually so that they will get used to seeing it in the cell and forget that it should not be there. I put it down next to my clothes. I adjust the angle, it must look as casual as possible. At that moment I hear voices outside my cell, I jump up, and remind myself that I must not look at my comb when they come in. 'Are you all right, Mr Sachs?' a voice yells at me. It took a few days before anyone started calling me Mister, now nearly all the policemen do so. 'Yes I'm okay, in the circumstances,' I shout back. 'Well, cheerio, then,' comes the answer. The footsteps, voices and keys cross the yard. Faintly I hear the yell, 'How are you, Dorothy?' and a little while after, 'How are you, Zollie?' Then the sounds of the guards move back past my cell, through the gates, and out into the world of beyond. Something is worrying me. Oh hell . . . now I remember, I forgot to ask for the oranges to be cut.

72

Dammit, my routine is upset, but that is not too bad for I can have my milk after exercise and the orange juice after supper. What annoys me so is the feeling of bafflement and frustration. Bah, foiled again! as the stage villains used to say. 'Dammit!' I yell out loudly. Again I wish I was less restrained and could swear more violently. Disconsolately I sit on the blankets. The comb has lost its magic properties; it now looks simply like a comb.

It must be after quarter past four. Soon it will be time for physical jerks. I hate the session of concentrated exercise every afternoon, yet I know it must be gone through. In twenty minutes of bending, stretching and pressing I must make up for a whole day's general bodily movement. The running at exercise time in the morning probably equals the amount of walking I would normally do in a day. I must, however, also make up for all the fetching and carrying, the reaching and bending that I would do, without even being conscious of any activity, in a day outside. Every single movement of limbs or trunk is now consciously undertaken and planned. My body is like an engine that has to be run at frequent intervals to keep it in running order. Shortly I will lift myself and start up the engine. I smile as I remember my efforts during the first few days to do yoga: my legs and back had ached, and physical discomfort was added to my mental distress. The spiritual peace I had hoped for eluded me completely; the only moment of joy for me was when I unscrambled my limbs, it was so nice when it stopped. Yoga, I feel, is for busy people who wish to relax, not for idle people who wish to be active.

The world looks odd from down here. Every now and then I develop a consciousness of being on the floor. I still cannot get over my amazement at living on the floor. It is as though mankind in the last thousand years has painfully struggled off the ground, and ascended to a plane two to three feet in the air, with the aid of chairs and beds and tables. Now with one cruel thrust the authorities have plunged me down to the ground and back a thousand years in history. It is true that many Africans today living in tribal society have no furnishing in their huts, but they live and work out of doors and use the huts only for

73

shelter. Huts are for tired bodies not active people. I am strongly of the opinion that the chair deserves to be ranked, together with the wheel and fire as being amongst the major achievements of mankind. Without the chair nearly all modern work would be impossible. Long live the chair and forward to the day when my seat will once more be raised. It is ironical that at present the only time my body experiences the ennoblement of being lifted from the ground is when it is excreting. I sit and I sit. The chimes ring out, half past four, time for exercise. Now that the time for physical jerks has arrived I want merely to sit. The exertion I am about to undergo is like a punishment I mete out to myself each afternoon. It is the hardest of my tasks, it requires the greatest self-discipline. I put on my sand-shoes and cross to that corner of the cell which is away from my mat and belongings. First I do loosening-up exercises, running on the spot—fifty steps with each leg. Then comes legs-apart and twenty-five arms-together, arms-stretched, followed by fifty swinging-arms. Next are the bending exercises, arms up together, swing to the right and touch my toe, up together swing to the left and touch my toe, twenty-five of those. I am panting now. Legs-apart, twenty-five forward-stretch, backward stretch. Then feet together, touch my toes twenty times. I am getting quite accomplished at this and can even press my palms on the ground without bending my knees. Now come the tiring bits. On my toes, arms out, squat, arms together, up, seventy-five times. By fifty my thighs ache and my brain becomes clouded. By sixty I feel dizzy. By seventy I am faint. The human machine carries on. On my toes, squat, arms out, up . . . seventy-five. It is done; good for me. I stagger round the cell, conscious of my thigh muscles, too tired to stand, still too activated to lie down. The worst is yet to come: press-ups. At first I could not manage ten, now I do twenty-five. I move the mat across the cell. I lie on my stomach and placing my hands upon the mat, press my body upwards: up, down, up, down. The first fifteen are not too hard. I use my system of significant fractions here. Five, ten, thirteen (halfway), fifteen, twenty—all are significant numbers. In the early days, with a view to sweetening the exercises, I used to try to recall happy moments of making love. The result, alas, was not to make the press-ups any more enjoyable but merely to depreciate my memories. Twenty, twenty-one, twenty-two, twenty-three. I am near collapse, twenty-four, twenty-five. I am exhausted and lie gasping on my stomach. The last exercise is easy—bicycle pedalling while lying on my back. I place myself on the mat and kick my legs into the air. I pedal at a steady, rhythmical pace. Sixty, seventy, eighty—how I hate all this counting—ninety, one hundred. Praise be, exercise is over. I return the mat to its usual position, stretch out two blankets, drink half a pint of milk, and lay my panting body between the blankets. I will not sleep now, for to do so would interfere with my sleep tonight. I lie comfortably tired, happy that I forced myself to do the exercises. Exercise, I tell myself, keeps me toned up, it is good for my bowel movements, appetite, and sleep, and prevents muscle cramp. The fact that I hate doing it is also in its favour, for hate is a definite emotion and I must do something each day that is as burdensome as the annoying chores of ordinary life.

It is nearly five o'clock. At a quarter past five it will be time to try to write with the cheese. I must think now of a few key words: *Caterpillar*, if they do discover my writing they will never know what I am referring to. *Song*—that will help me to remember my singing, and *Always*. What else is there? I must not forget the policemen, what they were like. I can write *Cops*. It is getting darker now and cooler. I stand up, reach for my long pants and jersey and put them on. Back between the blankets I try to remember what I had been thinking about. It had had something to do with my next activity. Now what was that? It was not draughts . . . oh yes, now I remember, it will be writing with cheese. I was thinking of words. What were those words again? It does not matter, they will come back to me later. Perhaps I will not be able to write at all. Only a few more minutes and then I will know. I lie and I lie. Have I missed the chimes? It is easy to miss the short peal for the first quarter hour. I lie and I lie. The ding-dong sounds once. It is time to try to write. I stand up and then empty my paper bag of junk.

I put aside a piece of cardboard and replace the remaining bits and pieces in the bag. Next I unscrew the cap of the tube of tomato-flavoured cheese and examine my *ink*. It is far drier than I had thought and a very pale pink. Still, if I can find a method of applying it, it should serve the purpose. What can I use as a pen? The fishbone comes to mind. I will prod and mould the cheese into letter shapes on the cardboard. The proof of the prodding will be in the writing, I say to myself, pleased that my mind is still agile enough to enjoy a pun. I squeeze a blob of the cheese on to the cardboard and poke at it with the fishbone. It takes a lot of patient rolling and pushing before a crescent emerges. It bears a resemblance to the letter C. Next I work on an A. The best way is to make a hole in the centre and push the blob out into a circle; then the right-hand side can be straightened and a little tail added. To do the T is relatively easy. Slowly I spell out the word caterpillar. The letters are large and ungainly, the words are spread right across the cardboard. Nevertheless I feel very proud of my handiwork. Writing may become an important source of activity for the future. For today it is as though I have just discovered the printing press. It is strange that although each letter on its own is almost unrecognisable, the word as a whole stands out quite clearly. I hope it lasts well. What were the other words I meant to write? Again I have that feeling of rage as I battle in vain to remember my thoughts of only a few minutes ago. Never mind, I console myself, caterpillar is a long word, and each day I can add a word or two. At least now it is guaranteed that I will not forget about the only other living things in my cell—the fleas, the ants and the caterpillar. There is no forgetting the fleas, it is true, because they constantly remind me of their presence. The ants, too, I should not forget, for I spent many moments following trails, envying them their facility for climbing up the walls and under the door. The constables one day killed them off with spray but I confidently expect, in fact eagerly await, the appearance of new ant-trails. The caterpillar was something special though. One day I noticed that some green peas I had received were bad. The cause was a tiny green caterpillar, not more than about a quarter of an inch long. I put the caterpillar and peas aside with a view to seeing how much it could eat in a week. The next day I heard a strange sound in the cell; any sound in the cell is strange, for I am the only source of noise. My sense of hearing has become so sharp that I would not be surprised if I heard fleas hop or ants crawl. This noise was most unusual however. It went crunch—silence—crunch—silence—crunch—silence. . . . I was quite baffled until I looked at my paper bag. Crawling across it was a caterpillar, swollen and long. I looked at the spot where I had left the peas—there was nothing save a few bits of husk. The peas were now crunching their way across the paper in the shape of an inch-long caterpillar. I put the caterpillar in the bag together with what bits of food I could find. Later in the day it was still there but when I looked on the following day the bag was empty. Where the caterpillar had gone to I was never to know, but I hoped that it had made it to the world outside. Inside the prison there was not a touch of greenery; the caterpillar would have had to negotiate long distances of yard, wall and roof to have reached its freedom. Even now I feel proud of the big, fat caterpillar which I helped to grow. Animal husbandry is obviously more my line than agriculture, for a green pea which I placed in a lump of bread and which I water each day shows not the faintest trace of germinating. Who would have thought that I would become sentimental about a caterpillar, or envy a worm? I put the cardboard in my clothing and replace the fish-bone in the paper bag. My writing session is over for the day and I am pleased with the results. It is nearly supper time and the worst of the day is over. At a quarter to six it will be Bible reading time once more. Today has been relatively rich in activity, so I do not feel my usual strong pre-reading excitement. Though normally I ration myself to two short spells of reading per day, when I feel desperately morbid I allow myself extra reading time. It is as though the Bible is a medicine which I normally take twice daily before meals, but if the condition deteriorates sharply I take a large dose immediately. This afternoon I am feeling unusually content and could dispense with reading altogether. My mind and body are relaxed and I am almost oblivious of my surroundings. Every few days this happens to me; I become unaware of my surroundings, or possibly I am still aware of them but somehow they seem unimportant. This mood of well-being may last as much as a few hours. It is equivalent to par outside, though of course it is far above the norm for my present world. Often I do not know exactly what brings it on, though it is usually associated with an event which I choose to regard as 'a good sign', or the discovery of an activity, such as today's comb-cleaning or cheese-writing. Though I welcome these periods as being times of relief from emotional pain, I sometimes wonder whether it is a good thing that I am adapting so well to an animal life. The pain I feel is a normal and healthy reaction to a cruel and distorted environment. Does the absence of pain signify a deterioration of my emotions to the extent that they no longer respond normally? Have I collapsed beneath the pressure of my environment? Or does it mean that I have momentarily triumphed over my environment by soaring above it? I am so absorbed in these reflections that the chimes come as a surprise to me—it is already six o'clock. Just as nothing succeeds like success, so nothing produces more activity than activity. It is not only the activity that is important, but the thinking about it before and afterwards, and the mental alertness which it generates. I take out the Bible and continue reading the Book of Judges.

And the men of Israel turned again upon the children of Benjamin, and smote them with the edge of the sword, as well the men of every city, as the beast, and all that came to hand; also they set on fire all the cities that they came to.

I read and later come to the Book of Ruth, where at least I find loyalty, virtue rewarded and a happy ending.

And when Boaz had eaten and drunk, and his heart was merry, he went to lie down at the end of the heap of corn; and she came softly, and uncovered his feet, and laid her down.

Twice I read it through. Then I close the book and lie back. One day, perhaps, I will once more know tenderness. Now I must fend for myself. Footsteps, voices and keys are outside my cell. In my reverie I did not hear their approach. I stand and wait for the door to be opened. I wonder if I know the policemen outside. The door swings open. A sergeant and a constable are talking to each other. They ignore me. The constable puts on the floor a plate of food which he has been carrying and then, at its side, a cup of coffee which he receives from the sergeant. 'Sergeant,' I say, 'would you be good enough to switch on the light.' 'Certainly, Mr Sachs,' he says. The last time he saw me was when he was on morning shift. His attitude had been neutral, neither hostile nor kindly. Though he himself would not talk to me, he did not stop the constable from discussing safe subjects with me. Tonight he does not intend to be harsh. He is merely too preoccupied with the conversation with the constable to spare me any attention. The light switch is outside, and as he puts it on, I ask if he will put it off at nine-thirty. 'Any time you like,' he says. 'I'd be very grateful if you could manage it at half past nine or round about then,' I repeat. I am worried that my request will be lost in his conversation. Lights-out at a regular time introduces some element of stability into the chaos of my life. Sometimes I lie for hours waiting for the light to be switched off. My dependency then on the guards is cruel. However tired I am, I dare not go to sleep for fear of missing the guards on their next round. I should hate the light to be on all night. So I must lie fighting off the sleep which I love, and prolonging the day which I hate.

My door is locked, the keys, voices and footsteps move across the yard and then back through the gates to the charge office. I look at the food on the floor. I am fairly hungry. Often I sit and stare at the plate without appetite. Eating then is like another form of exercise, something to be done not because I am hungry, but because it is good for me. Tonight the fare is not appetising—stringy beef, mealie rice and mashed up green beans—but I want to eat. As always the food is cold, but that no longer worries me. I eat the vegetables with the spoon provided and lift the meat with my fingers. The plate is soon empty. I try not to be too conscious of eating. What little savour the food has is lost when I am too aware of its size, shape, colour, texture and probable nutritious value. Often though, I find myself counting mouthfuls—nineteen, twenty, my plate's empty —much as though I had reverted to infancy. The jingle helps pass the time and there is something comforting and domestic about it. The tin plate grates on the floor as I push it in the direction of the door. Apart from flushing the lavatory, singing, and the occasional swearing, this is the only noise I make during a day. My foot plays with the plate a bit so that I can hear more of the noise. Then I return my attention to eating. I eat a banana, a guava and some dried fruit, and follow with cold, scummy coffee. As I reach for the milk I realise that I have again forgotten to ask for the oranges to be cut. I give way to frustration. 'Dammit!' I shout out. On the whole I realise that as far as food and clothing are concerned, I am not too badly off. If and when I get out I will mention that in these two respects, and only these two, the authorities have maintained civilised standards. For the rest, my conditions are barbaric. I feel a fantasy coming on. I am inspecting a prison somewhere in free Africa, speaking to the prison officials. I know you are short of funds for schools and roads and other necessities, I tell them, and you wonder why you should spend money on facilities for anti-social persons. Yet to lock a man up is a very drastic thing. I know, because I spent some time in a South African jail. And even if you cannot at first provide good living conditions for prisoners, you can at least ensure that their personal dignity is respected, that their rights and obligations are fully explained to them, that they are never kept in isolation, and that they have some useful activity to help them pass the time. In South Africa there was no excuse for the primitive conditions to which we political prisoners were subjected. The authorities boasted of the country's great prosperity and could easily have afforded to construct decent prisons. They deliberately made conditions harsh so as to further their aim of crushing us.

As always in my fantasies, my listeners are impressed by my remarks. The fantasy fades, and I am aware of myself sitting on the mat. My stomach is full and a drowsiness creeps over me. It must be about quarter to seven. The post-supper stupor usually lasts half an hour. That will take me to quarter past seven. It is as though my brain is happy to relax while my body goes about the business of digestion. I sit resting my back against the blankets, and loosen the top buttons on my trousers; my legs are stretched out in front of me. I am quite still, neither happy nor unhappy, a vegetable without intelligence, simply growing. I hear the chimes but hardly notice them. My brain is submerged by my stomach. Half an hour is soon past. I sit for a few more minutes and then raise myself to my feet. In another half hour, at a quarter to eight exactly, my evening concert will begin. This is something really special. I hope that if and when I get out I am able to do it descriptive justice. It is an integral part of the day's experience, yet it exists on its own, as a portion of a special relationship. Each day it marks for me a triumph of human determination and love. I prepare for it, and precisely at the end of the last chime at a quarter to eight, the concert commences. The hour goes quickly by, for this is the only portion of my non-sleeping hours that passes without my being aware of time. This is the brilliant, the happy part of the day. Goodbye, goodbye, the hour is passed. The day has drawn near its end. I will make my bed, do some more exercises, and wait for lights-out.

I turn the mat over, shake out the blankets and lay them out. My experience of camping out assists me here. I fold the blankets into a papoose which give maximum warmth and comfort. One blanket I roll up carefully to be used as a pillow. Next I do my evening exercises. They are less strenuous than those of the afternoon, the equivalent of a normal evening's movement. Thirty-five squats, ten press-ups, and fifty bicycles, and I am done. I perspire lightly, and pant a little. Then I undress, item by item. Since early schooldays I have always removed my trousers, underpants and socks in one movement. The habit is deeply implanted and it now costs me some effort of will to remember to take off each article separately. I fold my clothes carefully, and don my pyjamas. The guards will soon be here. The lights will be switched off, and I will sleep till morning. For the first few nights the guards used to come round almost every hour. They banged on the door until I answered them and frequently switched on the light and came into the cell. Perhaps they feared that I would hang myself, or try to escape. Escape was impossible, and nothing could have been more calculated to drive me to suicide than their interrupting my sleep every hour. Perhaps they had been instructed by the security branch to break into my sleep. Whatever the position, and I shall never know what their reasons were, after I had complained as forcefully, yet tactfully, as I could on every possible occasion, the night interruptions stopped. Now I have some consciousness of the guards checking on me after the early morning change of shift. I think I wake, answer them and go back to sleep, but it is so regular and such a firm part of my sleep routine that I am not sure whether it actually happens or not.

I sit with the lower part of my trunk in the blankets. Only when the lights are switched off will I creep right into my chrysalis and sleep. Now I must stay awake until the guards come round. Another day has passed, the ninth of such days. Each is almost identical. I seem by today to have explored every inch of my world and to have located all possible materials for activity. Once a week the magistrate sees me for a few moments, and every now and then my interrogators turn up. Otherwise each day is like the one before and the one to follow, and the next one, and the next. The days stand ahead of me in a row that vanishes into the far future. Behind me lie nine days like so many dominoes that I have knocked down. As I move forward along the column the pile of days behind me grows bigger, but the column in front of me still extends to infinity. I do feel proud though that I have lasted so long. The bewilderment and shock of the first few days has largely passed. I am now fully orientated to my new world. The days pass no more quickly now than they did at first, the emotional pain is as great as ever, but I am more confident of my ability to adapt and survive. Each day is a little victory for me and a defeat for them, even if, as is possible, they eventually do break me down. I must stick it out. I must not be dishonourable.

The footsteps, voices and keys are coming. They are at my door. This is the only time that I do not mind them seeing me on the floor. The door opens and the sergeant, who again is talking to his mate, sees that I am still alive and apparently not about to escape. 'Will you switch off the light, please,' I

82

ask. He carries on talking to his companion, slams the door, and the light goes off. The noises move across the yard and then back through the gates. The world is silent. I curl myself in the blankets, lie on my side, and close my eyes. It has been a wonderful day today, my best so far. I hope there will be more that are as good.

7 The Blankets

'CONSTABLE, WOULD IT BE POSSIBLE FOR ME TO GET CLEAN blankets sent in from outside? These are quite warm, but they're filled with fleas.'

The constable puts my food on the floor and, as he straightens up looks at the blankets to which I am referring.

'What's wrong with the powder we used?' he sounds offended.

'Well, it doesn't seem to have had any effect on the fleas, but it nearly kills me,' I reply. 'As soon as I lie down I start sneezing. My eyes water and I can't breathe properly. I have to have a handkerchief over my nose when I try to sleep.'

'You'll have to ask the sergeant.'

'When will I see him?'

'He'll come this evening.'

'Thank you, constable. I'll ask the sergeant.'

At intermittent moments in the afternoon I repeat to myself that I must ask the sergeant about the blankets. If only I could write it down. Eventually the sergeant comes, asks if I am all right, and leaves . . . I forgot to ask him. I keep on forgetting the simplest things. I must, I must, I must remember tomorrow.

'Sergeant, would it be possible for me to get clean blankets from outside? The flea powder in these is worse than the fleas. I meant to ask you yesterday, but I forgot.'

'You'll have to ask the station commander.'

'When will I see him?'

'He holds an inspection on Sunday before he goes to church.'

'Thank you, sergeant. I'll ask him then.'

The neat grey suit he is wearing makes the station commander look smaller than he does when he is in uniform. My door is open and the ringing of the church bells is no longer muffled. Standing with the station commander are two young boys also dressed in their Sunday best. Before setting off for church they are accompanying Pa to look at his prison and the new prisoners. Today I won't forget. How does one address a station commander? I suppose 'Mr' is best.

'Mr Kruger, would it be possible for clean blankets to be sent in to me from outside? These are full of fleas, I'm afraid. Your men have very kindly tried using insect powder, but it doesn't seem to affect the fleas at all. My clothing is all bloody from the bites, and I'm sure my mother can arrange for some new blankets to be sent in.'

The station commander is a man who carries out his instructions with neither special humanity nor special harshness. He is terse, colourless and efficient, but today, perhaps with a view to impressing on his sons how 'firm but just' he is, his reply actually runs to a few sentences.

'We do the best we can to keep the blankets clean,' he tells me, 'but you must realise it is very difficult, especially bearing in mind most of the prisoners we have. I am not allowed to let you have anything from outside except food and clothes, so there's nothing I can do.'

'But aren't blankets the same as clothes really?' I ask.

'My instructions only speak about clothes, not blankets. You had better ask the security men when they next come. They will have to decide.'

'If they give permission will you make the arrangements with my mother?'

'Yes, but only if they give permission.'

The first time the security men come I forget to ask them. Again I feel chagrin at the inability of my mind to hold such a simple idea.

The door opens and the two lieutenants are there. When they ask me how I am, I tell them about the blankets. 'The station commander said that if you did not oppose it, he would make all the arrangements,' I conclude.

'When you answer questions things will be much better for you. Then you can ask us for what you want.'

'But this has got nothing to do with whether I answer questions or not. Every prisoner has the right to certain civilised standards, no matter why he is being held.'

'There's nothing we can do about it. Only Pretoria can authorise it.'

'Pretoria, you mean my simple request has to go all the way to police headquarters in Pretoria? Surely they can leave a little thing like this to you people down here. Well, if that's the case, will you send on my request to Pretoria?'

'Our job is to question you, not to worry about your facilities.'

'Well, who can I ask then?'

'Ask the magistrate when he comes round. He has the direct ear of the Minister. If anyone can fix it up for you, he is the one. Ask him.'

Until now the magistrate has not been very helpful. He was only recently transferred to Cape Town so I have never appeared before him in Court. I am sure the other magistrates would not have been as harsh. When I told him of the warrant officer who on the day of my arrest had sharpened a pocket knife in front of me and told me, 'You know what this is for, don't you?' the magistrate's only reaction was to tell me the officer was probably only joking. These inspections which he has to do once a week are obviously very tiresome to him. As the cell door opens I see him standing with pencil poised ready to tick off my name.

'Have you any complaints?' he asks briefly.

'Yes, I'm being bitten to pieces by fleas. I can't sleep at night and my clothes are all bloody. I'd like some clean blankets from outside. There's no question of security involved. The security branch men said I should ask you.'

'Blankets are not in my department. My responsibility is merely to see that you are not being assaulted, that there are no Gestapo methods.'

'This is worse than the Gestapo.'

He smiles briefly. Obviously many prisoners tell him that. We do not mean that we are being physically tortured, though

86

possibly some get even that, but that the prolonged isolation is a more refined agency of personality destruction than many employed by the Gestapo. Because he does not see any bruises on us the magistrate has no idea of how we suffer. Also he does not realise that the mere fact of seeing another human being, namely himself, causes us to light up and be a hundred times brighter and closer to normal than we are during all the hours and days of being alone.

'There's nothing I can do,' he says brusquely, obviously impatient to get away. 'Ask the Security Branch men, perhaps they can help.'

'But they told me to ask you. They said you have the ear of Pretoria.'

'If you have any complaints which I consider to be reasonable I will make a note of them and see that they are properly investigated. It is not my function to deal with requests. Asking for blankets is not a complaint. If that's all, then I'll go.'

The pencil dips and ticks off my name. The magistrate leaves.

Who else can I ask? Perhaps Major Botha will come round again on inspection. He did not seem as harsh or petty-minded as all these others. I will try him.

Several days have passed and now the major stands at the entrance to my cell.

'Are you all right?' he asks.

'In the circumstances I'm not too bad. There was something I wanted to ask you though, but I can't remember. It should come back to me.' I turn to the sergeant. 'Sergeant can you remember, there was something I was asking during the week, and each person I asked put me on to someone else. What was it I was asking for?'

The sergeant agrees that I did ask for something but he can't remember what.

'I'm sorry to waste your time, major. Perhaps I'll remember next time you come. I'm afraid my memory is very bad these days. Thank you for your patience.'

The door is slammed. I look around the cell to see what it is I wanted to ask about. The blankets—oh well, being bitten by fleas is not the worst of my afflictions. At least the little insects provide me with some company, and catching them gives me something to do. I rather fancy the idea of the subject of my blankets penetrating through to Ministerial level. Perhaps the Minister and the general in charge of the police force will put their heads together over the problem. I must keep on asking.

8 Reflections

CONSIDERING THAT I HAVE A BACKGROUND OF INTENSIVE political activity I should have no difficulty in sorting out any moral problems which arise out of my imprisonment. The starkness of the situation in South Africa, as well as the fact that I am being cruelly punished by the enemy, should make everything very simple. Yet somehow it does not work out like that. On the contrary, the crueller my treatment, the greater my doubts. Doubt flourishes like a beard which is shaved away each day only to reappear on the morrow.

One of the main sources of concern is the intense selfishness which I have developed. Day after day I think of nothing but myself. Anything that happens anywhere, whether in fact or merely in my imagination, is subjected to the one question: how does it affect me? I am constantly on the alert for signs of what is happening outside. I snatch at what I consider to be straws in the winds, trying to build a whole piece of fact from a gesture or voice inflexion, just as a scientist reconstructs a mammoth skeleton from one tiny chip of bone. More and more I cease to regard the world as something existing independently of myself. I am the centre of the universe. It is my fate that gives significance to destiny. Events have value only as they affect my imprisonment. The rational centre of my brain has not ceased to operate, but its effective influence diminishes, so that it acts more as an observer than as a regulator of my conduct. I am aware of my selfishness and disappointed at its grossness. I know on the one hand that it is largely a by-product of my isolation, and a reflection of the struggle my personality is subjected to in order to survive the assaults being made on it.

I am being starved of stimulation, so it is natural for anything and everything that comes within my ken to be devoured and incorporated into myself, just as famished children are said to eat sand to satisfy their body's mineral hunger. On the other hand I realise that there has to be some link between my subjective will to survive and the objective world of action, responsibility and ideas to which I have always belonged and which, though ever-receding, has never slipped completely from my mind. Unless my will to hold out is sustained by the ideas I have held for so long, it will die.

The problem is by no means academic. It affects the relationship between myself and my captors and is crucial to my morale in resisting their pressure for co-operation. My rational brain constructs an ideal of how I should behave. This ideal is built on the examples set by two heroes, Julius Fucik and Henri Alleg, who respectively were killed and tortured by the Nazis in Czechoslovakia and the French in Algeria. Each had smuggled out from their prisons stirring reports of their resistance. I have often recalled them, especially in the early days of my captivity. The perfect political prisoner, I have decided, not only resists the efforts of his jailers to force him to talk, but attacks the enemy. He demoralises the enemy with his defiance. He lets the enemy know that only death can destroy him, that he and his ideas are invincible, that when he dies another will take his place, and another and another, that resistance will never end.

I know I can never attain this ideal, partly because of my temperament, for by nature I am conciliatory rather than defiant, my manner is gentle, my demeanour quiet, but mainly because of the tremendous pressure for survival, which works against the high standards I would like to maintain. All my strength has to be marshalled for the purely defensive action of holding out. I feel that to challenge my captors with anything more than my refusal to answer questions and my apparent buoyancy, would so add to my burden as to precipitate my collapse with the result that I would be unable even to defend myself. Thus I am always friendly to the guards, warming to those who respond and turning the other cheek to those who are rude. I am never hostile to my interrogators. I have rejected the idea of a hunger strike because I feel it would weaken me to a point where I would sink below the threshold of resistance. I am, I suppose, charming and chatty—on the few occasions that I have the opportunity to speak to a policeman, my jokes are remembered. I study my jailors, seeing them as individual men, and speak to my captors on the basis that they are working men doing their duty, an unpleasant one, but still that is their job. Looked at from outside it might seem incredible that I try to please and impress the authors of my wretchedness, yet curious human relationships develop in these horrid circumstances. I have become so dependent on the men who bring me food, let me wash, let me exercise, switch my light on and off, that I try to establish the best possible relationships with them, consistent with the maintenance of my dignity. In this way it is possible over a period of time to dampen the hostility of the captors and to secure utilisation of what few facilities are available.

9 Fantasy

MY MIND GRAPPLES WITH MY EXTRAORDINARY EXISTENCE. I have no control over my circumstances, but I can describe and interpret them. There is at least this measure of mastery I have over my fate. Thoughts flit and tumble elusively. Over the days and over the weeks I develop certain ideas. They have no solidity: fragments of dreams and fantasies drift, eddy and disappear through my brain. One day it is a whole theme that presents itself, the next day a vision of people, the third day merely a word that repeats itself over and over like a radio advertisement. The scaffolding of my thought is weak but gradually it assumes a meaningful form. Occasionally I manage to grasp a piece of the hurtling emotions generated by my imprisonment. A new insight, a novel experience, a startling reinterpretation of an old theme—the material acquires volume and demands form.

I will write a book. What happens to me will be mere chapters in the story. This is a way of fighting back. The worse the things they do to me, the more interesting the book will be. The more I suffer, the deeper the experience, the richer the book.

Yet a book is too flat, too controlled, too wordy and abstract. It requires pencil and paper and calm surroundings. In a book the material of life is rolled flat and sliced up into two-dimensional pages. I want something better, more immediate, with live people standing up and voices sounding. I must be active. The audience must not be a scattered and remote readership, but a thronging crowd which hears me directly. Only their living presence can draw articulate expression from me. I crave a response, a communication with live people. My present world has too much shape and volume to be compressed into a book; it needs air and height. The cells are too sturdy and real to be crushed into the flatness of words. These cubes must stand, each with its human inhabitant. There are three of them, each separate from the other but standing in some sort of relationship to each other.

My story, if it is to be told, must be woven around these three pieces of existence. The starting point is three living sentient beings, each in a separate concrete capsule. In the central cube is an African man. In the cube at one side is a Coloured woman, and in the cube at the other is a White man, who is myself. In addition to being in that cube, I stand outside and walk from cube to cube explaining to the audience what is happening to the three persons.

I cannot control the destiny of these three people, for each has his or her own fate. I cannot even control the person who is me, he is also subject to his fate. What I can do is to penetrate the concrete walls and describe to the audience what is happening to each. I can make our prison alive to viewers throughout the world. If I work at it hard enough, I can enable the three trapped people to speak to men and women in cities of all continents. The experience that each of us is undergoing will not be isolated and buried in concrete. We will defeat those who try to seal us off from humankind. We ourselves will tell our story, but I must provide the structure.

How slow thought is when one is all alone. It is two weeks, fourteen separate days, before my mind arrives at a point which, had I been outside, it would have reached after ten minutes. I will write a play. A stage has volume, people standing up, people talking, and a live crowded audience. I get up off my mat, put on trousers and a shirt and walk to and fro in the cell, thrilled as I develop the project.

On the stage will be three apparently opaque cubes. As the play develops, each cube will light up to reveal its inhabitant. I visualise the cubes. Perhaps they will be on different levels, so as to emphasise our present spatial disorientation. My cell could go anywhere, at any time, a space-capsule floating above

93

the earth, or a submarine resting below the icecap. No, on second thoughts I think that all the cells must be on the same plane for we are all in the same prison and subjected to the same discipline, and though we may be separate personalities, kept apart from each other, we share the same fate. There is a gravity that tugs us all down to the same earth. The vision of the three cubes fades and my thoughts tumble away from the stage. I try vainly to direct them back to the play I will write. I wish it were easier for me to concentrate. I have so much time for thinking and such a wonderful subject to explore, yet all I can do now is say over and over to myself the words:

I must think about the play, the play, the play.

I had better leave it for now. Perhaps later this afternoon or tomorrow I will be able to resume play-constructing. It seems to hold much greater promise than writing a book.

It is a pity I know so little about the theatre. Yet I feel somehow that circumstance itself shapes for the stage the material of our present lives. I will select from the material, and an expert can do the trimming and joining necessary for a smooth and interest-arousing production.

Each day I retrieve some of the jetsam floating on my thoughts and incorporate it in the play. On some days I add very little, on others I construct whole scenes. Sometimes I am able to visualise the space, movement and lighting on the stage. On other occasions I hear the people speaking. Long pieces of dialogue sound in my mind. Frequently it is I who am speaking. In the background there is singing: a deep African bass voice provides a ground rhythm for the drama.

The play takes place on African soil. In the centre background Zollie sings right through the play. Before the curtain rises he is singing and when the audience leave their seats at the end to go home he is still singing. During the play the singing never stops. For the greater part it is muffled and distant, but at appropriate moments it swells out more loudly. From time to time the singer's cube is lit up and the singer is seen. Tall and bearded, Zollie sings straight out to the audience, while in front of him the story between the dark girl and myself is played out.

In the beginning the stage is dark. Three massive shapes

94

can be dimly noticed. I walk to the left hand side of the stage and sit on a step-ladder. I talk directly to the audience. This is a play, I tell them, written by the people you see on the stage. My voice is warm, urgent but controlled. (The idea is to make the situation as immediate as possible to the audience. It is not just Mr X whose fate is being depicted on the stage, it is the man you see before you. Everything you will see is true. We will recreate our story exactly as it happened.)

I tell them that on 1st October, 1963, as I was entering my office a plainclothes man placed me under arrest. I asked him what for and he said under the Ninety-Day law. Seven officers searched my Chambers and then I was locked up in a police cell. The spotlight on me fades and the right hand side of the stage lights up. First the cube is noticed then a human figure inside the cube. The figure is myself (either I myself will act the part or else someone can be made up to look like me). The figure moves around the cell getting the feel of his surroundings. He does not speak to the audience, but his thoughts can be heard. 'So this is what it's like,' he begins. As he feels and prods the walls and floor, so he describes his new environment and his reactions to it. He flushes the lavatory, commenting that the wire juts from a hole in the wall like a snake's tongue.

He has escape fantasies and thinks about time. He sits on a mat and stands again. Frequently he wonders whether or not he will be able to withstand the isolation. The thoughts described are generally of an immediate and impressionist nature. The completeness of the isolation will be emphasised as well as the bewilderment and shock that I recall from my first hours and days in this cell. The voice used can be pre-recorded, or the figure on the stage can carry a tiny portable microphone into which he whispers the thoughts. One of the most difficult things to get across to the audience will be the horror of prolonged inactivity and deprivation of external stimuli. It is no good merely telling them of the mental disintegration that follows from staring at a wall for hours on end. The best thing to do is to give them a wall to stare at.

I reappear at the side of the stage and explain the problem to the audience. We shall lower a screen on the front of the stage,

I tell them, to give you some idea of what it is like. You are asked to look at it and nothing else for the time it is there. Don't speak to anyone or look at your programmes, or the person sitting in front of you. Simply stare at this screen, I will say, we have our walls to stare at day after day, you will have it for only three minutes. I fade and the screen is dropped. For three minutes exactly there is complete silence in the theatre. The members of the audience are surprised at how long it takes for three minutes to pass. They notice how their concentration flags, how difficult it is to hold a train of thought. They receive some taste, from an emotional point of view, of what it is like for us.

The screen lifts (perhaps it is gauze specially lit to appear opaque) and my figure is seen in my cell. I am lying on the mat staring at the wall. Faint whistling can be heard. The 'Going Home' theme from the 'New World' Symphony is fluted as if from a great distance. I jump up and whistle back. The whistling is the first sound which has been heard in the theatre for a few minutes. This should heighten the audience's appreciation of the miracle-like quality which in fact attached to my first hearing the whistling, and then establishing communication with the whistler. The curtain falls and when it rises again the left hand side of the stage slowly lights up. Another cell is seen, and in it is the dark girl. She has already been in the prison for some time. Her thoughts too are spoken to the audience.

Her cell has a feminine appearance. Although it is bare the few articles in it clearly belong to a woman. The dark girl is busy pinning up her hair. She tries different styles and wonders what each looks like. Her thoughts on various subjects come out all the while.

In constructing this part of the play, I always have difficulty. I can think of the themes which probably pass through her mind, but not in the idiom and language of her thoughts. If and when she gets out, she will write her own part so that the detail will be authentic and the emotions true. She will describe her immediate reactions to being locked up, and how she has got through the days. Her reactions to my arrival will be stressed—how she feels about a young man being brought into her world, and her thoughts about the fact that the new prisoner is White. Her feelings will be ambivalent—all prisoners must stick together, but what the hell is that White man doing interfering in our liberation struggle. . . . Eventually she decides to whistle to me. She whistles the 'Going Home' theme several times and waits for a reply. Finally the response comes and the curtain falls for the second time.

After that the play gets vaguer and vaguer in my mind. This far I can visualise very distinctly. I see the cubes and the people and hear the words being spoken, especially my own; the drama is inherent in the situation. Though I cannot see the audience I am very much aware of their presence. They are alert and eager to see how the play develops. Yet from now on, having merely presented the characters and the scene, my progress in constructing the play is very slow. The ideas lose their living character, and become more and more bookish. I tell myself what themes will be unfolded, but have only glimpses of the characters through whom the themes will be revealed.

The character who is myself will be something of a philosopher. One of his main preoccupations is remarking again and again on the quality of human isolation. So this is what the extreme existentialists feel—each individual is separate, alone, encapsuled in himself. They go through life aware of this all the time, even when they are at the dinner table, walking past people in the street or making love. Such a man lying wrapped in the limbs of his lover is lonelier than I in this cell; his intimacy is less than mine is with the unknown whistler. These thinkers are wrong to generalise as they do. Man is not naturally isolated and alone; the crowd is not his enemy. If that were in fact so, solitary confinement would not affect one so viciously. It would be a release, a happiness. No, man is interdependent in his very depths. He disintegrates in isolation, but flourishes through association. The urge for love and communication is the strongest of all drives. The thin line of music that connects me with the unknown whistler is more valuable to me than my food.

How strange it is that I, in this cell physically cut off from humankind, am less alone than all those people who are free for their whole lives to roam the streets and come and go from houses and speak to whom they will. Human solidarity gives meaning and warmth to life. There is more to living than merely striving to meet with nobility a pitiless fate.

Courage is not an abstract virtue; it is a concrete expression of love. Communication is not only not impossible, it is the easiest, most natural activity available to man. How strange it is that with our primitive means—a glance, a whistle—we in our prison reach one another far more meaningfully than all those people who are free to write paragraph after paragraph and to talk through the night.

I will also from time to time refer to details of cell life. One scene will open with me wondering what has happened to my caterpillar. I will describe the draughts, the cleaning of the comb, and the writing with cheese on cardboard. My thoughts on living on the floor: that the chair deserves to be ranked in the history of humanity with fire and the wheel, that greater than mankind's ascent into space has been his ascent from the floor.

The middle portion of the play will consist of a dialogue between the dark girl and myself. Both cells will be lit up. We will speak our thoughts in turn. While I am speaking, she will mime her activities. Similarly, while she speaks, I will shake my blankets, sleep, do my exercises, play draughts, read, dance. . . . Our existences border on each other but do not correspond exactly. Some of what each of us thinks is purely personal and unrelated to the other. Yet a lot of the thoughts of each will be about the other, even addressed to the other. Thus I will speak of my feelings about the dark girl, just as she will have spoken about me in the second scene. Some of the thoughts will be boy-girl, some white-black, some political. Each of us will have a line of thought independent of the other. Our dialogue will at first seem strange and unconnected: when she is talking politics, I will speak of my caterpillar, when I am philosophical, she will be thinking about the fleas in her blankets. We will address each other at different times. At one stage I will be wondering about her prison regime and facilities. Later I will wish to tell her something about legal procedure and the importance of holding out against her interrogators. At completely different moments in the play she will wish she could let

98

me know some of the things she has learnt about the prison, and wonder about the law and whether it is worth while to stand up to her interrogators. By the end of this section it will be apparent that our thoughts have covered substantially the same ground. The audience will know why each of us has been arrested, what our differences are, and what ideas we have in common. A relationship of great strength will have been built up between us, even though we will not have said a word to each other. The mere knowledge of the presence of another prisoner will inspire each of us with love and courage. The occasional momentary sight of each other and the communication by whistling will give intensity and depth to the relationship.

It is impossible at present to speculate even about the final section of the play. That belongs to the future: our story has yet to be resolved. Somewhere in the play will appear my decision to prepare our drama for the stage. The audience will be told of my first thinking about writing a book and then deciding on a play (not a play within a play but a playwright within a play).

The play may well conclude with the person who is myself actually starting to write the play. He will describe how the idea develops in his mind. He will start by referring to the concept of the three cubes, each inhabited by a prisoner. In one cube will be himself, in the second Zollic, and in the third the dark girl. In the background singing will be heard. And so—he will tell the audience—by writing this play I combat my isolation and defeat the attempts of my jailers to break my mind.

Without knowing how my story will end, I cannot complete the play. I do not know even what note to strike. The ending must to some extent colour the direction of the whole drama. All I can do at this stage is to picture in my mind the scene and the characters. As our fate unfolds, so will I add to the play. At present the days pass uneventfully. Each day is as wretched as the last and as horrid as the one to come.

Three weeks have gone and I find that I am not adding much to the play. They can keep us here like this for a long time, but eventually they will have to do something to each of us. Perhaps the dark girl will break down and give evidence against her friends. Perhaps she herself will be charged. Perhaps some serious charge awaits me, but it is no use my speculating. The play can only be finished when our story is in fact ended. For the time being I must try to remember what has happened so far, and to write up in my mind the first scenes of our play.

The rest belongs to the future.

10 Reflections

THOUGH I NOTE WITH REGRET THAT I AM NOT AS STRONG as my heroes, I am not unduly put out by the fact that the relationships I am building with my captors involve some measure of compromise on my part. At all times I keep my head up high, and must appear to the police to be remarkably buoyant. Behave like a worm and you will be treated like a worm, I tell myself. So I never crawl or abase myself to them. What does worry me is how the other political prisoners might view my chattiness with the police. My primary loyalty is to my co-prisoners and even though I am never able to communicate with them, I know that my conduct and demeanour becomes known to them just as theirs eventually becomes known to me. I am very anxious to avoid any appearance of being favoured because of my white skin.

If I could have spoken to them I would have said: Yes, it's true that the police converse with me at times in a way they never would with a non-White, and it's true that at last they've given me clean blankets, and it's true that they always want to let me have the big yard for exercise. But when I speak to them and make jokes, it's not only for myself, it's for all of us. It softens the atmosphere in the whole prison, and it shows them that we are bigger and more tolerant than they, that we can take it with a better grace than that with which they can dish it out. And note, I leave the blankets outside in the morning so that you can see them and ask for equality of treatment—I can be a lever to prise out better conditions for all of us. As for the exercise, well, you must have seen how I voluntarily go to the small yard so that you can have the big one. The choice of yards is an infliction rather than a blessing for it means I naturally always exercise it in favour of the small yard so that I have less than my share of the big yard. The only value to me of having the choice is that I can make this little solidarity gesture to you. Of course, I am favoured because of my white skin, and because of my standing as an advocate, but the favours are extended to all. Thus you all share in the extra food, you also get those few minutes added to exercise time, and when they come to switch off my light at a fixed hour, instead of whenever convenient to them, they switch yours off too. None of these extras came to me automatically—I had to push hard to get them.

There are many problems which beset a White person who joins in the non-White emancipatory movement. They arise from the fact that while he struggles against racial privilege, in his daily life he enjoys many of the amenities denied to non-Whites. This conflict pursues him even into the depths of prison and, when he is in a state of extreme loneliness, can be the source of considerable pain to him, especially as he will be virtually helpless to do anything to remedy the situation.

A not unconnected problem which causes me much anxiety revolves around the question of violence. Most non-Whites have for many years believed that the use of violent methods to achieve their liberation is legitimate. Their political leaders persuaded them that they should first examine and try every avenue of non-violent activity. By about 1962, however, the Government had, in word and deed, made it plain that it was determined to defend apartheid with the gun. Heavy penalties, including whippings, made passive resistance, strikes and boycotts ineffective as means of bringing about change, though they could provide powerful support for more direct challenges. While Africans throughout the rest of Africa were increasingly becoming masters of their own fate, in South Africa they were subjected to ever more burdensome legislation. All active African political organisations and leaders were banned, their newspapers closed down and meetings forbidden. No agitation was to be allowed. In the meantime the armed national struggle in Algeria was nearing victory, and open warfare had broken out in Angola. In South Africa itself Africans in a number of rural

102

areas had openly resisted Government measures, killing Government appointees and destroying Government property, whilst the African workers, in the locations sprawled along the outskirts of the cities, tired of being harried and beaten every time they tried non-violent activity angrily demanded counter-attack against the Government. The need for non-violence was no longer referred to, and bomb explosions throughout the country announced the start of a new phase of South African political life.

I have always loathed violence. From early schooldays I would be the one to break up fights and mediate between disputants. Violence might get rid of obstacles, but it did not solve problems. Yet I have never been a pacifist, intellectually I have accepted the right to use violence in self-defence, to smash the Nazi invaders, to force colonialists to release their grip. Imprisonment is a form of violence and even in socially advanced countries is obviously necessary, in some degree, for the foreseeable future as a means of dealing with serious anti-social conduct. Is it cowardice then that makes me recoil at the prospect of one day being called upon to kill and destroy? Not entirely so, of that I am sure. Nor is it, as many Africans would have it, that a White man can not be expected to kill another White man. It is simply that I find it difficult to hate any man, let alone kill him. What emotional sympathy I possess would in fact favour an African rather than a White on the ground that the Africans, at least historically, have justice on their side. If ever I am forced into the trenches I have no doubts as to which side I will be on. Yet I almost envy the Africans their simple and direct anger and their straightforward determination to thrust aside the human barriers to their liberty.

As I lie on the mat in my cell I think over these ideas in relation to the personæ of my restricted world: the police, the other prisoners, and myself. The more I get to know the policemen, the more difficult it is to contemplate ever trying to kill them. How surprised each one would be to know that as he bends to place my food on the floor I am wondering how I would feel if I plunged a knife into his back and, as he turns to go, I am speculating on whether I would ever be able to fire bullets into his body or crush his skull with some sort of club, or tear holes in his chest with explosives. I think too of the grief of his family. Then I ask myself how the African prisoner across the yard would think. His hatred would have started early in childhood with the first time the police burst into his home at night, searching for residence documents or for liquor, humiliating his parents and terrifying him before they moved on like invaders to the house next door. A hundred subsequent encounters involving himself or family or neighbours or friends would have reinforced this feeling. As the self-declared guardians of White supremacy, the police would have to be crushed and dispersed before the White supremacy could ever be destroyed. It was the police who beat and shot the people when they demonstrated. If, in the course of the struggle for African freedom, he were to kill a policeman he would be a hero in the eyes of his family, friends, neighbours and associates. Nobody was forced to join the police force and if someone chose to do so he must bear the consequences. No sympathy should be spared for the policeman's family, which happily enjoyed all the benefits of White privilege; it is more important to think of the African families whose parents are separated through the policeman's actions, whose fathers are kept underpaid through his actions. It is he or his colleagues who have been responsible for torturing African people, tying bags over their heads, running electric currents through their bodies, forcing them to drink water and then kicking their stomachs. The whole world knows who is right and who is wrong.

Is my squeamishness, I wonder, merely a cover for the fear that I myself might be killed, and is my lack of hate and anger due merely to the fact that I have never suffered directly from the indignities of apartheid, and what deprivations I have known have been voluntarily endured? It is perhaps fortunate for me, when one considers my moral difficulties, that I have never been called upon to join any active resistance group. I have, however, defended alleged saboteurs in Court, and have tried to explain to as wide an audience as possible why it is that a great section of a people has swung over from a policy of non-violence to one of violence. I have also from public platforms announced that I would go to jail rather than carry a gun for apartheid, expressing the hope that many other Whites would follow my example. I have often warned Whites that their refusal to meet and negotiate with the leaders of the non-Whites was leading the country to disaster, and judging by the Afrikaans press, I must have particularly scandalised a large number of Whites by stating what seems to me to be an obvious fact, namely that in the event of a showdown the Africans must triumph in the end.

Despite the long time I spend in reflection on the matter, I never seem to arrive at any firm conclusion. Looking to the future, I am convinced that the coming years will bring increasing hostility culminating in extremely sharp and widespread clashes. The only role I can see myself filling is that of a propagandist on the side of the Africans appealing to the Whites to lay down arms and negotiate. I would be able to do this with enthusiasm because this would help reduce not only African losses, but also the extent of destruction, both human and physical, in the country that the new Government would ultimately take over. It would be to the benefit of all if the Whites could be persuaded that they stood to gain more by submitting to multi-racial majority rule than by fighting it out to the bitter end. Though it seems inevitable that the greater part of the persuasion will come from the physical effort of a generation of African patriots resorting to armed struggle, I feel that realistic psychological propaganda could be of considerable supplementary value. At times I look even further into the future, and shudder a little at the thought of one day possibly being charged with the responsibility of locking men up just as I and so many others are being locked up now. May I never have to judge men and mete out punishment. Of one thing I am quite certain, and that is that I could never sanction prolonged solitary confinement as a method of punishment or of gaining information, no matter how desperate the situation.

11 Rondo

'GOODBYE, EVERYONE.' I AM IN THE CHARGE OFFICE, standing next to my belongings which are piled up on the counter. Behind the pile are two sergeants and four constables, who have crowded forward to watch my departure.

'I don't know where they are taking me, but all I hope is that wherever I go, the men there are as decent to me as you have been.' Whenever I see these policemen I have this curious urge to win their approval. To be quite honest, although the conditions for prisoners here are far more primitive than I had ever imagined they could be, the station is run with surprising efficiency. There are frequent inspections by senior officers, and the station commander seems to maintain effective discipline over his men. It would be dangerous to underestimate the South African police. Yet in the field of human relations these policemen could hardly be worse. They seem to make a point of abusing prisoners. Judging from the sounds I hear, some handle prisoners roughly, and nearly all of them yell at their captives. Only a small minority seem to show any measure of respect for the dignity of those in their charge. To me some have been harsher than others, but on the whole they have not been too bad. Perhaps they enjoy having an advocate under their control.

'It hasn't been a holiday camp,' I continue, 'in fact, this has been the worst time of my life. But I know you were just carrying out your instructions and that it wasn't you who made the Ninety-Day law.' It is a long time since I have addressed so many people in a group. They are listening with friendly attention. It is all so odd. Here I stand pale and tall in my suit,

106

wearing my white going-out shirt, open necked at the collar (they still refuse to let me wear my tie), and with my wrists pinioned in front of me by tight steel handcuffs. My hands are pale, my hair long, wavy and black. I must be the very picture of a political prisoner. In front of me is the station commander. He and his men have all paused in their work and I am now addressing them. I am making a farewell speech, and they are listening to me as though I were an officer retiring from the service, or being transferred to a new post.

'I hope you don't have too many of us Ninety-Day prisoners coming here to take up so much of your time,' I conclude. 'Goodbye, then, I hope the next time I come here it will be in my professional capacity and not as a prisoner. Goodbye.' The men do not actually applaud, but their farewells are hearty.

'Goodbye Mr Sachs.'

'Goodbye Mr Sachs.'

'Goodbye Mr Sachs.'

When the chorus dies down, the station commander takes a step back and raises his right hand in a half gesture of salute.

'Goodbye Mr Kruger,' I say to him, relieved that he has saluted, for I am not keen to shake the hand of my chief jailer. (What is the etiquette, I wonder, for manacled prisoners taking their leave?)

I take my bag off the counter, and walk to the White special branch sergeant who is waiting for me outside. It was ten minutes ago that he arrived at my cell to tell me to pack my things as quickly as possible.

'Where am I going?' I asked.

'You'll see,' he said. When I wanted to know whether handcuffs were really necessary he said those were his instructions. Now he is waiting impatiently for me to follow him. He curtly instructs the African special branch man with him to carry the rest of my stuff. Quick to be obedient, the African gathers my remaining belongings. Under close guard I step out of the charge office into a little lane that leads to the reception yard. Behind me walks the African bearing my most treasured belongings— a pile of soft blue blankets, some sheets and an air-mattress which, to my joy, I received the other day. A more kindly

107

magistrate had promised to discuss my request for clean, flea-less bedding with the colonel, and that same afternoon the bedding had arrived. So it had not been necessary to consult the Minister after all!

Although the manacles are uncomfortable and degrading, I enjoy my walk to the yard. The map I scratched on the wall was all wrong; it does not matter now. The area of my world increases a dozenfold with each step I take. Wherever they take me, things cannot be worse than they have been so far. The sun is shining and, although I am still enclosed by concrete surroundings, I am aware of a giant blue sky overhead. When we reach the yard my belongings are thrown into the back of a covered steel van, and I am ordered to climb in after them. The doors are closed and I sit locked inside.

It is dark, as though I am in the stomach of a whale. With difficulty I can see through the front where a glass panel covered with thick metal mesh separates me from the police in the driving cab. The sergeant and his African subordinate take their seats in the cab and the engine starts up. Brm—brm—the sound vibrates through the belly of the vehicle, drowning out the conversation of the two in front. The van reverses and suddenly moves forward. I am thrown off my seat but quickly resume my place and press my face against the glass.

With so many new colours and shapes, sounds and movements, vistas and expanses about I must not miss a thing. In a moment we will be out of the police station.

Goodbye Maitland. Goodbye Zollie. Goodbye Dorothy. I'm sorry I couldn't whistle you a farewell but I didn't know they were going to take me away to-day. Please be brave. Wherever I am taken I will think of you. One day, perhaps, we will meet in freedom, and hug each other. Until then goodbye. Goodbye Dorothy, goodbye Zollie.

We are in the street now. I can see ahead for hundreds of yards. Yes, for the first time in twenty-three days I have a view that is unobstructed for hundreds of yards. My eyes delight in looking at the long pavements and the tall lamp posts stretching into the distance. We are in a back street between the main road and the railway line—brm—brm. The van goes into a lower gear as it climbs the bridgeway that crosses the railway line. The sound is rich and exciting, a roar of movement, a clarion of activity. We are on the great new freeway: cars speed by, vast lush fields of green stretch on either side. I see trees, their tall swollen curves silhouetted against the wide pale sky. In the distance looms Table Mountain, a solid colossus, with the crags and broken lines which nature imparts to its structures. Glorious golden daisies glow in dazzling flower patches that flank the road and separate the lanes. There on the left is a pool of water in which white birds stand. Grey, black, salmon pink—cars of all colours and shapes whizz by. We enter a built up area. The houses, with their walls of cream and their roofs red in the sun, look sedate and warm. They have windows and gardens, and low green hedges. Often their gates are open. I see a small brown dog, and there are some children in tidy multi-coloured clothes. In front of us a car is dawdling: woman driver! Next to her on the front seat is a jumble of groceries, and in a carrycot at the back sits an infant waving his fists. With an exciting rush of speed we overtake the car and the van accelerates along the well-banked curves of the expressway. Where can we be heading? Will they take me to the airport and fly me to Pretoria, where the first Ninety-Day prisoner to die was found hanged in his cell? He too had come from Cape Town. We have stopped at a traffic light. How ordered and civilised all these drivers are. They stop when the light is red and move when it is green. A coloured nursemaid wheels a blue-grey pram across the road. On the corner to the left stands a grocery shop, bright and ugly with advertisements. The light is orange and now green. We surge forward and I press my hands against the panel to prevent myself from toppling. Are they taking me to Court? Anything would be better than being on my own again. They can charge me with treason, sabotage, anything they like. Only let me come out into the open again, where I can see my accusers, where I can speak to the world, and where there is some sort of law and some sort of rules. Cars dash past. Treelined avenues lead off on either side into a vast suburbia of houses and side-streets. Perhaps they are taking me to another cell, or they are going to put me on an

identification parade, but then why take all my stuff along . . .
or perhaps—dare I hope—they are going to release me, but then
why the handcuffs? The people on the pavements do not even
look at us as we pass. Their clothing, especially the dresses of
the women, is so colourful that I almost gasp as we shoot by.
How casual these people are, idling along, not in a hurry, each
walking freely neither ordering others nor being told where to
go. They are not even curious to look inside the van to see who
is being conveyed past them.

They do not know that this van is really a mobile cage
carrying a Ninety-Day detainee along this road. It is obvious
from the carefree way they stroll that they are not even thinking
of prisoners. But it does not matter, people, I am not cross with
you. You do not know that this is I, a Ninety-Day prisoner who
has already spent more than three weeks in solitary confinement,
who am being carried past you. And if you did know, you
would not pause for long: for how can you, who have never set
foot in the cruel world into which we have been flung, possibly
appreciate the horror of our lives. One day, perhaps, I will
write it all down. Maybe you will read it then, and wonder if
you perhaps were in the road that day in 1963 when a police
van drove by with a prisoner in it.

PART TWO

Wynberg

The Station Commander

12 The Centre Bar

UGLY BROWN WALLS SURROUND ME, AND OUTSIDE THE noise is violent. I lie on a bed, I am wretched and jangled. So this is my new cell. It is oblong-shaped, like a loaf of bread, the dirty brown paint extends from the floor to a line six feet up and above that the wall is white. Rather, I should say, it was white before countless prisoners scrawled their filth on it.

My bed is to one side, on my right is a long bunk that stretches the length of one of the short walls. On my left is a washbasin with running water, cold, and next to that in the corner is the lavatory. In front of me looms a massive steel door which when opened leads on to a tiny yard. High above the door are three glazed windows, heavily barred and covered with a thick metal mesh. In some ways my facilities have improved—I have a bed, a bunk and running water. But the cell is so ugly, and the yard outside so small. I long for the mat on the floor, for my old cell.

It took me a long time to get to know my prison-world at Maitland: its geography, its time-rhythm, its personnel, and especially its prisoners. Now I have to start all over again. Here everyone shouts at me and even after they have locked me in the shouting continues outside. The din is unbearable. Droves of mumbling and shuffling prisoners are constantly being shunted from one passage to the next, doors are slammed, engines rev violently. Policemen scream harshly at the prisoners, volleying curse after curse at them for being too slow, or being too fast.

I suppose the Court proceedings must be over. The police

113

station in which I am now lodged is at the back of the Wynberg magistrate's court buildings. The prisoners convicted during the course of the day, as well as those whose cases have been postponed and who have been refused or cannot afford bail, are being sorted out and dispatched to their various prisons. A nearby door is constantly opened and then slammed, and this is done with such violence that a tremble runs through my cell. I hear a series of loud metallic raps. Heavy steel key-rings clatter; a child is crying; a voice screeches hysterically and subsides to a moan, and then soars again with raging self-pity and anguish. The sounds are merged and cacophonous, and I shudder and tremble inwardly as though I am being physically assaulted by the noise. My eyes travel around the walls. Previous inhabitants have hurled their aggression on every inch where they could reach. The violence of their scribblings on the interior of my cell matches the hideous din outside.

My senses are being crushed by this harsh new world. I am horrified at my lack of resilience. Gust after gust of misery blows through me.

Be patient, I tell myself, it takes time to adjust to a new place. Perhaps after I have been here a while the warders will stop shouting at me. Day by day I will explore and map this strange universe, penetrating the chaos with my ears and eyes, building up an ordered existence out of bits of information the guards may let slip from time to time.

A loud tapping coming through the far wall causes me to sit up as though I have been shocked. There it is again, a vigorous tattoo of taps. I move over to the wall and slap it with my hand. There is no response. I slap again, harder and harder. Still no response. A battered tin mug stands in the basin. I pick it up and tap softly. No answer. I tap in different rhythms, wait, and then bang furiously. The general row outside continues but at the wall all is quiet.

I return to the bed. My nerves are exposed like electric wires pulled out of their sockets. My emotions have fallen apart, disintegrated. Now I hear whistling. Someone is whistling near my cell. I stand up and whistle back, at first softly, then boldly. I whistle the 'Going Home' theme, Beethoven's Fifth,

114

an African song, one, two, three pop tunes. The whistler out-side carries on with his repetitive melody. Suddenly the whist-ling stops. A voice barks out an order. The whistling resumes. It was a policeman! Probably the tapping I heard was also that of a policeman, perhaps smacking his pipe against the wall. I have no friends here, only enemies.

Waves of prisoners sweep back and forth. Now I am truly alone. The wash of humanity around my cell emphasises my loneliness without assuaging it. The fact that they have gone to the trouble of moving me here means that they plan to keep me for a long time. Never in my life have I felt such unhappiness.

The yard door is being opened. The locks to my door are unfastened and I stand up and face the doorway. As the door swings open a tall policeman enters. He is elderly, roundfaced and balding, his body appears to bend backwards, as though it is still sustaining a vast belly which has been reduced by dieting. There is something strange about him which I cannot place.

'Have you got all your stuff?' he barks at me. His voice is metallic and harsh, like a loudspeaker at a fair. It is also heavily accented. I am bewildered by his question. What stuff does he mean? He shouts out the question again. 'All the stuff you brought from Maitland, have you got it all here?'

'I hope so,' I tell him. My things lie in a jumble on the bunks. I cannot focus properly. I feel completely disorientated. I hardly remember what things I had in my other cell. The pile looks about the right size, but at the moment I am too dazed and upset to work out if everything is there.

'You people always come along afterwards and complain that your stuff is missing and then you blame us,' the man says sharply. 'You must tell me now, have you got all your stuff?'

'It seems to be all here, but I'll make sure just now.' I speak politely, barely maintaining control. 'I don't think you'll find me a troublesome prisoner.'

'You'd better not be.'

'To whom, may I ask, am I speaking?'

'I'm Warrant Officer Snyman. This is my station here, I am the station commander. You will be under my control and I don't want any nonsense from you.'

'You can ask the people at Maitland, I try not to cause any unnecessary trouble.'

'I'm not interested in Maitland. This is Wynberg. Now, for the last time, have you got all your stuff?'

I go over to my belongings and start to separate them. My hands move the items and I pretend to be taking stock of what there is but I cannot concentrate. All I know is that I must make some show of co-operation if I am to satisfy the station commander, who is clearly intent on some gesture of submission.

'I can't think of anything that's missing,' I say eventually.

'Yes, well don't come along afterwards with a lot of lies.'

I pause to allow my anger to subside. 'I take it I get three meals a day here,' I say.

'Well, what do you expect? Do you want us to make special food for you?'

'May I ask when I get my exercise time?'

'Whenever we can find the time. We're very busy here, and can't worry about you all the day long.'

'In Maitland . . .'

'I've told you I'm not interested in Maitland. I'm interested in here. If that's all, then I'll be going.'

'Just one more thing, please. Does my mother know I've been moved here? She'll be very worried if she goes to collect my washing in Maitland and they don't give her anything.'

'That's got nothing to do with me.'

He turns round and slams the door. As he leaves I realise what it was that made his appearance strange. Although he wore full uniform, he was bareheaded. He is the first uniformed policeman I have seen not wearing his cap. He is also the rudest. No wonder the men under him are so unpleasant. And to think that he is the person to whom I must make my complaints and requests.

I sit down on the bed. Outside the din continues. The obscenities high on the wall are as thick and menacing as a plague of flies. My head is dizzy. I feel I want to lie down and block out the world but as soon as I stretch out my body and lay my head down I feel worse. I stand up and walk around looking for

116

something on which to focus. I am overcome with lassitude. A great fatigue settles on me and I rest myself on the bed again. For how much longer is this to go on? Twenty-three days have passed. I am not even a third of the way to my first ninety days. I thought it might become easier as the days went by, but now I realise how fragile the self-control was which I built up at Maitland. I am fragmented, bereft. I am going down, down. Can it be that I have not touched bottom yet, that there is worse to come?

Another ninety days, and then another. They will close in on me, move me around all the time, perhaps even subject me to physical violence. Is this what I was born for? I cannot give way, yet for how long can I endure this? If it continues to get worse, if they take me in for another ninety days . . .

I look carefully at the window above the door. The centre bar is planted solidly in the wall. It is a relief to know that a girdle or piece of sheet could be tied round that bar. It should easily hold my weight should it become necessary.

13 Interrogation

'YOU REALISE THAT YOU FACE A CHARGE WHICH CARRIES the death sentence.' Captain Rossouw's face is stern, his manner brisk and hard as he threatens me. We are sitting around a table in the station commander's office. The captain opposite me and Lieutenant Wagenaar sitting to my right. 'You must know that your position is very serious indeed. You face the death sentence.'

I sit impassively, but feel my adam's apple twitch. I hope they did not see it.

'We can make no promises, but if you make a full statement, tell us everything you know, we can put it up to the Attorney-General with our recommendation. Now will you tell us what you know?' The captain glowers at me.

'My position remains the same,' I reply.

'What is that?'

'I am not prepared to answer questions. Take me to Court and I will answer all the questions you want.'

'You realise that your life might be at stake?'

'If you think you've got a case against me, then bring me to Court.'

'Look it makes no difference to us but it can make all the difference to you. The Attorney-General will have to decide, but we will make a recommendation which might help you.'

'My position remains the same.'

'What have you got to gain from sitting here like this simply repeating the same thing over and over again?'

'I am not prepared to say anything which might have the result of landing myself or anyone else in further trouble.'

118

'So you admit that you know things?'

'I admit nothing of the sort. Possibly I know something which as far as I am concerned is quite innocent, but which might be the piece you need to complete your jigsaw puzzle. Then you will use it to put someone else into this hell. No, I'd rather suffer here for the rest of my life than have that on my conscience.'

'I don't understand you. All the others are talking, and yet you keep quiet. We've got plenty of statements from others, we can show them to you if you like.'

'Really, captain, what do you think I am that I would be impressed by that kind of thing. You think I'm some sort of . . . skollie that you've picked up on the street corner? I'm not interested in what anyone else has said. I know what my attitude is.'

The captain looks perplexed. The lieutenant laughs and explains that the captain is from Pretoria and doesn't know what a skollie is, it's a Cape Town word.

'I'm not some cheap crook who would be frightened by your talk of statements by others,' I explain. Actually I feel indignant. That he should try such an elementary trick on me!

'What is your attitude?' the lieutenant now asks.

'I'm not prepared to answer questions, for a number of reasons.'

'What are your reasons?'

'Well, for one thing, how could I ever face anyone again if I bought my freedom at the expense of someone else's?'

'If you tell us everything you know, then no one outside of the police need know. We promise you complete secrecy.'

Again I feel indignant. 'If I had anything to say I'd rather say it openly than in secret. Why, that would be worse. What kind of a person do you think I am?'

'If you don't want to be a witness, we promise you that you won't be called to give evidence.'

I say nothing. These men are rats, they deny me even my honour.

'Don't you trust us? If we give our word as senior police officers, you can be sure that we will keep it.'

119

'It's got nothing to do with that. I trust that you will honour what you say, but I don't trust what you would do with any statement I might make.'

'Look here,' the captain resumes the interrogation. He is intimate, confiding. 'You can be out of here tomorrow.' He bangs his hand on the table. 'Yes, tomorrow,' he repeats.

'If I do what?'

'If you tell us everything you know.'

'I'm not prepared to make a statement.'

'It would be worth your while to speak out.'

'What have I got to gain?'

'Well, that depends on what you tell us.'

'No. I'm not trying to bargain with you. It would be against my honour to make a statement, and that is that. No decent person would do so in my position.'

'One would think that any person worried about his honour would realise that it was his duty to assist the police in detecting crime. He would try to help protect the State, and not help those who undermine it.'

The argument proceeds back and forth. The captain does most of the talking for their side, but every now and then the lieutenant jumps in to support him. They are sarcastic, confidential, hectoring, indignant. Above all, they are tough. This is a no-nonsense interrogation. They interrupt me, and jeer at me. They pretend that they are about to leave, and then fling a new volley of questions at me. They are intense, driving, relentless. I am slightly exhilarated, but feel a great physical exhaustion overcoming me. I notice that they are starting to repeat themselves, that they have lost their inventiveness. They have to struggle to continue, yet do not wish to let me alone. For my part, I wish they would stop their verbal punishment, yet I do not want them to leave. If only we three could just sit here and talk in friendly fashion about something non-controversial, just person to person. I repeat my refrain, I'm not prepared to answer questions. I'm not prepared to make any statement. I appreciate your spending so much time with me, but you're wasting your time. My position remains the same. I'm not prepared to answer questions. In some ways it is easier for me—I need give only the

120

one reply each time, while they constantly have to think up fresh lines of approach.

'It's a quarter past one already,' a new harsh voice suddenly interrupts. We all look up to see the station commander standing in the doorway. 'We have to have our lunch, you know,' he booms out to the captain. 'Will you still be long?' He gate-crashes the group, and the tension breaks.

'No, we were just going,' the captain seems relieved at the interruption.

The questioning is over. It lasted several hours. They told me definitely that they have enough evidence to charge me with a capital offence. I'll cross that bridge when it comes to me. Yet why were they so keen for me to do a deal with them? They want to use me for something. If they've got evidence which they think they can use to get a conviction against me, then sooner or later they will have to bring me to trial. I must hold out until I get to Court.

My legs are unsteady as I walk down the corridor and back in my cell I pace round and round for a long time before I can sit down to eat my lunch. The food is cold, but I hardly notice what I am eating. I see myself, in fantasy, in the witness box facing my accusers. I answer them firmly, speaking in the direction of the judge. The crowded court is impressed.

14 Reflections

I HAVE BECOME QUITE ALARMED AT THE FACT THAT ALTHOUGH there are people outside who might love me, there is nothing of mine which can carry on without my being there. In particular I long for children, who would be a part of me that would grow irrespective of what might happen to me. My children would be the answer to my captors who wished to annihilate me. At times I grow quite morbid as I contemplate my younger brother and me, neither having married, both being wiped out at an early age, my brother on the operating table and I through the activities of the present South African rulers. It may well be that loneliness, like pain, can never be properly compared. I feel, however, that my loneliness is greater than that of prisoners who have wives and children. I have always been sceptical of the theory that unmarried people should be able to cope more easily with imprisonment than those with families. Thinking of your children can be as much a source of support as it can be of worry. People who worry will always find something on which to fix their anxiety, whether it be having children or not having children. People who search for a source of support, on the other hand, cannot make just anything serve the purpose: there must be something real and growing, that has an existence independent of themselves, that will carry on no matter what happens to them. My longing for children stems basically perhaps from an unconscious attempt to resist the efforts of the police to extinguish my personality. Yet I do genuinely feel that if I had a wife and children I would be in a far better position to cope with my solitude. As the days pass it becomes increasingly difficult for me to think coherently about any sub-

122

ject. I find it easier to make up situations belonging to the future than to recollect with clarity past happenings. A major preoccupation is what I will do if I am ever released. The key problem is whether or not to leave the country. This problem has worried me for years prior to my detention. Keen to get rid of 'White agitators' the Government would not prevent my departure, subject to the condition that I never returned. The pressures to leave have been tremendous, but I have felt it would have been a betrayal of myself and my associates had I run away merely because the going had become difficult and dangerous. Nothing has happened to justify my leaving; on the contrary South Africa is my Spain, and the harder things become, the greater the challenge. It is a question of loyalty both to people and to principles. With each crisis a further wave of anti-apartheid Whites has quit South Africa. Some have been sent abroad by the political movements in South Africa, but more have, in effect, deserted and run. Their decision was understandable, but can not be justified or excused.

Fairly early on during my imprisonment I decided that should I ever be released, I would leave South Africa. This was a tremendous decision for me personally, not only because of its import, but because of the manner in which it was made, namely by myself alone and not after collective discussion and decision. In any political movement a certain measure of discipline is required, but more important, the persons belonging to such movements must never forget their responsibility towards each other and the cause they wish to advance. Where such movement is up against a Government as powerful and determined as that ruling South Africa, the responsibility is even greater. Personal problems become acute, and the temptation becomes strong to give way to considerations of immediate self-interest. Ingenious rationalisations, involving appeals to a range of fine principles, can always be relied upon by way of excuse for what is in essence a selfish and cowardly action. Balanced discussion gives way to gossip and recriminations, while honesty of purpose is replaced by opportunism.

The right thing to do is to stay and fight to the end. Inside prison I have decided that I am not strong enough to do what I know to be right. The prospect of never-ending punishment is more than I can face. I will see my solitary confinement through to the end properly, I will never betray anyone, I will stick to my principle and refuse to answer questions, even if it means endlessly prolonged agony. If necessary I will die rather than give in. In order to protect the ideas and people at the centre of my thoughts I will endure almost anything, certainly death and possibly even torture.

Without doubt I prefer the horror of continuous isolation and the terror of an early death to the shame of a life bought with betrayal. But without doubt, too, I feel that should I survive this imprisonment I will desert the field.

Negative considerations, such as the avoidance of shame and defeat, provide more powerful support for resistance in my case than positive ideology. I do not feel that holding out is noble and glorious; I do feel that to give way is dishonourable. To sustain myself I need a positive reward however. The mere fact of doing the right thing is insufficient, as is the expectation of approval from those whose opinions mean most to me. Weakness of character makes me demand for myself the prospect of a happy ending in the personal sense. I dream of peace, and of children. This can only be attained outside South Africa. Accordingly the bonds of discipline and responsibility have snapped, and I have decided on my own that, come my release I will quit the country. I feel ashamed of this decision, but it does provide some relief for me during the periods of greatest suffering, for I feel that the greater my suffering the less unjustified my quitting will be. Prolonged solitary confinement, with its consequences on my health and career, could provide some measure of excuse for leaving, nothing else could do.

A happy ending, peace and children. These have become poles around which my thoughts rotate. In imagination I woo and marry a South African girl living in London with whom I have corresponded for some while. She is rich, beautiful, fairly sensitive and not very committed. The richness I forgive her, to the extent that it guarantees her independence. She will love me sufficiently to respect my committedness, as I will respect the world of aesthetics which is central to her existence. Life

with her becomes the counterpoint to the life I am leading.
The greater my desolation, the more I transport myself in fantasy to London. I travel with her to Algeria, where I write a
book on the Algerian Revolution, to Northern Rhodesia (Zambia) where I edit a newspaper, and back to Europe where I start
up a magazine similar to *Encounter* but with a left wing spirit and
containing the writings of young radicals and revolutionaries
from both East and West. I continually weave fantasies around
her, at the same time suppressing obstructive memories and
glossing over points of incompatibility. In the early days,
when my fantasy apparatus was not working well, and when my
values came closest to collapse, I turned in my mind for support
to someone much nearer physically, a girl saintly in her goodness
and generosity. The memory of her courage and spirit helped
tide me over the critical early period, just as the prospect of a
quiet and peaceful happiness with the girl in London has assisted
me in coping with the onerous days that have followed.

15 The Station Commander

WHY CAN'T HE LEAVE ME ALONE? EVERY DAY NOW HE comes to provoke me. Surely as station commander he has better things to do than to pick a quarrel with one of his prisoners. There he stands, with his open jacket and loose belt. He carries a tin plate which contains my supper—the usual meat ball, pumpkin and mealie-rice. Perhaps his harshness covers a greater humanity than the dour and correct station commander at Maitland possessed. In books it would be like that, the tough, unpleasant commander turning out to have a warm heart underneath it all. Yet for all I can observe, neither his heart nor his food is warm.

He puts the plate down on the bunk.

'Where's your mug?' he asks in his rasping voice. I bring the mug to him; it is dented and stained.

'I know that a White man shouldn't have a mug like that,' he says. 'When I took over here five years ago I was shocked to see that the White prisoners also had to eat out of tin plates and mugs, so I bought five proper cups out of my own money for them,' he pauses. 'You know what happened?'

It's obvious what happened, I want to tell him. The ungrateful prisoners broke them all. Instead of doing this, I shake my head and say:

'No, what happened?'

'They bust them all within a week. That was how grateful they were. Look at that stain on the wall.'

I look at a wild splash of brown on the upper portion of the wall. It has the vigour of an action painting, but it always

126

depresses me, as though it is a perpetual dark cloud lowering at me.

'That stain came from a girl who threw her coffee at the wall. They break the light and the windows. We've had to fix the lavatory I don't know how many times. Anything they can get their hands on they destroy. That's all they know, how to break things. Then they come here and complain that we don't treat them properly.' He looks accusingly at me as he pours coffee from a kettle into my mug. I notice that there is a Coloured policeman standing behind and carrying another plate of food as well as a piece of paper containing half a dozen slices of bread. That must mean that there is another Ninety-Day prisoner somewhere in these cells. The bread will be for the ordinary prisoners.

'There's a woman outside who says she will send in whatever food you want. Aren't you satisfied with the food you've been getting?'

'Mr Snyman, I'm sure you would like me to speak quite honestly with you.'

'Yes, man, speak out from your heart.'

'Well, to tell you the truth, the food I've been getting is quite good, there's plenty of it and so on, but it's a bit more starchy than I'm used to.' Try as I would to praise his wife's fare, I cannot bring myself to do so.

'What's wrong with starch? A good plate of porridge in the morning sets you right for the day. The old Bantu at the back, he doesn't complain about the food, he's very happy with it.'

'I'm sure it's much better than he was able to have at home,' I reply.

The station commander blushes. It occurs to me that the Afrikaners and the Africans have not unsimilar diets, though the Africans can hardly ever afford meat while the Afrikaners eat large quantities of it. He would be horrified if I pointed out that the African could better appreciate his wife's cooking than I.

'Mmmm . . . too much starch, hey? Anyhow, you're entitled to food from outside, and I'll make arrangements for you to get it. I see you've got the Bible there. Do you read it?'

127

'Oh yes, every day.'

'Well, you must read the Bible. It's all there. You think you are in trouble, well, read the Bible and you will understand. You don't think I understand you,' he continues, 'but you're wrong. I also used to be a rebel, so I know. It's your unconscious, that's what it is, it's your heart that rules.'

Usually he searches for words in English, so I am surprised that he should use the word 'unconscious,' perhaps he is not as unsubtle and clumsy as he first appeared to be.

'Yes,' he continues in his piercing voice, 'I was nearly in here myself. Then I read the Bible and that saved me. It's all there, I tell you, it's all there in the Bible.'

He turns round to the Coloured constable, shouts at him, and walks away. Well, he was not too bad today. How lacking he is in insight—imagine not knowing that I do not want to be treated preferentially 'as a White man'. Then how stupid he was the other day when he gave me my shaving kit to keep in the cell.

'It's untidy having it in the charge office,' he said then. 'If you're going to cut your throat does it matter if you do it when anybody's watching or not,' he added. I felt like replying, No, you stupid clumsy fool. I have thought of suicide, but I won't cut my throat, I'll hang myself on that bar over there, and then you'll be sorry for speaking like this.

It is a few days later, a Wednesday after lunch. The station commander appears wearing long white flannels. His shirt collar is open and his blue uniform jacket unbuttoned.

'I won't see you this evening,' he rasps, 'I'm off to the bowls now, and I'll be back later. The sergeant-in-charge will see that you get your food. He's a good man. Most of them are shit, but he's a good policeman. There's a lot of real rubbish that I've got to control here. If you don't watch them every minute of the day they're causing trouble.'

'Here, you rubbish,' he shouts at the Coloured constable standing quietly behind him, 'go and fetch the broom from the office. Hurry up, man, don't stand there, fetch the broom.' The constable hurries away and the station commander turns to me again.

'Some of these Coloured police are very good, very good. This one has been here for twenty years, and the other sergeant has been here even longer. I could trust them with anything. They're very good policemen. In fact, these two are so good, they're almost as good as White police. That sergeant, he may be Coloured, but we understand each other. I can shout and swear at him as much as I like; he just stands there and smiles and it's all over. Ah, here comes the broom. Here, take the broom, man. You've got to be clever in the police force. Now sweep out your cell. Go on, sweep it out. I'll be back in a few minutes. I'll leave the door open into the yard so you can sweep it out. You understand? You've got to be clever in the police.'

As he finishes talking to me he starts abusing the constable and, still talking and swearing, disappears into the heart of the building.

It takes me five minutes to sweep out my cell. I sweep the floor a second time, then a third. Still the station commander has not returned. I stand in the doorway, enjoying the sun, with my hand on the broom. Several more minutes pass. In the distance I hear the station commander's voice approaching. He keeps up his shouting until he reaches the door of my yard. I quickly start sweeping again and, as he enters the yard, he sees me busy as though I have never stopped sweeping.

'That's the idea,' he says. 'Perhaps tomorrow I'll let you sweep out your cell for a little while again. You've got to use your head if you want to get anything in the police force. Now tell me, how's the Bible reading going?'

'I'm learning a lot, but there are some things which I don't understand that I'd like to discuss with someone who knows more than I do.'

'As soon as the Police Widows and Orphans Ball is over, I'll be able to spend a little more time with you. I'm a bit of an expert on the Bible, you know. I've been studying it for thirty-five years. This ball is a big nuisance! I'm Secretary of the Committee. They make me secretary of everything, then I haven't got time for my own work.' He looks at his watch. 'Yirrah, it's late. Here, give me the broom.' He takes the

129

broom and I am locked up again in my cell. I enjoyed those extra minutes in the sun. I suppose he meant me to have them.

Outside my cell is a special tiny yard which is even smaller than my cell. It connects through a heavy door on to the main passage which joins the other yards in the station, all of them small. For my exercise time this afternoon they take me to the yard which adjoins the cells in which the ordinary White male prisoners are kept. As I run round and round, I notice that the cell doors are open. They have no fittings for padlocks, so there cannot have been any Ninety-Day prisoners here.

'Look what's up on the wall here,' I say to one of my guards. Someone's written:

IF YOU WANT TO F—K THEN GO TO 279 SMITH STREET
LANSDOWNE AND ASK FOR ANNIE JUSTIN

This is my only reading matter apart from the Bible. Some of these things are quite funny. He moves over to have a look.

'Hey, look what some bugger has written up here,' he yells in Afrikaans to his mate, who also walks up to see what is so amusing.

'Ag, it's only Annie Justin,' he says, with evident disappointment. 'That whore, she's about five foot wide. You can have her. She stays there in that house with the brown gate in Smith Street.'

Turning to me, he asks how I am finding things in Wynberg. I tell him that it is taking a little while for me to get used to things.

'It's because we're so strict here,' he says. 'Every little thing you've got to be careful of.' He watches me for a while as I run round and round.

'I suppose you have had all sorts here as prisoners,' I say.

'Oh yes, doctors, lawyers, even ministers. I was almost in here myself, just last week.' I had thought he was moody and aggressive. Now he is quite pleasant.

'What for?' I ask.

'Immorality: a Coloured woman laid a complaint. The case was supposed to be the other day, but the Prosecutor withdrew it before it started.'

130

I am puffing now as I run and hoping that he will continue talking.

'You can't do anything right in this place,' he goes on. 'The station commander is never satisfied. If you want to arrange your night shifts so that you can go out for something special, he just tells you to go to hell, yes, just like that, he tells you to go to hell. Last year, you know what happened?'

'No, what happened?'

'Well, this other chap and me were on patrol duty and a Jewish doctor here in Wynberg went away on holiday. Well, he asked us to look after his house while he was gone, and we made a point of checking up every day. Well, when he came back he came to the police station and asked for us, and then he gave us each a bottle of whisky, for looking after the house you know. Also it was nearly Christmas time. Well, he was just putting the bottles down on the counter when old Snyman came in. You know what he did?'

'No, what?'

'He just walked up to the counter and picked up both bottles and said *he* was taking them. He didn't even leave us one. Just like that, he took them. It wasn't him who looked after the house, it was us. I mean, we made a special point of checking up every day. The whisky was meant for us, not for him, and he just took it, both bottles, just like that.'

Fortunately running makes it easier to contain laughter, but I feel I must show sympathy to the aggrieved constable.

'I can see he's not an easy man,' I say. 'Imagine, just taking the bottles, just like that, when you were the ones who looked after the house. I must say, he was very hard to me at first when I came here, but he seems a bit better now. Perhaps,' I add, 'it's better to be one of his prisoners than one of his men.'

16 Convert

I AM A CAPTIVE AUDIENCE, LITERALLY. EVERY EVENING after supper the station commander gives me the benefit of his erudition, and of his deep experience of the world. At first he would stay for a few seconds only, then for five minutes. Now sometimes we stand talking, or rather he talks and I listen, for as much as a quarter of an hour at a time. There is no subject on which he is not an expert. When I mention that I am fond of playing bridge he tells me that he used to play the game for many years, but that now unfortunately he no longer has the time, otherwise he would take me on. He had, apparently, made a very thorough study of communism. There was a time when he used to read everything there was on the subject, from both sides. To give him credit, I am sure he knows who Stalin was, and it is possible he has heard the name Lenin somewhere.

I tell him that actually I am sick of politics and would very much like to hear his views on the Bible because I am sure he has so much to teach me. When he was a young man he read widely in general literature, he informs me, but now he has time only for the Bible and Westerns. He enjoys a good Western for you can relax with it better than with all that heavy stuff. The subject on which he really is an expert, however, is the Bible. You can never know it all, he tells me. He has been a student of the Bible for the past, well, here the period varies. On some days it is the past thirty-five years, on others the past twenty years. In any event, it has been a long time. Seeing that this is the only subject in respect of which he does not claim to be the complete master, I feel that he probably does know a lot about the Bible.

132

'It's all there,' he tells me. His voice rasps on and on, pausing only as he searches for a word. In ordinary conversation he speaks reasonably well in English. When he thinks of the Bible, however, he thinks in Afrikaans, and he has to translate every word. 'A Christian is a Christian, and a Jew is a Jew. King Salomo . . . what's his name—yes, that's right, Solomon, sinned with the heathens and that was the beginning of the fall of the house of Israel. Even before Solomon, Abraham had for himself Hagar, who was not of his race. Their son was Ishmael who went south to the land of Cush, where he mingled with the descendants of Ham. Now Ham's father Nooach . . . what do you say—yes, that's right, Noah was drunk and Ham saw him with his skirt up and laughed. In those days the men used to wear a kind of skirt instead of trousers. Anyway, God punished not Ham but his sons and their sons. Well, the Ishmaelites and the sons of Ham had mixed marriages in the land of Cush. This land is now the land of Abyssinia, and just look today at the trouble they are causing us.'

He pauses a moment to make sure that I am listening, and then proceeds with the lesson. I stand with my arms folded together, grateful to have someone talking to me, fascinated by his interpretation of African history, and curious to know how the theme will develop.

'Yes, just look at the trouble they are causing us, with their conference against South Africa and so on. In the war they wanted us to fight for them. I said I would fight for South Africa, not for Abyssinia. King . . . what's his name, the King of Abyssinia, he claims he is the son of David, but look what he's like. You can't trust them. They are just like snakes. They will stab you in the back. I grew up with them. We even had some in the house. That was my Grandfather's place, he had a farm before the British took it away, and he even allowed a few Hotnots to sleep in the house. Yes, I know what they're like, they stab you in the back, just like snakes. You can't trust one of them, not one.

'It's all there, I tell you. It's all there in the Bible. I've got a Biblical ensiklopedia—how do you say it—oh yes, encyclopedia —which explains everything very nicely. If there's anything you want to understand you'll find it in the encyclopedia. It's all there.'

It occurs to me that the station commander may be almost as lonely for company as I am. He has eighty men working under him, so he tells me, but he is obviously unpopular with them, and he is always reminding me how he has to watch them every minute of the day. Whenever I am taken out of my cell for interrogation he insists that I have my cell door locked, for he does not want anything of mine to be stolen, and he knows that the only persons who have access to my cell are the police! He tells me too of his family, his wife who has stood by him loyally all these years, and of his sons and daughters. Two of his sons are about my age. The younger of the two is a great disappointment to him, for although he was brought up in a very strict Christian home he seems to spend far too much of his time at the University 'in pleasure'. This year they won't even let him sit most of his exams because he hasn't been doing his work.

One day the station commander brings the district surgeon to examine me. As I take off my shirt he tells the doctor to look at the pimples on my chest. 'Don't you think a bit of fresh air would help him?' he asks the doctor. The doctor says yes, he recommends that I get some sunlight to dry out my skin. As they leave I hear the metallic voice of the station commander telling the doctor that if they wish to ill-treat his prisoners they must send them to another station.

I now am allowed into the yard outside my cell for upwards of an hour each morning and each afternoon. The yard is minute, about three-quarters the size of my cell. Its walls are high, so that I see only a small patch of sky above me. I am still completely alone, and at weekends I am not allowed into the yard at all. Yet it is an exciting venture each day to cross the threshold of my cell into the sunlight. Both literally and metaphorically it brings more light and shade into my life.

I notice that the broom is still brought to me every day. I lean it against the jamb of my cell door where I can grab it quickly should any senior officer come round on inspection. Whenever anyone enters the yard during my sunlight hours he sees me with broom in hand, sweeping vigorously. Although

134

'doctor's orders' alone would provide sufficient authority for my cell door being unlocked, it is safer to have additional justification.

The station commander seems to be impressed by the attentive hearing I always give him as he expatiates on his knowledge of the world and of the Bible, the two being to him almost interchangeable.

He tells me the story of the Samaritans. 'They were a mixed breed of people, partly of Jewish blood,' he relates. 'They were just like the Coloureds here in South Africa, and they also caused trouble all the time. When the Jews arrived in Canaan after wandering through the desert they were very tired and hungry and thirsty. Now the people they came among had strange sexual customs. The girls were not allowed to marry anyone from their own village; they had to marry strangers. When the Israelites arrived in the area and asked the people for food, the older men had a plan. They told the Israelites they would give food provided the Israelites sent young men for their daughters. Well, the Israelites accepted the offer. They needed the food, and the young men had wandered in the desert a long time without rest. The Israelite women by then were all hard and tough from the years in the desert, whereas the girls in this area had soft flesh. So the young men of Israel went to the daughters of the village and sinned with them. And that was how the Samaritans came into being. Afterwards the Samaritans and the Israelites developed side by side. They lived in the same land but they never mixed. The Samaritans always gave the Israelites a lot of trouble, but that was God's punishment because the young men of Israel gave in to temptation when they came from the desert.' I wait for him to continue with the parable of the Good Samaritan but his story is over.

I notice that a new theme has crept into his talks to me. He tells me of a very interesting book he read by a Jewish man who was an atheist for forty-five years before he started to study Christianity. This man was so impressed with what he learnt that he decided to become a Christian. He was converted and then wrote this book. It really is most interesting.

Another day he stares at me for a short while and says,

'You know, *I* can't convert a person. Only God can convert a person. But if God so chooses, he can use me as his instrument to convert someone.' I look straight back into his eyes without showing emotion. 'You know,' he continues, 'that reminds me of the story that our Dominee tells. He really is a very fine man our Dominee. He is a very good Christian, but he is a warm person and can tell a joke too. Well, he tells the story that he was walking down the street one day when a drunk person all dirty and unshaven bumps into him and says, 'Dominee, does Dominee remember me?' So the Dominee looks at him and says no, he can't remember him. So the drunk says: "But doesn't Dominee remember me, Dominee converted me five years ago." ' As he begins his harsh, hearty laugh, I realise that the story is over and grin back at him.

'So you see,' he adds, 'only God can convert somebody. We human beings can only try, but it is God who decides what is to become of us. We cannot decide a thing for ourselves. It was God who saved me on a number of occasions. In fact when I was nearly in here myself for being a rebel, it was God who saved me, right at the very foot of the door. I have also been through many difficult times, but it was God's help that let me get through those dark days.'

He is at pains to show me that he is not old-fashioned in his views on the Bible. He has read many books on the Bible written by modern scientists—what do you call them? Yes, archæologists, that's right—and they prove that the Bible was right.

'Of course, you mustn't take the Bible to be exactly right. When they wrote it in Moses' time they didn't know things that we know today. For example according to the people who wrote the Bible the world was created exactly 5,724 years ago. Now you mustn't take that to be exact. They didn't know then what we know today. Scientists have gone into the question and they have come to some very interesting conclusions. They have finally worked out, for example, that Creation was at least three hundred years earlier than the Bible says.

'You see the people who wrote Genesis gave a list of all the families. Well that was just the history of people, it wasn't really the Bible, and they left out two important families. They got the names mixed up and only put them in once instead of a few times because their names sounded the same. And you must remember that in those days people lived much longer than they do now. Methuselah, for example, lived for nearly a thousand years. So you see, you mustn't take the Bible exactly.'

I am now in possession of his encyclopedia—this means that my reading matter has been doubled—it is an Afrikaans translation of a Biblical encyclopedia brought out in Holland by two Dutch Fundamentalist theologians. I sit in the sun and read it through alphabetically, paragraph after paragraph. At my present rate of progress I should reach L after another month and Z more or less at the end of the first ninety days. I am particularly interested in its commentary on the life and teachings of Christ, to which the station commander never refers. It is ironical that I, the Jew, am more interested in the later prophets, especially Isaiah, and in the Christian doctrine of love, whereas he, the Christian, is obsessed with the tribal nationalism and fierce hatreds of the early Jews. Quite clearly he regards the Israelites as being merely the precursors in history of the Afrikaners, who after their long sojourn in the desert have at last entered the land of milk and honey. The big danger now is that as the Jews sinned with their neighbours, so the Afrikaners might give in to the pressures all around them, as well as the promptings of the weak persons within their own ranks, to worship false gods. Only once does he ever mention the word 'Love', and that is when he says to me: 'Why should I hate you because you are a Jew and a communist and an agitator? Doesn't the Bible say I should love my enemy?'

If ever his superiors ask him why he worries about me, he can use this Biblical authority as justification. I think he is developing a certain fondness for me. I am his prize prisoner whom he shows off to visiting superiors. If needs be he can rationalise his new attitude towards me by saying that he is being a good Christian by loving his enemy.

It is a Friday evening, and the station commander is even heartier than usual. His shirt is open at the collar, and his long pale legs stick out beneath a pair of short pants. I notice

137

that he is barefoot. As he comes closer I smell alcohol on his breath.

'Here, give me the keys,' he says to the constable with him. 'You can go back to the charge office. I'll be along just now.' The constable leaves. I can see that the station commander is in an expansive mood. He notices that I am looking at his bare feet.

'It's good for my Athelete's foot. The doctor says I should walk barefoot as much as I can. You say you also used to walk barefoot as a child? Hell man, we didn't even know what shoes were. We were very poor then, but that wasn't the reason. We used to like it barefoot, and our feet were hard as steel. Well, how are you getting on? The same as usual, hey. We had a bit of a party this afternoon to celebrate the Police Widows and Orphans Ball. It's over now, we had a record attendance. Now I can have more time for my work. They make me secretary of every damned thing. The officers came down from the divisional headquarters, and we had quite a bit to drink. You want to know if I went to the ball? No, I don't much care for that kind of thing. All they do is drink all the time. I'm not a man who cares for drinking.'

I think of those two whisky bottles being lifted off the counter, and cannot suppress a smile.

'No it's true,' he continues, 'I'm not a drinking man. Of course I occasionally have a drink or two at home, but I don't go to the bar.'

He looks round the cell, pausing for a moment to stare at some random object, then to look at me. I ask him if he would care to sit down for a while, and absentmindedly he seats himself on my bed, with his long, bare legs dangling to the concrete floor.

'Yes,' he starts up again in his harsh voice, 'I was almost in here myself. It was at the beginning of the war; they tried to get us policemen to join up, but I said I was prepared to fight in South Africa for South Africa, but not overseas for other countries. Well, they tried to trap me. They sent a blind man to visit me, and he invited me to the pub. We had a few drinks, and then he suddenly stood up and said "Heil Hitler!" Well,

138

after that, the next day, they sent other police round to arrest me. I told them to ask the barman. Yes, I was saved by an Englishman, mind you. The barman was an Englishman, he used to be a policeman too: he was a sergeant before he left the force and I knew him up at Kuruman. That was fifteen years before. I said to him in the bar, don't I know you from somewhere, I never forget a face. Then I asked him if he had ever been a sergeant at Kuruman and he said yes, how did I know, and I told him I was also in the police force and I had once been sent there and I never forgot a face. Well, when the police came to arrest me I told them to phone that barman who was an Englishman and also used to be in the force, and he told them that what the blind man said was a lot of nonsense, so they let me go. After that I decided politics was a waste of time, and I started reading the Bible. I always read the Bible before, but now I started reading it properly. God had sent me a sign, and I took notice and became a student of God's word. Since then my life has been much better. What's the use of politics: they never get you anywhere, they only let you down.'

'You must have been in the police force a long time,' I say to him.

'Yes, man, it's more than forty years. Life was very hard when I was a youngster. My grandfather had seven farms, he was a rebel, and the British confiscated every one of them. We had nothing. I remember we had to work on the roads with a pick and shovel. Before the war the Cape was a separate colony and my grandfather was a justice of the peace. Then there was the Cape mounted police. You know where my grandfather used to tell them to go? To the back door, yes, they had to go round the back if they wanted to speak to him. They also used to sleep at the back with the Hotnots. Well after the war the British confiscated all my grandfather's farms because he was a rebel. Life was very hard and we were very poor. After the war the South African police force was formed and so I joined.

'All I used to get was ten pounds a month then, and I used to work damned hard, much harder than they work now. Mind you, things were much cheaper then. You could get a whole snoek for threepence and now you've got to pay six shillings.

'Well, in those days the police force was run by the English, the Irish and the Scots. The English hated the Irish, and the Irish hated the Scots and the Scots hated the English, and so on. But one thing they all hated, that was the Afrikaner. Whenever I used to ask the English sergeant anything he had one answer only. He would tell me to "f . . . off". Just like that. There's one phrase you'll never hear in my station, and that is "f . . . off". I remember one sergeant we had. He couldn't even read. We had to write his reports for him. Yes, he was a sergeant and we were just constables but he couldn't even write his own report. And all he used to do was swear at us. One day there was a wedding amongst the Coloured people up in district six. I mean, they were a real respectable couple, nice people, not like some of them. Well, two of the constables were sent there afterwards to check up, and see there was no trouble and help with the traffic and so on. So the people there said have a cold drink, and they put these paper hats on their heads and said have a sandwich. While they were eating the sand- wiches and they had these hats on their heads—everything was finished, there was just them and a few people over, and they were only being friendly after doing their duty—this sergeant comes along. Well, he couldn't even write his own report, but he had them both dismissed, there and then, just like that, just for being friendly.'

I shake my head to convey appropriate sympathy.

'It was very hard for us Afrikaners then, I wrote my sergeant's exams before the war, and they failed me. I wrote again, and they failed me again. So then I protested; if you want anything you mustn't be scared. Well, I wasn't scared of them. I sent a telegram to the Commission that was sitting then, and they said now I must send another telegram saying everything is all right. So I said no, I've already sent that telegram and I want my rights. You know there was another one of us who wrote that same exam, and his best subject was English. Well they failed him in his best subject. I could understand if he failed in one of the other subjects, but in his best subject. . . . They made me a special service sergeant, as they called it then, after that. After the war, in 1947, I wrote the exams again, and again they failed

140

me. In the next year the Nationalist Party came into power, and then I expected things to improve. But I was disappointed. They still wouldn't pass me. The people who went ahead were the OBs,[1] the ones who were mad during the war and cut wires and blew up things. It was then that I lost interest in politics and took up the Bible.

'Then things began to change a bit. First they put me in charge of a small new police station in Milnerton. When I started there were only four men under me, but by the time I left there were sixteen. Here there are now eighty Europeans. When I started here in 1953 there were only thirty-five, now there are eighty under me. You've got to watch these young men all the time though. You have to be strict and tell them what to do. They're a lot of shit. I'm past the optional retiring age. When I turned fifty-five last year I could have retired. My brother was Brigadier Snyman, he was in charge of eleven districts. He told me to stay put. If you move around you have to pay for your house each time he said. No, it's better that I remain only a station commander. There are lots of advantages too in being a station commander.

'I know this area very well. I've been in charge here now for ten years. I'm completely straight. My friends are eighty per cent United Party, you know. The English, the Jews, the Indians, the Natives, the Coloureds, they all come to me from all over this area. If I wanted a thousand pounds I could get it to-morrow. Yes I could get a thousand pounds, just like that, tomorrow.'

He stretches his arms out and yawns. Even his yawn is harsh and rasping. 'Ya-ya-ya-ya,' the yawn draws to an end. 'Well it's been a busy day for me. I think I'd better be getting to bed. Yes, all right then, I'll be going now. You've got everything here, hey?' As he plants his feet on the ground I see his soft white toes spreading out. He starts to stand up but before he can straighten he suddenly lurches forward. I put out a hand to steady him, but just as he is about to topple, he clutches the blankets and steadies himself. I remember his having told me

[1] From the Afrikaans: *Ossewa Brandwag* (oxwaggon sentinel); a fascist pro-nazi organization which engaged in sabotage during the 1939-45 war.

one day that he is troubled by low blood pressure when he straightens up at bowls. For an instant I am urged to knock him down and snatch the keys from him. What shall I do if he faints—the thought flashes through my mind—he might be very ill. I'll run outside and tell his wife, and then run away down a side street. No I won't run away afterwards. I'll just wait there till the ambulance comes. I'll tell them that I could have run away, but this man was sick and I preferred to save his life. Yes, in his own clumsy way, for all his initial harshness and all his attempts to convert me to his incredible beliefs, he has shown more humanity to me than any of the others. And not only to me, but also to Esme who apparently had this cell before me and has now been released, and to the non-White detainees as well. This is clear from little things he lets slip from time to time. He has done more than he needed to. No, I couldn't push him to the ground and lock him in here. While these thoughts flit furiously through my mind, I do no more than make a gesture of supporting him. He mumbles something about his damned blood pressure—I can see he is scared—and I tell him he must take it easy, he's had a busy day.

'Good-night then,' he grunts as he locks the cell door and then the padlock. He crosses the tiny yard, lets himself out into the passage, and locks the yard door. His bare feet are quiet on the ground but I hear the keys clinking as he moves. The clinking grows fainter, and as it disappears in the direction of the charge office, I hear in the distance his metallic, loudspeaker voice starting up again. Presumably he is back to telling the shit who work under him what they must do.

About two hours later I am sitting on the bed waiting for the men to come to switch off the light when I hear the passage door being opened then the padlock on my cell door. I am about to ask that the light be switched off for the night when I notice a tall red-faced man, with a thick-knit blue jersey, short pants and muscular legs, approaching me. He smiles, puts out his hand and says:

'I am Warrant Officer Van der Merwe. How are you? I am also one of those responsible for looking after this police station.'

I shake his hand and wonder what has brought about this visit.

142

I notice that he too smells of liquor. He is very affable, yet I sense something strained in his manner.

'Oh, by the way,' he goes on, 'I believe Warrant Officer Snyman was here earlier this evening. They tell me he was alone with you for a long time. Is that correct?'

It's not my fault if anyone stays here to talk to me. Oh, now I get it, it's not me he is after it's Mr Snyman.

'Well, he was here a short while,' I say.

'Yes, but he was alone with you, wasn't he?'

'I think that if you want to know what he did you should ask him rather than me.'

'That's all I wanted to know. You don't deny that he was alone with you. Goodbye.'

'Would you mind switching off the light after you lock up.'

'The men on cell duty will do that just now. Good-night.'

The door is locked, and he is gone.

The next morning has arrived. Every Saturday morning the colonel comes down from divisional headquarters to inspect the station. About an hour before the colonel arrives the station commander invariably pays me a visit and peers around the cell to make sure nothing is amiss. Whenever I know that a visitor is coming I make my cell look as austere as possible. If it is the magistrate who comes then the station commander is annoyed, for he likes the magistrate to see how well he treats me. When the colonel comes, however, the barer my cell appears the better, for he wants the colonel to know that he is not mollycoddling me. As far as the colonel is concerned, I get the impression that, for himself, he could not care one way or the other how I am treated, but he is anxious that the security branch do not get the impression that my conditions are too easy. But immediately the station commander appears today I can see that his attitude towards me has changed. He is very correct, almost formal. I notice that he is in full uniform, he is even wearing his cap.

'There's been a bit of trouble,' he says gruffly. He does not look at me as he talks, but paces around restlessly, fixing his attention on little objects in the cell which he moves from place

143

to place. 'One of the men made a complaint behind my back. He said I had been alone with you here.'

I tell him about the visit I received last night from the warrant officer, stressing what I had said about asking Mr Snyman and not me.

'I'm glad you said I was here for only a short while. I told the colonel that surely after my forty years in the force I was above suspicion. There are some people in this station who are supposed to be colleagues of mine, but they will never lose a chance to stab me in the back. They're jealous of me, and they think it will help them if they make reports behind my back. I'm not scared of them mind you. If you're scared in the police force, you'll never get anywhere. In all my years I've had much worse things than this happen to me, and I've always come out all right. So I'm not worried. Fortunately some of the men here are loyal. One of the sergeants told me last night about the report, so I knew all about it.'

'What did the colonel say?' I ask.

'Oh, of course, he said he had known me for many years, he's a very good man that colonel, and he would never have the slightest doubts about me.'

'So it won't make any difference to your visits?' I continue.

'The colonel trusts me completely, that's what he says. These jealous young men will never tell me what to do or what my duties are. I'm the station commander here, and it's my responsibility to check up on you every day.'

The words are buoyant, but the tone in which they are expressed is flat. I imagine that the colonel told him something to the effect that his trustworthiness was never in question, but he should set an example to the men and never see me without being accompanied by another policeman. I notice now that he has a Coloured constable with him. He always speaks more freely when his companion is non-White, as though he is then not afraid of being reported. For all his nasty racial theories, he clearly has a much warmer personal relationship with the non-White police than with the Whites. Perhaps it is simply because non-Whites are used to being shouted at and can shrug it off more easily.

144

So our daily conversations have come to an end. A week ago I would have grieved as though over the loss of a limb. I feel now that I have by now heard all he has to say, about anything. Having told me his views on politics, the Bible, his family, and the police force, I think his entire store of knowledge has been revealed to me. To hear it once is fascinating, but to hear it all again and again could be worse than complete isolation.

The station commander leaves, and returns an hour later with the colonel. Usually he is very bluff and hearty with the colonel, showing him around the cells as though taking him on a tour of his estate. Today they are both silent and abrupt and the visit is over quickly.

17 The Law

EVERY AFTERNOON FROM MONDAY TO FRIDAY IT IS THE same. On Saturday I hear it at noon, while on Sunday there is silence all day, with the station as quiet as a deserted battlefield. The sunlight creeps down the tall sheer slope of one wall, across the tiny asphalt square that constitutes my yard, and up the steep wall opposite. The yard is still warm as though it is a giant flue glowing with heat after its fire has gone out. I have put my air-mattress and blankets back in the cell and I begin pacing round and round, waiting for the ordeal to begin. I find it easier to cope with if I am upright and moving about.

The last of the prison vans has roared out of the dispatch yard into the silence of the outside world, and for a moment there is a hush over the police station. Doors in various parts of the building are slammed, footsteps and voices can be heard congregating in the passage on the other side of the wall of my yard. A harsh scraping sound must be the noise of a bench being moved. A series of names are yelled out each followed by a faint 'Ja baas.' Next a single name is called and a moment of silence follows. There is a lot of confused shouting and guffawing. Then it comes: a smack followed by an instantaneous scream. A terror-stricken boy's voice soars into a strident, swooping yell which tails off into a beseeching, hysterical-like series of yelps. I hear it not only through the wall, but coming up, echoey and distorted, from a drain in my yard like the spirits of the earth. The drain is connected to the passage by a large tube and this tube funnels all loud sounds made in the passage through to the base of my yard. Thus the boy's screaming reaches

146

me from two angles in hideous stereophonic sound. His wild soprano shriek is partly drowned out by great bellows of vigorous male laughter. My fingers clench tightly and I find myself practically running as I frantically try to ward off the ballooning din of pain, supplication, mockery and cruelty that assaults me. Smack! The yell grows into another fierce screech. Smack! The blows are falling quickly now. Smack! Smack! The screaming is fixed in one long continuous spasm of agony, counterpointed by successive waves of broken, raucous laughter. Smack! I cannot block it out and will never get used to it. The world heaves up new cruelty each day and I am chained here as if to be its witness. Smack! Smack! The blows cease and the screaming drops to a piteous blubbering moan. I imagine the bloody and torn back, the convulsive, trembling hands as the thrashed boy tries to put his short pants on again. Society has tried to teach one more youth that he must respect the person and the rights of others.

When the magistrate comes round on his weekly inspection and asks if I have any complaints, he would laugh at me if I told him I had a serious allegation to make: every afternoon three or four hefty adult men get hold of young boys, aged anything from eight to eighteen, and beat them mercilessly with canes. The beating is so severe that when I go out for exercise I see broken pieces of cane scattered on the floor. But you're a lawyer, the magistrate would tell me, and surely you know that the police are carrying out sentences imposed by the magistrates who in turn speak for the whole of civilised and ordered society. And how can you talk of cruelty, he would continue, when it is the law that orders that these boys be caned. They have broken the law, without which there can be no civilisation, and in any event it is better that they have a quick beating than that they be sent to prison or reformatory. And I would have to concede to the magistrates that, prisons and reformatories being what they in most cases are, he would in this respect be right.

Thus all I do say when the magistrate comes round is: 'One good thing about being locked up here is that I'm getting a worm's eye view of the law. We advocates normally never know what happens to our clients before and after they reach Court.

147

At least I'm learning a bit more about the machinery of the law, even if I do so the hard way.' The visiting magistrate smiles at my remarks but says nothing. It would not do for me to be too blunt. I would like to say: In a way I am glad that I am getting this view of the law. I think every lawyer and every judicial officer should be forced to spend at least one weekend in the cells before he practises or enforces law. In Court we see Law's smiling face. Even there at times it can be ugly but at its worst it is never as bad as here in the cells. Ninety-nine per cent of practising lawyers would be shocked if they experienced law the way most South African prisoners do. And perhaps the magistrates and judges would not be so sanguine about the sentences they dish out if they knew what they entailed in practice. For most prisoners the time spent in Court is only a small portion of their period of captivity. The law as they know it is not represented by the judge or magistrate, defending counsel or prosecutor, but by the policeman and the prison warder. The courtroom is an important part of the law, one of its vital organs, but the crucial part of the system is the police station and the prison. Whatever jurisprudential theorists might say, as far as the overwhelming majority of people directly affected by the law is concerned, law is an instrument of coercion and punishment. The officers of the law are seen as inhuman agents of retribution. Individual policemen may vary a lot, but it is the general attitude that is appalling. Policemen in charge of awaiting-trial prisoners seem to work on certain assumptions, one of which is that, by virtue of their positions as officers of the law and the State, they are entitled to demand absolute submission from those in their custody. They also assume that only guilty people are arrested. If some prisoners manage to 'get off', it is only because the evidence against them is insufficient or because the defence lawyer is too cunning. All prisoners are evil and deserve to be punished, the assumptions proceed, and all prisoners must share responsibility for those who assault and kill policemen and those who escape from custody. Policemen are good by virtue of the fact that they are policemen while prisoners are wicked by virtue of the fact that they are prisoners.

I cannot tell all this to the magistrate now but perhaps, when

148

and if I am released, I can give my colleagues some idea of how the law appears from the point of view of a prisoner. Yet I know my descriptions will be inadequate. How can I convey the hard feel of wall and floor, the indignity of being utterly dependent on the police, the stoic murmur of batches of prisoners being shuffled around, the whip-like screeches of command of the warders and, worst of all, the periodical screams of terror and anguish of the boys being beaten and the yelling of the new prisoners being brought in.

It is my hearing that enables me to probe the prison and that connects me with life outside my cell. In the normal world one sees further than one hears, but here it is different. My range of vision is only a few feet, but I can hear sounds coming from beyond the walls. In the morning the vans arrive from the smaller police stations. Prisoners are disgorged like loaves of bread being delivered and are then sorted according to the courtroom in which they are to appear. Lists are read out and, presumably, lists are ticked off. White men, White women, non-White men, non-White women, name after name is screamed out. Prisoners shuffle to and fro. Doors are unlocked, doors are slammed. Prisoners move when ordered, stop moving when ordered. It is as though the breath of life has to be yelled into them by the police. Every morning, except Sunday, it is the same. I see no people but only hear the sounds. I realise that every day brings new batches of prisoners but from what I hear it could be the same people brought in again and again, as in some awful charade. They have no faces, only sounds, and the sounds are the same, like a long tattoo repeated every morning.

In the afternoon the whole process is gone through once more only now in reverse sequence. The screaming of orders is a little louder, the rush of prisoners a little more frantic, for the policemen in charge of the courts are anxious to finish work so as to get home as soon as possible. The prisoners emerging from the tunnels beneath the courtrooms, sorted according to sex, race and whether convicted or still awaiting trial, are finally dispatched in vanloads to the central prison in town.

Next comes the caning of the youths. Perhaps I should be grateful—I do not hear the adults being whipped. The flogging

149

is done elsewhere. On average four or five children get six to eight strokes each a day. About twenty-five boys a week receive a total of up to one hundred and fifty strokes. In a month hundreds of cuts are given and over a year it must run into thousands. Some afternoons the boys take it stoically, grunting their pain not screaming, but usually the strokes are followed by ghastly shrieking and wailing. Much seems to depend on the first victim: if he bears his beating in silence, those that follow remain silent, whereas if he yells they all yell. Frequently the police in charge of the boys burst out laughing during the caning. Whether they are amused at the antics of the terrorised boys, or whether they find the breaking of the cane funny, I will never know. Sometimes the boys scream out the number of each stroke. Sometimes they beg desperately to be spared the thrashing. Sometimes they repeat the same ejaculation of pain after each smack—*Eina Eina Eina Eina Eina Eina*. But usually it is one long wild yell, as though the violence of the assault strips them of all self-control and brings out infantile or animal-like terror responses from them; possibly vocalising their pain provides some relief. Long after the caning has ended the screams continue to vibrate in my mind.

Later in the afternoon when all the prisoners have been moved and new prisoners have not yet arrived, I am taken into the passage for my exercise. This is the quietest time of the day in the station. The cells are empty and my guards usually sit eating sandwiches and drinking coffee from a Thermos flask. The only noise is the soft padding of my feet as I run up and down the passage or round and round in the yard. A long bench lines one wall of the passage. Bits of broken cane lie on the floor. On a table is a sheaf of paper containing lists of names. Every movement of every prisoner is tabulated in duplicate or triplicate, or rather, the prisoner is moved according to the entries on the paper. The bureaucracy is efficient. For umpteen years policemen on court duty have been counting, moving, sorting and shouting at the prisoners. They now do it with an efficiency which would be envied in many a factory turning out motor cars or furniture or processed food. Like all workmen, they have their good days when they manage to shunt the prisoners

150

around quickly and their bad days, when everything seems to go slowly. They are used to me by now and some of them, especially those who saw me appearing in Court as an advocate, are not unfriendly. One old man complains to me about his arthritis, another says to me 'nice day, isn't it?' every day, whether it be sunny or raining. Who the screamers are I will never know, nor the persons who give and supervise the caning. The faces I see are those of ordinary men preoccupied with the minutiae of living. In the context of family or neighbourhood many must be highly respected and kindly fellows. Each probably thinks that at heart he is a soft bloke, and each can probably remember some incident in his career which proves how lenient he really is at heart.

After supper the cells start filling up again. The police on patrol duty, the modern fishers of men, bring in their haul in a series of single captives. Many of these prisoners submit quietly to their fate, but others resist captivity as fiercely as they can. Screaming and yelling bodies are dragged along the passages and through the doors, and thuds are frequently heard as if kicks or blows with the fist are being given. Some prisoners shriek hysterically all the way from the charge office to their cells and then even after having been locked in they continue with their cries. They pummel the cell doors until they are tired in a vain and desperate attempt to secure their release. The banging has a definite pattern. First it is fierce and staccato, then long loud blows are delivered, then a coda of sharp bangs is heard, finally there is silence. The silence lasts for about half an hour during which time the prisoner recovers sufficient strength for a new wave of desperation to send him once more to the door. So the rounds of pummelling continue right through the night until eventually the prisoner grows too tired to carry on and falls asleep. The law never sleeps; just as women give birth to babies day and night with complete impartiality, so the police bring in prisoners throughout the twenty-four hours. The wheels of justice are in perpetual motion.

Being so close to the Courts and hearing the ebb and flow of prisoners to and from Court, emphasises to me in a special way the peculiar harshness of my personal lot. Those prisoners may be constantly abused and insulted, but each one of them knows that within forty-eight hours of his arrest he must be brought before a Court, that, if he can afford it, he can engage the services of a lawyer, that he can only be convicted if a specific charge is alleged and proved against him and so on.

I have been entirely abstracted from the judicial process. The courtrooms are only a matter of twenty or thirty yards from my cell, yet I have less right of access to them than would a murderer, a rapist, or a thief who may be captured twenty miles away. I live in a little world of non-law. And it is the law that has done this! The law says that the police may take me out of the realm where law applies and keep me for as long as they like under their personal control. So as far as the police are concerned, in holding me without recourse to the law they are merely carrying out the law. The tyranny could hardly be more complete yet it has the full sanction and authority of the law. The fact that I am a lawyer is not really important, but it does add a measure of piquancy to the situation. What a joke! Time and again I am driven to conclude that law is a mere façade which hides tyranny. Tyranny is the reality, law the illusion. I am confined by a superior power. If I am released it will be because that power decides it has more to lose by holding me than by freeing me. Only pressure will force my release, pressure from the outside world and from inside South Africa. In some ways I am more fortunate than most detainees, for I can expect some pressure to be applied on my behalf. My father can be relied upon to do something in London, and in Cape Town at any rate I am known in quite wide liberal and progressive circles, to the Press and to the legal profession. The legal profession—will they do anything? The Bar Council passed an excellent resolution condemning the Ninety-Day measure: after it had already become law. Now one of their members has been snatched away from his chambers in terms of this law. Will they do battle for me? Or will they find some excuse for avoiding a confrontation with the Minister? I fear they have already done the latter.

In the early days of my detention I was allowed certain visits from outside. First, on the second day, a young attorney was permitted to see me to make arrangements about cases which I had in hand and which would have to be given to other counsel. It was a business visit, but he was able to gather the essential facts of the circumstances in which I was being forced to live. Next, two days later, one of my colleagues and friends was allowed to see me to make arrangements about fees outstanding to me, my chambers and so on. His visit was some solace. On the question of the Bar and what stand it was taking he indicated that the Bar Council would do everything it felt itself able to on my behalf. In fact, he told me, one of our senior colleagues, a recently appointed 'silk', was going to Pretoria and would make a point of speaking to the Minister. My colleague who has the ear of the Minister spoke to the Minister personally, and when he got back to Cape Town shortly after my detention, told me that the Minister had promised to keep a personal eye on me. And, he continued, as I know the Minister I can tell you he is a man of his word. Fool that I was to rely on my colleagues. Law to them is essentially a money-making career that might culminate in a judgeship. Some of them are undoubtedly fine craftsmen with a passion for their work. But how many have a passion for justice, without which law becomes a paper set of rules, a game, a mockery. And how hard are they prepared to fight to preserve the legal profession as a fearless and independent body dedicated to the defence of those in need? It is not for myself that I feel sad, though certainly I long to be out of here, but for the profession. All they need do is demand that I be brought before Court or be released. They need not support my politics nor proclaim my innocence.

Charge him or free him: that is all they need say, and if they were to do so publicly, it would embarrass the Minister considerably, and make it more difficult for him to have me detained indefinitely. Instead they take the coward's way out.

If my colleagues have been disappointing in their lack of positive action, the visiting magistrates have turned out to be surprisingly sympathetic. The first one to see me at Maitland was very cool and uninterested to the point of being harsh. Since then a number of different senior magistrates have come round, one each week. I have in the past appeared before all of

153

them in Court and I detect in their manner towards me now some measure of kindliness. Our interviews are very brief, lasting a minute or two at the most, and our discussions very formal and correct. Yet I sense that each of them is saying to himself: well, I'm glad I'm not in that poor bastard's shoes, he's not a bad chap really, always conducted himself well in my Court, won't do his practice any good, must be tough on his family. It is also probable that a couple of them would even feel sympathy for the non-White detainees. Perhaps unconsciously they resent the usurpation of their authority implied in no-trial detention. Yet solitary confinement is so unnatural and inhuman that only the most hardened official would fail to have some sympathy for us detainees. Even the ordinary policemen, emotionally calloused as they have become, occasionally drop remarks indicating some distaste for Ninety-Day imprisonment.

One magistrate made an interesting statement two weeks ago. He is a short man with a yellow bald head and a long face that is normally fixed in a cross glare. In court he is notorious for his rudeness to defence lawyers and he and I have frequently had sharp forensic clashes. Of all the magistrates to visit me now, he has been the warmest. His voice is soft, his words are gentle; perhaps it is only on the Bench that he is fierce. A fortnight ago he casually told me that my application had been postponed for a few days. What application? I wanted to yell at him. Yet I merely nodded, knowing that if I asked that question he would realise that I am not supposed to know of any application. Last week and this week I asked casually how the application had fared (I wish I knew what the application was!) but on both occasions he skirted the question. When I asked again yesterday I noticed an exchange of glances between him and the station commander. Something is in the air, but if there has been any application it has certainly brought me no fruit and honey.

It is later in the afternoon. The door is unlocked and I see the station commander with a piece of paper in his hand. He clears his throat and addresses me in the harsh, querulous voice he used during the first few weeks. 'Someone was here from the

Court,' he says, 'and served this order on me. He ordered me to show it to you, which I am doing now.'

'Is it good or bad?' I ask apprehensively.

'Read it and then sign over here that you have received it.'

As he passes the paper to me I notice it is a formal document bearing an official seal. I give it a quick nervous glance so as to gather in one glimpse its main import. On the top is my name— Oh joy—entitled . . . reasonable supply of reading matter and writing material . . . costs—I've won an application which I didn't even know I had brought! I read the whole document now, slowly. I cannot focus well. I am too excited, and after all these weeks I am not used to reading legalese any more. How unjust I have been to my colleagues. There *is* scope for law, even in the midst of tyranny:

IN THE SUPREME COURT OF SOUTH AFRICA
(CAPE OF GOOD HOPE PROVINCIAL DIVISION)

CAPE TOWN: *Wednesday, 13th November, 1963*
Before the Honourable Mr Justice van Winsen, and the Honourable Mr Justice Banks

(Thank you Louis, thank you Basil—I know you were acting strictly as judges, but still, thank you, thank you.)

Between

ALBERT LOUIS SACHS

Applicant

And

CAPTAIN D. J. ROSSOUW
of Security Police, Cape Town

Respondent

I read on:

Having on Wednesday the 30th October, 1963, heard Mr Snitcher Q.C. (Thank you Harry) *and Mr J. Aaron* (Thank you Jack) *Counsel for the Applicant, and Mr Burger, South Africa, with him Mr Kleynhans*

155

(it's all right Alwyn, it's all right Ernst—someone had to appear against me, and it's Counsel's duty to accept any brief offered him, however unpopular—I'm not cross with you)

Counsel for the Respondent;
Having read the documents filed of record
THE COURT *postponed the matter to the 6th November, 1963*
THEREAFTER, *on Wednesday, the 6th November, 1963*
THE COURT RESERVED JUDGMENT
THEREAFTER, *on this day,*
THE COURT:
1. *Declares the Applicant entitled while detained under the provisions of Section 17 of Act 37 of 1963 to be accorded reasonable periods of daily exercise, to be supplied with, or to be permitted to receive and use a reasonable supply of reading matter and writing material.*
2. *Orders the Respondent to pay the Applicant's costs; and*
3. *Directs the Registrar of this court to transmit to the Applicant a copy of this Order.*

This means they have to give me books, pencil and paper, and not only me but all the detainees. Now the whole public will know—I'm sure the Press covered the application fully—how we have been treated. This is one in the eye for the security boys.

'Now you've read it, sign here.' The station commander's harsh voice interrupts the growing ecstasy of my thoughts. 'If they'd listened to me, this whole case wouldn't have been necessary,' he grumbles. 'Some policemen are so obstinate. I would have given you a few books and there would have been no case. Now they come and serve this order on me.'

I sign and return to him an acknowledgement of receipt. As he is about to leave I ask for it back for a moment, and add in bold letters the words 'With Thanks'. For the first time this afternoon the station commander smiles. 'Well, I hope your people leave me alone,' he says rather petulantly. 'It won't help to keep at me. I can only carry out instructions. The

156

lawyers were here last night, but I told them I don't go by what's in the newspapers, and I hadn't got my official notice of the judgment. When I got it, I said, then I would consider the matter. There were also people from the Press ringing up all the time and I told them the same thing. It won't help you at all if these people make a fuss. They tried to tell me what I must do, but I don't listen to them.'

'The judgment does say, though, that I am entitled to books and writing materials,' I tell him.

'If they're not satisfied,' he continues, 'they can take me to Court. I'm not scared. I carry out my instructions.'

'But surely you will carry out the Order of the Court?'

'No one has to tell me how to do that. I will send you pencil and paper later on and I will speak to security in Cape Town about the books.'

'Will it be possible for me to see the whole judgment? You can make that my first bit of reading matter.'

'Security said I could let you see it if I wished. Tomorrow I'll give it to you. There's a page missing, and I'm waiting for that.'

'Well, anyhow, I'd like to say thank you now for having let me read your encyclopedia and so on, when you didn't have to. I'll always be grateful for that, though of course I'm very happy now that the judges have said I am entitled, as a matter of law, to get books. If you are too busy now to let me have books, may I speak to you about it tomorrow?'

He agrees sulkily to my request, and locks me in again. Oh my colleagues, how I maligned you. You were doing something which will help not only me, but all the detainees, for the Court has interpreted the Ninety-Day clause in such a way as to give all of us certain rights. The judgment will not affect the fact that we are being detained without trial, in indefinite solitary confinement, but it will transform the conditions under which we are held. The mental torture will be mitigated. We will have something to do.

It is the next day, and I have the full judgment in my hands. I feel like crying. In clear and vigorous prose the judge sets out the arguments of both sides and states why I am entitled to the

157

order claimed. (Fortunately I had signed a General Power of Attorney at the time of my detention so that it was possible for the application to be brought on my behalf even without my knowledge.) The judge states: *In the terms of our common law every man has certain fundamental rights of personality to which he is always entitled unless Parliament takes them away in clear terms. The Ninety-Day legislation says nothing about the conditions under which a detainee is to be held, and unless by necessary implication a detainee can be deprived of the elementary amenities of life such rights of personality must be held to remain intact. When I refer to deprivation (of the rights Applicant claims) being necessary for the purposes of detention, that is, interrogation, I do not mean to imply that deprivation can be inferred to have been intended by the legislature on the grounds that it would constitute a useful or necessary instrument to compel the detainee to speak. The section is not open to that construction. The only sanction that the legislature has prescribed in Section 17 against the person who refuses to answer questions satisfactorily is the sanction that he will continue to forfeit his liberty by being subject to continued detention.* I read the judgment through again and again. It is a thrilling document, couched in strict and correct legal terminology, but infused with the spirit of liberty and respect for the rights of man. An important issue was whether my conditions should be purely within the discretion of the officer in charge of me, or whether the Court has jurisdiction to ensure that my treatment accorded with certain objective standards regulated by law. In deciding in favour of the latter view the judge re-affirmed the duty of the judiciary to protect citizens from having their rights taken away, arbitrarily and without lawful sanction, by officers of the executive. I know it is only a matter of time before Parliament alters the law so as to give the security police absolute power to determine the condition of detainees, but it will be a few months before this can be done. Yet even if the Court's decision is nullified by legislative action, I shall always remember the terms of the Supreme Court judgment, especially this one passage, which has done so much to restore my belief in the value of law:

I venture to suggest that the approach [which favours interpreting the law so as to infer wide power to the executive in times of emergency] is open to the criticism that it might tend to deprive a citizen of the protection of the law at the very time when he is likely to need it most, that is, when emotions are running high and the danger of arbitrary executive action being taken against him is perhaps more real than in the settled times of peace.

18 Pencil and Paper

THE PAPER IS DAZZLINGLY WHITE AND IN MY HAND IS A pencil. The wood feels clumsy between my fingers. I must use it, but to do what? I rest my hand on the pad and wait for my fingers to start moving. Should I write my name? But that would be silly. Should I draw something? But I am hopeless at drawing. The pencil point is on the paper now at the top right hand corner of the page. Slowly it presses up and down on that spot. The lead markings are like a small pit of charcoal. My first creation is taking place. There it is: a tiny black blob. Is that blob me, all hunched up, secretive and anonymous? Is it my cell, so small, sealed and impregnable? I know what the trouble is: I am frightened, scared that I will reveal myself for them to see. This blob is an adventure, a probing. How ridiculous I am! I do not want to waste paper so I start off in the corner. Yet I have plenty of paper and can always get more. The law has now guaranteed me my supply. I have hidden a bit broken off from the pencil and they will never find it in its fluff-covered cranny in the corner of the window frame. I will keep it there, just in case. Ah, that is a bit better. I have now drawn a square, small but with an empty space of white in the middle. I suppress an urge to black it in. I must draw more freely, more happily, for am I not blessed to have pencil and paper? Yet my fingers are unpractised and stiff, as though the nerves which lead from them to the brain are stiff with dirt and decay. In addition there is an unseen rein holding my hand in check, stopping it from crossing the page in the bold, sweeping movements that would more accurately represent the conscious excitement of my mind. I am unused to the freedom of writing; I have the opportunity

160

but am helpless to utilise it. I am early man learning to write, a child making its first marks. How strange that with my thoughts flowing so rationally, my body should be so primitive and slow. Yet my body is right. My mind leaps backwards and forwards, lofted high by hopes, flung down by despair, slowly assimilating new experience, carefully incorporating in me the externals of my existence. My body knows that I have plenty of time for writing. My body also knows that the pencil and paper came too easily. It was like a gift from outside: not earned by myself. What the law gives the law can take away. All I can be sure of is what I gather in for myself.

Two weeks ago I made a find. I was favoured by luck, but still I had been confronted with the task of taking advantage of my discovery. There was an element of risk and effort involved, so that when I was finally able to savour my trove, I had no difficulty in doing so to the full. The find consisted of a double leaf of newspaper. It was lying in the far corner of the exercise yard, crumpled up and sodden with beetroot juice, fish oil and vinegar. For twenty minutes I ran round that yard, waiting for the attention of the guards to be distracted. I did not look straight at the paper, but its presence burned in my mind all the time. Finally the moment arrived. I kept on running and as I reached the spot where it lay, I bent and scooped up the paper with my hand. Round a few more times and then I swiftly popped the paper in my pocket. Nothing had been observed. It is in prison that I learn the coolness and cunning of the thief. Who says that prison does not reform one's character?

Later, back in my cell, I spread the magnificent loot on my bed and quickly worked out how I would enjoy it. It consisted of four pages from the magazine section of a week-end paper: three pages of advertisements and a back page of crossword puzzles, chess and stamp news. How lucky I was; there were no less than three crossword puzzles. Here was a week's reading material at least. One crossword puzzle every other day and in between a page of advertisements. Every day for a week I had something to look forward to. I read the *Births* and the *Marriages*, and even the *Deaths*. So the world had not stood still. I read the *Cars for Sale*, and the *We want to Swop* columns. For

161

one whole glorious week I dipped into my treasure, each day carefully restoring it to its hiding place under the mattress or in my clothes. Special savour was given to the crossword puzzles by the fact that I had to fill them in with a pin and Marmite. Eventually it turned out that getting rid of the paper proved to be nearly as hazardous as getting hold of it had been. I flushed it down the toilet and as it disappeared from sight felt a sense of loss at its departure. But it had not gone far. Two days later I noticed that the water in the pan was flushing out very slowly and had taken on a muddy, discoloured appearance. The next day the position was even worse. With horror I realised that the outlet pipe was blocked. I could not ask the police to clear it; I realised I must open it myself before the police became aware of the smell. I had no option but to strip off my shirt and plunge my arm into the pool of fæces. There was no instrument for me to use, so I had to scrape with my fingers. Lumps of loose, foul-smelling turds floated around my shoulder only inches away from my face. I was like a victim in the Inferno flung into a river of excreta. My arm could barely reach the sodden paper, and as the putrid water lapped around my neck, I felt as though I were submerged in it up to my chin. Gradually my nails managed to shred the paper and finally I was able to push the whole ball through. I flushed the pan several times and scrubbed my arm and shoulder till they shone. Alas, there was no one with whom I could share the joke, for joke it now was. I was thrilled at having encountered and surmounted the danger. I had enjoyed that piece of newspaper to the full and now felt I had fully earned my enjoyment.

Now, with pencil and paper officially granted to me, all I can do is scratch a few puny lines on the vast white surface which rests on my lap. I recall Sir Thomas Beecham's reputed remark to the lady 'cellist: Madam, you have between your legs an instrument capable of giving pleasure to millions, and all you can do is scratch on it. Yes, I have in my hands an instrument which for millions is a tool of liberation and creativity, and all I can do is scratch with it. Never mind, I tell myself, in time you will uncoil and after a few days you should be able to make better use of writing materials.

162

The days pass as slowly as ever but some of the worst agony is gone. If I have queries or requests I make a note of them so that when the appropriate official comes I can remember what it is I wish to ask. I am receiving a trickle of reading matter. It takes time and patient explanation on my part, for they will not let me receive any printed matter from outside. No newspapers at all are allowed. They tell me that some public-spirited citizen read of my application in the Press and presented security with several books for me. I am elated by the gesture until I see the books. *The Decline of Communism* is the first one given me. The writing is dull, the content dated (published in the year before Sputnik, it forecasts complete scientific collapse in the Soviet Union) and the subject about as unappealing to me now as any they could have found. The next is *The Case against Communism,* subtitled *The Christian Answer.* The quality of the writing is better and the presentation of what the author calls 'The Christian approach' to social problems is not without interest, but it is only sheer lust for reading matter that drives me through the remaining tedious pages. Thirdly I am given *An Outline for Sanity* by G. K. Chesterton. The first page contains a rather conventional critique of socialism and communism, but then the book leaps into a sustained and exciting plea for the abolition of capitalism, the scrapping of machinery and a return to pre-industrial society. The most preposterous ideas are presented so divertingly and with such masterly assurance that in my heart I fervently cheer each paragraph. What gives me particular joy is that Chesterton is arguing for a Society organised on Catholic lines. If there is one thing that the station commander, and probably three-quarters of the police, hate more than a Jew, a Communist and an agitator, it is a Catholic. Why only the other day the station commander gave me three pamphlets issued by his Church on the danger of Rome and the insidious techniques of Popery. He also gave me a fundamentalist Protestant pamphlet which, he assures me, I can have each week. As I hand the Chesterton back to him he mutters:

'Yes, he's a very interesting author. What's his name again— Ches . . . Oh yes, Chesterton; when I was younger I used to read

163

a lot of his books. Now I haven't got the time any more.'

'I found it very interesting the way he argues for a Catholic society. Chesterton was a Catholic, you know.'

For the first time the station commander is at a loss for a comment. The strident voice is silent now. He takes the book from me and departs without saying a word. I want to laugh out loud but pretend I have noticed nothing.

To get other reading matter is proving very difficult. The main problem is not so much that the police wish to defy the Court order, but that the world of books is so strange to them. One policeman on seeing a couple of books on my bunk went so far as to sympathise with me, not for having so few books to read, but for having so many! Obviously he regards books as a sort of punishment, and given the choice would rather be locked up without than with them.

To prevent the question of message-passing being used as a pretext for circumventing the Court order, I have suggested that the police buy books for me directly from a nearby book-shop. I will supply the money, security can vet the titles, and the police themselves can buy the books. The police are unhappy in bookshops, that much is obvious. The constables on cell duty delay passing on my requests so that the next shift will have to deal with them. They know how to capture criminals, but to get a book, well there was nothing in their course about that. Comics, photo stories, a Western or two, and the occasional newspaper seem to form the sole reading diet of the majority of policemen. I order the best known books of two leading Afrikaans novelists. No one in the station has heard of them; little wonder that so many Afrikaans writers have to depend on doing translations for their livelihood.

The station commander is alarmed at the amount of money I am spending on books. I tell him it is nothing: I'm getting free board and lodging, and books to me are like food and drink. Yet he is upset at seeing so much being paid out for reading matter, to him it is a waste. He tells me he has spoken to his wife and she doesn't mind if I use one of the family's library cards. The next day I write my request and smile a little as I visualise the sergeant on patrol sending the constable under him into the library to ask for *Swann's Way* by Marcel Proust. (I write it out carefully so that there can be no mistaking which is the book and which the author.) I am not sure which thought amuses me most: the idea of the gun-holstered, blue-uniformed constable entering the library with the paper trembling in his hand, or the amazement of the librarian on hearing the constable ask for Proust. It might justify to her all those years of casting bread upon the waters.

It is not easy to think of book titles. I am in the position of the man selecting ten books to take with him to a desert isle. I do not wish to re-read those books which made the greatest impact on me, yet I struggle to remember the names of books and authors I have not read. With ten hours a day completely clear for reading, I can easily finish a six hundred page novel each day. So I still ration myself, always trying to keep some reading matter in reserve. There is no doubt about what kind of books I want. I want to read novels, books alive with people, people who talk, mingle with each other and undergo all the normal emotions of life. I want to escape, but escape into the world of reality. Books of philosophy, or politics, or criticism have no attraction for me now. I want people, not ideas, the living, not the abstract. With books I could be happy almost anywhere, and having been denied them for so long I now appreciate them doubly. One day they will take away these books from me again. Until then I must make the most of what I have and what I still can get. Stone walls do not a prison make, that is if you have company or books. They deprived me of books just as they deprived me of human association so that I would suffer the torture of inactivity and loneliness, and so that they could make themselves my sole source of ideas and information. But now by means of the pages which I hold in my hands I am restored to mental activity and, above all, I resume my position as a member of humanity.

19 Reflections

I HAVE COMPLETELY UNDERESTIMATED THE EFFECTS OF isolation. It is not simply a case of not having like-minded people with whom to discuss matters. Prolonged solitude and inactivity produce emotional effects whereby rational thinking is displaced. The mind that is brought to bear on problems is not normal and, worse still, even where it does function logically, it seems to be impotent to govern behaviour. You know what is right and wrong, yet feel powerless to act accordingly. Being useless and inactive for so long drains my will so that after a while I begin to feel useless and discarded. At first I used to semi-consciously identify myself with the mat in the cell. I felt depersonalised and anonymous. My political ideas, the philosophy and aspirations of so many years, seemed remote and cold in this situation. They were words, formulations, phrases, not descriptions of a life that bore any relation to the one I was experiencing. Now, having become more active, I feel I have evolved from something as inanimate as a mat into something that lives, but merely at an animal level. I hoard things and am suspicious all the time. My emotional reactions are grossly exaggerated—a sharp word depresses me for hours, even days, whereas if the guard says 'Good night' when he switches off the light, I feel correspondingly elated.

My greatest problem is to keep my dignity and self-respect, and to feel that resistance is worthwhile. This is the crux of the duel with my captors. I sensed this fairly early on, and have taken certain measures which prove to be of great assistance. There was nothing I had read or heard which gave me any guidance but, almost instinctively, I felt that proper care of

166

my body was essential to the maintenance of my self-esteem. This has involved working out a regime of exercise and activity for the day, building up good eating and sleeping habits, and keeping clean and tidy at all times. It is more than a case of healthy body, healthy mind. By keeping bodily activity as normal and regular as possible I hope to keep my mind and emotions as normal and regular as possible. In fact I have found that the physical discipline, which I imposed on myself at a time when my mind was rational and my emotions near par, has remained effective throughout. Sound bodily habits provide an element of regularity in my life, something which is controlled by myself and which provides me with a continual source of self-confidence. The guards laughed at me when first I insisted on shaving each day. 'You won't be seeing anyone,' they said, 'so why not grow a beard, it's less trouble.' Precisely what I want is more trouble, something to do, in particular something which I can control and which is regular in time and a valuable relic of the world outside. I do not dress for dinner; I do dress for interrogations. However impatient the guards may be, whenever I am called for questioning I make a point of putting on shoes and socks, of wearing long trousers, a white shirt and a jacket. My clothes are neatly folded and my cell kept clean. From the start I used valuable minutes of my exercise time to wash thoroughly from head to toe, even though on some days the wind blew and the water was icy. I force myself to do a certain amount of vigorous physical exercise at fixed times every day. I eat as much as I can, even when I do not feel hungry, but do so only at mealtimes. I arrange for my light to be switched off at a fairly regular time each evening and try to have my exercise at more or less the same time each day, rather than simply when they can fit it in. I plan my activities every day and build up a regime to which I adhere strictly. In this way I am able to effect some degree of control over my life. I have constructed an order to operate within the order imposed on me from without. This inner rule helps me to bear my thoughts and emotions.

On the intellectual side too I have had to make conscious adjustments to save my self-respect. It is as though I feel

167

called upon to justify to a primitive part of myself a course of action which brings on me constant deprivation. A simple appeal to my philosophy and outlook on the world is insufficient. Similarly, imagined dialogues with my closest friends and associates do not help much. Both seem too distant, too abstract, too far away from me. Yet I know that I must stick to the principles associated with my philosophy and friends in some way or another, and relate them to the actual life I live. They have to be personalised; the objective factors have to be presented in immediate subjective terms. The ideas alone would be worthless without the will to utilise them, and my will is constantly being sapped.

My will was first hit by the shock which followed immediately on my imprisonment. I was bewildered and amazed and badly orientated in my new environment. Later I became more adjusted to the world of prison, but felt my scale of values being challenged. Though I have known all along that it would be wrong for me to answer questions, what I do seems increasingly less important to me. That is the major problem: to reassure myself that it does matter, that it does make a difference. The realms of experience I have entered are entirely new to me. The world seems harsh, lonely, absurd. Human effort appears to achieve so little. There is so much pain, so much sacrifice and so little to show for it all. I feel a kinship for people who have been near to death, who have seen humankind stripped of its bluff, who have achieved a certain philosophical insight and calm through their suffering. The life I have led in the past takes on a new perspective. It seems less important somehow. The person I have been outside has been so vain, so presumptuous. When faced with a real challenge I have proved to be so weak, my good only just outweighing my bad. I feel my pride being crushed; a new and purer personality emerges, but one much feebler.

20 Interrogation

FOR THREE WEEKS NO ONE HAS TRIED TO INTERROGATE ME
unless one could call the visit of the local lieutenant an attempt
at interrogation. He called in after five one evening 'just to say
hello', as he put it, 'I was going to get petrol here anyway so I
thought I would drop in.'

His manner was genuine and he was extremely personable.
He chatted to me about my position, stressing that this was not
an official visit. Did I have any complaints or queries, was there
anything he could do, was there anything I wanted to tell him?
I enjoyed his visit. He was at ease and natural compared to
the others. Funny though, he kept calling me by my first name,
as though we were old acquaintances. Apart from him, no one
has been to see me. Perhaps they are leaving me here to stew.

I am sitting again with Captain Rossouw and Lieutenant
Wagenaar in the station commander's office. 'Well, how are you
feeling today?' the captain asks.

'The same as usual. Nothing much changes for me.'

'Let's get down to business and not waste time. We have
certain questions which we want you to answer. If you don't
know the answers, then just tell us so. Now can we continue?'

'I'm afraid I'm not prepared to answer questions.'

'If you don't know the answers then just say so.'

'I'm not prepared to answer any questions.'

'Well we won't waste your time and we won't waste our time.'

He makes as if to go.

'I'm only too happy to have my time wasted, so don't leave
on my account.'

'We've got lots to do, and we can't waste our time because of your attitude. It might interest you to know that almost all the Ninety-Day prisoners in the Western Cape are no longer in detention. Why you want to be the last, I don't know. At the moment in fact there are only six left.'

'Out of how many?'

'Over sixty.'

'Whew, were there so many? And of those released from Ninety-Day detention, how many have been kept on in jail as awaiting-trial prisoners?'

He hesitates for a moment, as if caught off guard, and then smiles as he says: 'Well, that's not an easy question to answer off hand. The fact is that there are only six still being held under the Ninety-Day law. This I can tell you: some are now completely free, they were released unconditionally.'

I say nothing but inwardly I am overjoyed. They will have to do something with me now, they cannot just keep me. If they thought they really had a case to bring against me they would have put me on trial by now. I am glad I stuck to principle and held out all this time. The fool, he thinks that by telling me all the others have been released he will weaken my morale, when in fact it is the greatest news I've had since I was arrested.

'Well if you've got nothing to say,' the captain continues, 'we won't waste your . . . I mean we won't waste our time any more.'

On the way back to my cell I want to dance. When I get there I see the station commander standing in the little yard. After interrogation he always watches me as I return to my cell. He asks me how it went. 'Oh, the same as usual,' I tell him, 'we don't get very far.' He says nothing. Is it my imagination or is he pleased that I refuse to give in? Perhaps he does not want them to break me down. After all I am really his prisoner, not theirs. Whatever I might have done in the past I speak very respectfully to him and I read the Bible regularly. I make jokes and I can't really be evil. Must have been bad company that I was in. Perhaps too he enjoys seeing someone stand up to the special branch, the new glamour boys of the force. They think they know everything and they try to run the show even in

170

police stations which are being run by people who have been in the force much longer than they have.

It seems that we are back to the routine of weekly visits. This time the captain and the tall lieutenant come to speak to me in my cell. They are jovial today. We chat in Afrikaans, which seems to make them very happy. I soon let them know that my attitude to answering questions remains unchanged, and they do not press me on that score.

'What do you want pencil and paper for?' the tall lieutenant asks. 'Are you going to write a book?'

'I'm not allowed to write a book, my ban[1] prevents me.'

'Yes, here in South Africa that's so. But they could publish it overseas. The people there would buy it like a shot.'

'Well all I do is make up crossword puzzles and work out word games.'

'You've got everything you need here, I see. The facilities aren't so bad, and you seem to have lots of books, and plenty of food. It's not such a bad place to be in really.'

'Any day you want to swop with me I'll be only too pleased.'

'I suppose when you leave here you'll tell everyone how badly you were treated?'

'You can be sure I'll tell the truth, and only the truth. Some things have been terrible, like being alone all the time, while other things have improved a lot. It's been quite an experience for me and, however it turns out in the end, I will have learnt a lot. When I get out, whenever that might be, I'll speak of the good as well as the bad. I might mention that I think I understand the police force a lot better than I used to before. Many things about the way it is run, its discipline and so on, have come as quite a surprise to me.'

'He's not such a bad chap, you know,' the captain says of me

[1] This was the second Banning Order against Albie Sachs (the first was applied when he was an undergraduate at Cape Town University and a supporter of the Passive Resistance Movement). Under the terms of the ban he is not allowed to leave Cape Town; to enter a school or university; to publish anything he writes, to write letters to prohibited persons except to his father who is in England. It also forbids him from being in the company of two, or more, people—a restriction which makes a game of bridge as illegal as a political meeting.

171

to the lieutenant. 'If he promised to give up all his nonsense, we could even think about letting him go.'

They are at the door ready to leave. The sun beats down. We are so friendly, such good chaps together. The only feature which spoils the show is that after we have bidden each other hearty farewells they will leave me behind locked up in my cell.

'It depends on what you mean by nonsense,' I say.

'All your subversive activities. You know very well what I mean.'

'What would a promise be worth in these circumstances?'

'It seems you don't think very much of your own promises.'

'No, what I meant is that I can't make any promises from here where I know nothing of what is happening in the world. If I did make a promise, then I would stick to it. But I would rather not make a promise which I would regret later.'

Why did I pursue the subject of the promise? If they let me go, it won't be because of any promises, but because they have no further use for keeping me. I must learn to control my tongue.

One morning the station commander stays longer than usual with me. We have finished discussing the porridge I had for breakfast, and the weather. He stands near me, looks me in the face, and says:

'It won't be long now. You'll soon be out of here.'

I have been hoping for something like this. The atmosphere has eased so much over the last two weeks that my expectations of being let out have soared.

'You mean they are going to charge me?' I ask cautiously. 'Or will I be completely free?'

'No, they've decided to let you go completely. I've heard from a very reliable source. They've had trouble with witnesses because so many have left the country. So they're letting you go. The papers should be on their way to Pretoria and it shouldn't take long. Once they decide, they can arrange everything in a day. With Esme they decided to let her go in the morning, and the next day they got a telex back authorising her release. So it shouldn't be long now.'

172

'Well, thank you very much for letting me know. I'm very grateful.'

'I haven't told you anything. Don't forget that. I am just in charge of looking after you. I'm not supposed to know anything about when you will be released.'

'All right then,' I smile back at him, 'thank you for not letting me know. I won't forget.'

As he leaves he grins back at me, grateful that at last I am getting into my head some of the ways of how they do things in the police force.

I have been in now for exactly sixty days. If they let me out this week, let's see it's the beginning of December, I'll just have time to go back to Chambers before the end of the Supreme Court term. It will soon be vacation, and I will rush down to Clifton beach and lie in the sun. There will be lots of people there and they will say: who is that pale youth? Someone will tell them that he is Albie Sachs and he has just come out from Ninety Days. And the people will crowd round me, and I'll tell them all about it, and they will be impressed. I've made it, I've made it. Three cheers for me! I've made it. And they've lost.

Two anxious weeks have passed. I no longer leap to my feet every time I hear the keys. Something has gone wrong. It is a week before Christmas. My ninety days will be up four days after Christmas, so if they are going to let me go, they will do it this week. From their point of view it would be a gesture which would look good in the press.

I am called into the station commander's office. As usual I put on my best clothes for the occasion: suit, white shirt and shoes. Normally the station commander is the one who tells me to go to the office. Today a young special branch sergeant has come. He was the one who arrested me two months ago as I was entering the advocate's building. Now he is quite friendly.

'You were the bloke who started it all,' I say to him jocularly. 'It's all your fault. If you hadn't arrested me I wouldn't be here now.'

'That's right,' he laughs back, 'I'm the dirty bastard.' He

173

looks round the cell, and noticing the bag of oranges hanging behind the door, says,

'It's just like Patel's shop[1] in here. Okay, are you ready now? Let's go.'

Sitting in the station commander's office is the tall thin-faced Vlok, the warrant officer who threatened me with the knife the day I was arrested. His teeth are large and brown stained. They seem to block his words as they come out, so that his voice sounds thick and clumsy. His speech is deliberate and emotionless, yet its dryness gives it a slightly hypnotic quality. Although he speaks loudly, I have to strain to follow what he is saying. The only way he reveals any emotion is by occasional movements of the corners of his mouth, which he pulls out to show pleasure and contracts to show displeasure. His long, taut cheeks never seem to move. The one feature which betrays that he possesses a nervous system is his eyes, which are bloodshot as though all the nerve endings under his mask-like face have crowded there to reach the air.

Our conversation begins with the standard preliminary verbal sparring. He enquires after my well-being, I make a careful reply to the effect that solitary confinement is cruel but I will survive it. (I am sorry in a way that the captain is not here. I have got used to the captain. There is a sort of relationship between us. I know his face so well, all the inflexions of his voice, his idioms and speech idiosyncrasies. The battle is really between the captain and myself. Why does this man have to intrude?)

'Now, before I put certain questions to you, I must warn you according to the judge's rules. I don't have to repeat them to you, I'm sure you know them well enough.'

'My memory is a bit hazy, so I'd like you to repeat them to me, please.'

'Oh come on now, you're an advocate, you know them better than I do.'

'In any event, there are different warnings for different situations. Am I merely suspected of a crime, or am I under arrest and facing a charge, or what?'

[1] Called after the Indian who opened it.

He sighs, and the corners of his mouth contract. He looks pained that I should be such a stickler.

'You are being detained under the Ninety-Day law at the moment. What will happen afterwards depends on the Attorney-General. He will decide whether to prosecute you or not. In the meanwhile I warn you, in terms of the judge's rules, that we are going to put certain questions to you and if you answer them your answers will be recorded and may be used in evidence if you are brought to trial.'

'Am I obliged to answer the questions?' I ask. I know well enough that the main point of the caution which, the judges have laid down, must be administered to all suspects, is that suspects need not answer questions if they do not wish to do so.

'No, you are not obliged to answer any of the questions,' he replies dryly.

'But if I don't answer the questions then you will continue to keep me locked up under the Ninety-Day law.'

'The two things are quite separate.'

But I am only one person, I wish to say, on the one hand you advise me that I need not answer questions, on the other you tell me that if I don't answer questions, I'll never be released from solitary confinement.

'Now let's get on with the questions,' he continues.

'I'm not prepared to answer questions.'

'We'll read them to you anyhow.'

He takes out from a briefcase two bundles of typescript, one of which he gives to the sergeant, the other he holds in front of him. Then he begins reading. The questions are in Afrikaans.

'When you were arrested on 1st October 1963, a copy of the May 1962 issue of *Fighting Talk* was found in your office. Did you know it was banned?'

'I am not prepared to answer at this stage.'

'Two: for how long had you possessed it there?'

'I am not prepared to answer at this stage.'

'Three: did you have permission from the Minister to have it in your possession?'

'I am not prepared to answer at this stage.'

The questions drone on and my replies—always the same—

are copied down by the sergeant. I am asked about lecture courses given in a room in Athlone. I am asked about multiracial groups which were said to have been given training in mountain-climbing. I am asked in great detail about my participation in a camp held in December 1962 near the village of Mamre. Did I know that instruction was given on sabotage? When did I arrive there? Whom did I bring with me? In which tent was I going to sleep? Who was in charge of the camp? What did I say there? Why did I tell people there that they must be careful of police spies and of agents and provocateurs? I am not prepared to answer at this stage. I am not prepared to answer at this stage. . . .

The final group of questions relates to an address given to a house-meeting of Africans in Nyanga Location[1] on such and such a date.

'Twenty-three: who was present there with you?'

'Twenty-four: why did you tell the Bantu there that freedom would soon come. That they would get support from Ethiopia, Ghana and Algeria. That they must keep up their sabotage activities. . . .'

'I am not prepared to answer at this stage.'

Finally they are done. Three pages of questions have been put to me, and my declining to answer recorded after each question.

'Are you not prepared to answer *any* of the questions?'

'When I'm in Court I'll be happy to answer *all* the questions. Until then, there is no point in picking and choosing. I suppose this does mean that I will be charged?'

He looks gravely at me with his long, stiff face. 'You've got friends,' he mumbles through his teeth.

His speech is so flat and unrhythmical that I hear the sounds but am not sure of the sense.

'I beg your pardon,' I say.

He seems sad and tired, as though the proceedings are boring him.

'But surely, you're a clever man,' he says, 'you must have

---

[1] A location near Cape Town where, after Sharpeville, tens of thousands of Africans demonstrated and a number were shot. Later Albie Sachs successfully defended some of the demonstrators.

worked out a defence to the Possession of Banned Literature charge.' He does not repeat the bit about my having friends.

'Of course I've got a defence, but I didn't work it out, it's the truth.' The sergeant seems pleased by my answer.

I am thinking carefully now. These questions will be placed before the Attorney-General who will have to decide whether to prosecute me or not. In fact I am not guilty of any crime in relation to these questions. Now for the first time they have put specific questions to me. When I am charged, I can make out an affidavit for the Attorney-General explaining everything. It won't involve anyone else and it should persuade him to withdraw the charges against me. If not, I will speak out in Court.

'There's just one thing I want to say. I'd like you to write it down.' The sergeant gives a faint sigh, which sounds like the inrush of air into a newly-opened tobacco tin.

'Wait, let me write it first so that I get it quite straight.' I borrow pencil and paper and make jottings.

'Okay, here you are: I can say quite honestly and on my honour as an advocate and officer of the Court that I am not guilty of any offence in relation to any of the questions put to me.'

'Is that all you are prepared to say?'

'Yes, that's all.'

The warrant officer puts the typescript back in the briefcase with weary movements, as though all this questioning is very tiresome to him. We chat for a while, about Christmas and about the hot weather we are having. He is slightly more animated now. The sergeant comes into his own. 'I hear you've been studying the Bible,' he tells me, 'have you learnt anything from it?'

They all ask me about the Bible now, as though the mere fact that a person reads the Bible makes him good.

'Yes, I've learnt a lot,' I reply. 'It's given me a new insight into things I knew very little about before, and there are many things I understand now which I did not understand before.'

The sergeant seems happy with this reply. It is as well that I do not elaborate. He would not understand me if I told him what my new views were. That, as a portrayal of the gradual

177

development of a philosophy which culminates in an assertion of the power and glory of love, it contains a magnificent truth. That as an historical record it presents a picture of virtually unrelieved barbarism made all the more horrible by a purported divine sanction. That the Book of Job is perhaps the most compelling piece of writing I have ever read and that, take away its false happy ending, the riddle it poses negates all religion, based on theism. That it is ironic that the Afrikaners, who in recent times, to a large extent have made themselves a party to the persecution of the Jews, as continued in the present day, should draw so heavily on ancient Jewish history in creating their own national ethos. That the Old Testament both in letter and in spirit (apart from the Book of Isaiah) does not support apartheid. That the New Testament, both in letter and in spirit, is utterly and explicitly in opposition to apartheid. To him no doubt the Bible is quite uncomplicated. It is literally true and deals with sin, nationalism, crucifixion, and redemption for the chosen few. It would not do for me to add a religious dispute to my present difficulties.

We chat on about other subjects. Christmas is in the air even here in the police station. There is an informality and lack of tension about our discussion that reminds me of school breaking up at the end of the year. 'I'll be round again soon,' the warrant officer tells me. 'We'll see what we can do. Unfortunately the final decision does not lie in our hands. Oh by the way, here are the questions. You might like to think them over.' He hands me a few pages of typescript.

'No thanks,' I reply. 'I'm not really interested.' I return them to him. He replaces them in his briefcase and they leave.

I have much to think about as I return to my cell. It seems that they are planning to charge me with possession of banned literature and with sabotage. It will be strange appearing as the accused in the Court where I have so often appeared for the defence. I wonder who the judge will be? I hope it's the Judge-President. He will believe me, especially if he knows I have put myself on my honour. As far as the banned periodical is concerned I shouldn't have any difficulty with that. I had no idea it was in my office, and could have had no motive for keeping it

178

there. It was quite legal when first published, and must have got stuck between some papers of mine after I had finished reading it. They can't possibly get a conviction against me on this score. The camp might be a little trickier, but surely they know that I was there only for a morning. They found us there at the time and if *they* could see nothing suspicious to justify arresting us, there is no reason why *I* should have been suspicious. If sabotage was discussed it certainly was not done in my presence or to my knowledge. As far as I could see it was an ordinary holiday camp with talks and lectures on physical fitness, motor car engines and so on. The funny thing is that I cannot remember the subject on which I gave a talk! Was it my talk on precolonial Africa? Or was it the elementary one I give on economics, in which I say something about the production of wealth, the operation of banks, how companies and the Stock Exchange work and so on? All I can remember is that there were two young Africans who fell asleep while I spoke. Someone gave them a crack with a switch so as to wake them up, and I said, 'No, if the teacher sends the pupil to sleep then the teacher deserves the hiding.'

Hell, it would be ludicrous in Court if that is all I am able to remember of the lecture I gave. Yet there it is. My talk was routine and could have been any one of a couple of routine lectures I have worked out. I had no need to remember it afterwards and my memories of that day are taken up entirely by the arrival of the police and my attempts to prevent them from arresting those Africans present who did not have their passbooks with them.

It is two days later, and I am closeted in a small office alone with Warrant Officer Vlok.

'Look here,' he says to me, 'I'd like to try to help you. The present position isn't getting you anywhere, and it's not getting the police anywhere. As a matter of fact I'm due to retire in a couple of weeks and I'd like to get this matter finished with as soon as possible. To me personally it doesn't make any difference. I've had a long career and I can see you are no ordinary criminal. In fact, we don't like to see a chap like you here. You don't belong here at all.'

That's easy, I feel like saying, open the door and you don't have to see me here any more.

'Isn't there anything you can suggest to get out of the deadlock? Headquarters are absolutely adamant that we cannot let you go until you make a statement,' he continues.

'Well, Mr Vlok, I've been thinking about the matter a bit, and all I'm prepared to suggest is as follows. I'm prepared to clarify to the Attorney-General anything he wants to know about those questions you put to me the day before yesterday. I will do it either through one of my colleagues—you can choose anyone you like—or through one of the assistants of the Attorney-General.'

'Good.' His mouth extends outwards. He is pleased. 'I can't promise you anything. I will put it to my superiors this weekend and I should be able to let you have an answer by Monday or Tuesday.'

'Wednesday is Christmas, so I'd be glad if you could get it done right away.'

'Certainly, I'll do my very best. I'll see you again soon.'

As he leaves me I realise that, apart from the occasions for which the station commander was subsequently reprimanded, this is the first time I have been spoken to by one policeman alone.

It is Tuesday morning, Christmas eve. I am tense with apprehension as I approach the office in which the warrant officer is waiting for me. As I open the door, I see his face is longer than ever and his lips are pursed so that the corners of his mouth are drawn in.

'I tried, really I tried,' he tells me, 'but they said nothing doing. Someone has just been to Pretoria and he reports that they cannot possibly allow you to speak to anyone on the Attorney-General's staff. I'm sorry.'

Oh well, that's that. I am glad in a way. I was a bit unhappy about making a clarification to the Attorney-General, even if by agreement it was restricted to the written questions put to me and related to my own actions only. On principle I should never say anything at all, to anybody.

180

'I'll tell you what I'll do for you, though,' he continues, 'write out whatever statement you want and I personally will see to it that it gets to the Attorney-General.'

'Thank you for the offer, but I'm not prepared to go any further than my suggestion of the other day.'

'Don't you trust me?'

'Please don't feel insulted, but . . .'

'I feel very insulted.'

'It's got nothing to do with you. I'm not prepared to make a statement to any policeman, not even you.'

'But what's the difference? Anything you told the Attorney-General we would get to see anyhow.'

If that is so, then why wouldn't you accept my original suggestion. I've already put myself on my honour as an advocate. Does that mean nothing to you people? I feel emotional. My eyeballs are pricking. It is so humiliating to have these people scorn one's honour like that. He watches me closely.

'I must say I admire you, I admire the way you are prepared to take the rap for the others.' I want to shout at him, What do you take me for? Gangsters take the rap for each other. I'm not a gangster, I'm a principled person who cherishes his honour. You don't agree with my views, obviously, and right now I'm not questioning your right to have me here, but why do you insist on speaking to me as though I were a jewel thief or a bag snatcher? My cheeks feel warm and when I do speak, it is all I can do to remain calm.

'Well, thank you for trying. I don't think there's anything more to discuss, unless you want to get on to something else.' A tremor of anger gives a slightly hysterical edge to my words. I relax for a moment as a thought occurs to me. 'Oh, and let me wish you Happy Christmas.' He too has been growing tense, but on hearing my greeting the corners of his mouth push outwards.

'I extend the compliments of the season to you too,' he answers, 'and, as my Jewish friend says, well over the Fast!'

One of your best friends, no doubt. He is too mean even to wish me a proper Happy Christmas. I want to get back to the security of my cell. His smile bares large tobacco-stained teeth.

181

For the first time I wish to be alone. I cannot wait for him to stand up. He stares at me for a long time in a fatherly, admonishing way, draws in the corners of his mouth, shakes his head slightly from side to side and raises himself from his seat. I notice that his eyes are more bloodshot than ever. Then he goes. The station commander is waiting for me outside my cell.

'Well, how was it today?' he asks jovially.

'I was hoping we could arrive at a compromise,' I mutter back at him, 'but they refused. So it's back to where we started.' I feel bitter, ashamed of my offer to speak to the Attorney-General, yet angry that it was refused.

'I showed Vlok your Christmas card when he came this morning. We had a good laugh over it.' He chuckles in a harsh, honest, self-satisfied voice. 'You can talk to Vlok you know, he's quite straight. I've known him for many years.'

I say nothing. They are not going to release me. It was you, you bugger, who told me I would soon be free. Now they will arrest me again when my ninety days are up, and again and again. I know it's not your fault, and that you believed what you said and were trying to bring me some cheer. But you don't have to stand there looking so smug. This wonderful world of yours, it won't last all that long. You think that South Africa is one big police station that you people can run how you like for as long as you like, but you're making a big mistake. You people are asking for it. You stupid, dumb, obstinate people. You say you are trying to preserve yourselves but all you are doing is inviting destruction. Yes, total destruction. You will go under in the debris of your own constructions. And it will be your own fault.

'What are you looking so serious for all of a sudden?' The station commander bursts into my angry reverie. 'You're usually so cheerful.'

'No, I was just thinking,' I reply. 'I suppose they are going to charge me after all.' He looks slightly embarrassed, and nods his head.

'Yes, they're going to charge you.' He rattles the keys and moves towards the door. 'I've made arrangements for Mrs Cleminshaw to bring you a special Christmas dinner tomorrow.

182

My wife will also be cooking you a special lunch. You will have food from our own table. I hope you like it. I'll come in the morning to see you. I must be going now, I can't wait around here all day. They're waiting for me up at divisional head-quarters. We're having a little party you know. We have them every year. Well, cheerio then.'

He slams the door and I stare at it bitterly, letting my eyes run along the criss-cross pattern of its bolts. Cell of mine, it looks as if you will have me for a long, long time.

21 Soliloquy in Blue

JAIL IS FOR THE BIRDS.

Scratching these words on the inside of my cell just above the door gave me a lot of pleasure at the time. It was fun to watch the police walk in and out of the door oblivious of the slogan above their heads. But today it fails to amuse me for my melancholy is too deep.

The wishbone from the chicken I received at Christmas is wedged on a bolt just below the word BIRDS. It is dry and warped, and looks rather silly. I can't say it has brought me much luck.

I look at the calendar which I have scratched out day by day at the side of the door. It extends in a long column and is already halfway down to the words which I wrote, in jest, just above the ground:

HOPE I DON'T GET THIS FAR

At the top of the column is the sentence:

... A. L. SACHS WAS DETAINED IN SOLITARY CON-
FINEMENT WITHOUT TRIAL AS A NINETY-DAY
PRISONER FOR STANDING AS ADVOCATE AND
CITIZEN FOR JUSTICE FOR ALL

Was it I who wrote those words? My mood must have been braver then than it is now. How many times have I gouged into the paintwork with the end of a tube of toothpaste?

Today is my eighty-ninth day. Tomorrow my ninety days will be up. My first ninety days. It is the middle of the holiday season, halfway between Christmas and New Year. Why can they still be holding me? I had hoped to be lying on the beach by now. Perhaps I was silly to believe the station commander when he said I would soon be out. Yet all the signs pointed in that direction. I am sure he was genuine. Imagine, he even went so far as to tell me I should join the police force. Said that with my University degrees I could be an officer within eight years. And when I told him tactfully that I was too soft to be a policeman, meaning that I would always sympathise with the suspect, he said:

'Never mind, we won't send you out on patrol. We'll give you work in the office.'

I think he really is quite fond of me. I have the feeling that he even tried a little pressure of his own to get my release by telling security that he wanted to do certain repairs and cleaning work to my cell! That would explain why the Public Works Department men came here the other day. He really does have a fixation about cleanliness and order though, which is surprising considering that his jacket is always undone and his belt loose. Every time he sees a tiny bud of green pushing its way out of cracks in the asphalt, he orders that it be swept away. And how can I tell him that I love the little plants, even if they are only weeds growing from seedlings blown in by the wind.

I'm sure one of the reasons he likes me is that I seem to put the colonel in a good mood whenever inspection time comes round. For example, on that day when it was raining, and the colonel said I wouldn't be getting much sun, and I replied:

'No, not even the Supreme Court can order the sun to come out.' That had become the big joke. I am sure, though, the colonel must have got tired of hearing the station commander repeat the same joke each week. I wonder if he showed the colonel my Christmas card? It was addressed to the men at the station, but I should imagine he would have passed it on:

ALTHOUGH I HAD MY TWENTY-FIRST SIX YEARS AGO OR MORE, ALL I WANT FOR CHRISTMAS IS,
and then on the next page,

THE KEY OF THE DOOR

Not that my home-by-Christmas campaign got me anywhere. Still, it was fun working out the card.

It all comes back in such detail. It's amazing how clear my

memory is. That is, for things that have happened since I was detained. I keep forgetting things that I have to do, and my recollections of the world outside are extremely faint, yet the events of my detention stand out sharply. I suppose it is because life here is so pure in a way. There are no distractions whatsoever, none of the trivia of ordinary life, the preoccupations which normally clutter the mind. It is as though the air is clear, like a scene at night after the rain, when distant lamps throw out their light firmly and without any twinkling. The peculiar thing is that I tend to forget all the horror of my life here. The loneliness, the spells of near despair, the hours and hours of aching unhappiness, the contemplated suicide. Those I take for granted. Also the—how shall I describe it—the disintegrative processes in my mind. The inability to develop a thought, the apathy. The desperate longing to do something, as though I am chained down by idleness, the craving for stimulation, the feeling of neutrality, of depersonalisation and the ridiculous terrors. At least I hope they are ridiculous. That so-and-so is pregnant, that so-and-so is seriously ill.

Yet if one looks out after dark one doesn't see the night, one only sees the lights. Or if one swims under water one doesn't see the salty, choking, bitter water. That is merely one's habitat. One sees the fishes that pass by, the streaming seaweed, and the refracting rocks that are embedded at the bottom. If someone asks what it was like down there, you don't say it was wet, you tell them of the things you saw.

I often seem to think of the sea these days. When I run in the yard, I think, in fantasy, that I am running to the sea. When I lie in the sun I dream I am drifting on an open raft in quiet soporific doldrums, far from land. The whole period of detention often seems like a journey into a different physical dimension, an existence in a strange element, a rapid evolutionary reversion to primitive submarine life. Perhaps it is having read *Moby Dick* that has made me so sea-conscious. I must find that passage again. Ah, here it is:

The sea had jeeringly kept his finite body up, but drowned the infinite of his soul. Not drowned entirely, though. Rather carried

186

down alive to wondrous depths, where strange shapes of the un-
warped primal world glided to and fro before his passive eyes, and
the miser-merman, Wisdom, revealed his hoarded heaps; and
among the joyous, heartless, ever-juvenile eternities, Pip saw the
multitudinous, God-omnipresent, coral insects, that out of the
firmament of waters heaved the colossal orbs.

This has a sweep and majesty that equals that of the Book of
Job. And to think that if I hadn't been in jail, I might never have
read either work. It's an ill wind. So many things about my
detention are strange. The policemen who at first shouted at me
now ask for legal advice. Some even call me 'Sir'. I must be
the first prisoner ever to complain of receiving too much Roquefort cheese and olives in my food packages!

It is wonderful the way the people outside have been organising food for me. Five times a week now I receive a meal from
outside in addition to daily milk and fruit. Three times a week
at least I get Roquefort or olives. I used to like both so much,
and now I can't eat either. The station commander tells me that
Mrs Cleminshaw has done all the organisation. How lucky I
am to have such a fine friend. Yet how ungrateful I am in some
ways to my benefactors. I examine each pot of food as though
I were an overzealous food inspector or a cookery school exam-
iner. How much effort and imagination has gone into its
preparation: a cold meal? Don't they know it is cool in the cell,
are they too busy to think about me, has sending food become
a tiresome chore, am I just part of the week's routine? A well-
prepared fancy dish can make me extraordinarily happy, whereas a plain plate of supper leaves me downcast for hours. I am
such a baby about food. I know it, but I can't help it. Also I
am always hoarding things. I have a whole carrier full of junk:
string, paper, plastic cartons, paper cups, fruit wrappers,
aluminium foil. I must throw it out. All of it, even the aluminium foil which I have pressed into a ball and which I fling into
the sunny air. And I hide things: a piece of pencil, a blade, writing paper, food.

I suck up to the police. There is no other phrase for it. I
don't actually crawl to them, but I am so eager to win their

approval, and so deferential in my manner. I wonder what they think of me? I would say most of them now would like to see me released, though they were pretty hostile at first. The one who cuts hair wouldn't accept payment for the haircut he gave me. 'Have it as a Christmas present,' he insisted.

Then there was the sergeant who came into my cell on Christmas day, took off his cap, gave me a vigorous handshake, and wished me the best of luck for the future even if the present wasn't too bright. I don't think they like some of the security branch men too much, though they don't seem to like the station commander either.

In fact, this is a very unhappy police station. There are constant intrigues and accusations and counter-accusations. Two weeks ago the station commander was charging some of the men with having stolen blankets. The men often seem to be rubbing things out in the books and changing the entries. They do it during my exercise time when they are guarding me as I run round the yard. Probably they don't realise how closely I observe them and listen to their conversation. I'm always jumping to conclusions and am nearly always wrong. Like the time when the blankets were stolen. I had seen one of the sergeants scratching out an entry with a blade a few days earlier. Then later I heard the constables talking about a policeman who killed himself with a gun. The sergeant did not appear for a whole week, so I assumed that he was the one who had committed suicide because he had been caught out in his theft. Then one day he turned up again. He had merely been on outside duty for a week. I am always trying to fit little pieces of information together to form a story.

I'll never forget those newspaper headlines that I tried to read. That was different, it was during exercise time, on a Saturday afternoon about the middle of November. As I started running round the yard I noticed that the two policemen guarding me were both reading newspapers. They sat at a table in a passage which led off the yard, and for about a third of my circuit round the yard I was able to see them. The newspapers were flat on the table, and I was moving all the time so I wasn't able to see much. Yet I could not miss seeing the huge type in which the headlines had been set, the biggest I have ever seen. The rule against my receiving news from outside was so strict that if the policemen had seen me trying to read the headlines they would have folded the papers and reprimanded me. Accordingly I had to keep up my normal running pace all the time. I was able to angle my run, however, so that I could look straight at the papers without turning my head. For the full half hour of my exercise time I tried to make out what was in those headlines. The first letter was clearly a K. Then I thought I saw an E, but I couldn't be sure. The third letter looked like an s or was it an N or a w? K-E-S? or K-E-N? That must be K-E-N-Y-A. How would it be in Afrikaans, K-E-N-I-A? Also K-E-N. . . . Oh hell, does that mean that there has been a Congo-type development in Kenya? That will panic the Whites in South Africa even further and give the Government the chance to keep us locked up for as long as they like. Or is it that there's going to be an election? The only time they have head-lines that big is when there is a General Election announcement. What is the Afrikaans word for election again? Oh yes, VERKIESING. Is there such a word as KIESING (a choosing)? Perhaps it was K-I-E that I saw. So I speculated as I ran. At the end of the half hour they folded the papers and led me back to my cell. On several occasions that day and the next I tried to work out what the headline could have been but could make no progress. After a few days I forgot about the matter altogether. Then, about five days after I had seen the headlines, as the captain and the lieutenant were leaving my cell (they had come for a brief interrogation), the lieutenant suddenly turned round and said to me:

'I suppose you've been told about Kennedy?'

Kennedy—K-E-N, that's it, it was KENNEDY, I thought. I told him no, I had heard nothing.

'Didn't you know then that he has been assassinated?'

'What?'

'Yes, he was shot last week.' As the lieutenant speaks he grins with excitement.

I must have been the only person in Cape Town who hadn't yet heard the news. I could imagine what it must have been like when it first broke—everybody stopping everybody else and asking, with the shocked laughter that accompanies such news, whether they had heard. Now he had again found someone to whom he could be first bearer of the story.

'You're not pulling my leg are you?' I asked suspiciously.

'No, of course not. And what's more, not only was he assassinated, but his assassin was also assassinated.'

I looked at the captain, who was also grinning.

'No, it's true,' the captain said.

'Who did it? Who killed Kennedy, I mean?'

'One of *your* people,' the lieutenant smirked back at me. He seemed very pleased.

Hell, how terrible, I thought; they were delighted, and I was shocked. Then, it occurred to me that this might mean war . . . war! nuclear weapons, and no holds barred. The world blown up, humanity wiped out.

Now comes the part of the story of which I am particularly ashamed. Of all the things they have done to me, this is the worst: they have made me think of everything that happens in the world in terms of how it affects me. The world, as I saw it, faced destruction, yet all I could think was: if there is war, it will be terrible for us detainees. We will be lined up and shot. Yes, after the initial feeling of shock and distress at hearing the news of Kennedy's death had subsided, I started in fantasy anticipating myself being taken away by rough guards, put against a wall and shot. For the first time since the early days of my detention I began to think about escaping. I was in terror of being shot, and yet was too integrated into my new life to think in practical terms of how to get over the wall. Then as I ran round and round during exercise time a beautiful daylight dream would overcome me.

I would imagine that the police station had once been a school, and hidden away in my cell was the end of a gas pipe which had formerly led to the science laboratory. I would open the nozzle of the pipe and fit it to my air-mattress, which would be inflated like a lighter-than-air balloon. Then I would tie myself, with the girdle of my gown, to the air-mattress and float slowly out of the yard. I would soar high, high above the

190

police station, way up into the sky. There I would be, floating above Cape Town, looking serenely on the houses and green far down below. Then, letting the gas out bit by bit, I would descend gently to a soft green lawn where no one would trouble me any more. My fantasies when I am running are always happier than those I have when lying down. I seem to dream more during the day than at night. In the early weeks, I remember, I did have a few vivid dreams at night. Some were sex dreams, and I recall that in all of them consummation of the sexual act was frustrated by the intervention of some external occurrence. Now it is as though there is insufficient material to occupy my mind when I am awake, let alone when I am asleep. As for sex, I hardly ever think about it. I would like someone to hold my hand and tell me I am nice, certainly, but not to go to bed with me. If they allowed a girl to spend the night with me here, I think I would refuse the offer. It would only upset my routine and make for a painful readjustment afterwards.

When one is deprived of external stimulation, the erotic drive apparently is not very strong. If it were not for stimulating passages in some of the books I read, I think I would forget about sex entirely. Poor old station commander: he is so worried about sex and immorality. Yet he interprets the Bible as though it were a history of sexual encounters and of apartheid. When he saw that Lawrence Durrell described the *Alexandrian Quartet* as an examination of love, he clearly considered withholding the series from me on the grounds, as he put it, that it was about immorality. I'm afraid I lied a little to prevent the ban: I told him that the books were not immoral but an attempt to expose immorality.

Durrell, Henry James, Proust, George Elliot, Racine, Melville, Moss Hart, Mary Renault, Jan Rabie, Venter, C. P. Snow and Lampedusa; I have certainly got through quite a long and varied list of authors. I wish sometimes I could bring together the various characters of their books. I'd especially like to fling some of James' fussy old ladies and gents with their 'ambiences' and 'relationships' into the Nile mud, or put them to sea with Captain Ahab. None of them ever seem to get their hands dirty or do any work—just like me now!

191

I suppose idleness is a sort of prison in itself. Whatever the effect of stone walls and iron bars might or might not be, empty hours do a prison make and idleness a cage. The only work I do these days is running. I must have covered quite a distance by now. Jogging at the rate of say ten minutes a mile for half an hour means that I run about three miles each day. Three miles a day for eighty-nine days—say ninety—is two hundred and seventy miles. I wonder if I would have been able to run non-stop to Muizenberg beach if they had released me? The sergeant said it is about eight miles away. He said I should easily make it if I kept my head up. Apparently he used to be a bit of an athlete himself. He is one of the nicer ones here. He never shouts. I bet he is an ex-serviceman.

That other quiet sergeant, I wonder if he is a homosexual, said I should go to a party with him when I was released. They have nice parties, he told me: no girls, mind you, but they drink and have a lot of fun. I wonder how he got those two scratches right down his cheek? That was on Christmas day. His companion, the very young constable, had been sick that same day. Vomited all over the yard. That was a most peculiar morning I remember. All the prisoners were released on bail save for one woman who they said was a prostitute. She couldn't raise the five pounds. It was a stroke of luck for me, for it enabled me to give someone a Christmas present, and to do so in true Christian style, without the left hand knowing what the right hand was doing. I must look up that passage again. I wonder what that woman looked like? In the end they let her out on her own recognizances, and my money was returned to me. So I had the best of both worlds—the satisfaction of liberality, and my money back.

On Christmas eve they must have had a staff party for the officials at the magistrate's court. Or rather, two parties, one for the Whites and one for the non-Whites. As though two Christ-children were born that day in Bethlehem. The yard allotted to me for my exercise that afternoon adjoined the Court building, and through the windows I could hear the chatter of the non-Whites—the interpreters and cleaning staff—and could sniff the fragrant perfume worn by their wives. Every few minutes I heard the voice of the Chief Magistrate asking if they were still enjoying themselves. This was followed by obsequious assurances from them that they were very happy. I was but a yard away, if that, and felt like yelling:

No, we're not happy. Why the hell must we stand around here on our own in the passage when you Whites are all having such a good time in the courtroom? And what are we celebrating anyway, the thousands of people we sent to jail this year, the hundreds of boys we beat with canes? Court is an awful, solemn place, where human dislocation is dealt with, it is not a fitting locale for festivity.

Of course I said nothing, but simply ran on and on in the little yard, intoxicated by the rich aroma drifting through the windows. It was the first feminine smell I had known for nearly three months. Together with the gift of the lovely rich Christmas cake, a friend so thoughtfully sent in to me (wot, no sixpences), it made Christmas a special day for me, which it never really had been in the past. I remember I nearly cried when I received that cake.

My emotions are obviously extremely fragile. I cannot cope with anything unexpected, particularly if it is pleasant. Then when I had finished eating the cake I felt sad. It was all gone and I was still in prison. I remember lying in the sun on the wall-enclosed patch of asphalt outside my cell, and thinking about families parting after heavy convivial meals, with each member voluntarily seeking solitude and sleep. I am lucky to be able to lie in the sun each day. It makes me feel healthy. When I am in the sun I don't mind not doing anything, even not thinking. It is as though that is an activity in itself: merely to be in the sun; when the sun leaves the yard I always feel melancholy. I notice the insects that beat against the wall, they are trapped and batter themselves in spasmodic and futile efforts to reach freedom. Eventually they die, and their small carcases lie hollow and dehydrated on the baking ground. Dainty parachute seeds float down past the high wall and land on the hard asphalt. Nothing grows here. The faintest trace of green is regarded as a weed which must on discovery be instantly swept away by the broom. This is a place of death. I desecrate it with my living.

One day I too will turn to dust and be swept into the asphalt by the hard spiky bristles.

I wonder what they will do with me tomorrow? There is a faint chance that they will release me on the exact moment that my ninety days are up, but it is so slight as hardly to be worth hoping for. Perhaps next week they will bring me to Court. Anyhow, it is no use speculating. I have waited so long, I can wait another few days. I feel rather proud that I have stuck it out for nearly three months. That takes me halfway to the end of the next ninety days. I hope I can hold out till then.

This heavy steel door is so formidable, so enduring. I have to be fed or exercised every day, but the door just stands there, like my personal destiny. I must take down that wishbone. It looked rather jaunty when first I put it there, but now it seems silly, a dirty piece of bone. I might as well break it and wish.

I remember outside how difficult I found it to wish. Once I stood for ten minutes after my coin had sunk to the bottom of the pool, hesitating over an appropriate wish. It had to be something for the good of all, yet personal to me: of general value, but not too abstract and remote. It had to be not too unrealizable yet at least in some measure fanciful. Thus in the end my wish had all the requisite characteristics of a good wish, save the most important of all: it lacked spontaneity.

Today I won't hesitate. With each hand I grasp the wishbone, and pull. My left hand wins: it does not matter if my right hand knows.

I wish I were set free.

I wish it.

I wish it.

PART THREE

Caledon Square

Sufficient unto the Day

22 Vivat Libertas

AT LEAST I DO NOT FEEL SUICIDAL THIS TIME. I HAVE learnt to cope with being transferred from one cell to another. My standard of living has dropped somewhat. I am back on the floor, though I do have a mattress, and there is a narrow bunk on which I sit occasionally. The cell is small, only nine feet by six, and has so little natural light that the electric light has to be kept on all day. Fortunately my watch has been given back to me otherwise I would have difficulty estimating the time here. There is no lavatory in the cell and no running water. I will have to get used to a completely new set of guards. I will no longer see the sun, though for half an hour in the morning and half an hour in the late afternoon I will be allowed to exercise in a small yard at the end of the passage which runs past my door.

It is only a few hours since they brought me here to the Caledon Square police station from the Wynberg police station. Again they did not tell me where they were taking me.

'Pack your things as quickly as you can,' Lieutenant Wagenaar had said. 'These days,' I had replied, 'I am not used to doing things in a hurry.' 'Well, you'd better hurry now,' he had answered. They keep me doing nothing for eighty-nine days, but when they want to move me, they expect me to rush at their command. I suppose that is one of the laws of prison life: endless time-wasting punctuated by an occasional absurd sprint, on the prisoner's part, to demonstrate obedience.

The journey to my present cell was a little disappointing. I was conveyed in a car this time, a sign perhaps of my improved status. Though the colours and movements of the world were exciting, they were not as thrilling as they had been on my trip from Maitland to Wynberg. I suppose that having reading matter to occupy my mind has to some extent assuaged the extremeness of my hunger for visual stimulation.

My guess is that they have brought me here to the central police station at Caledon Square so that I will be in the same building as the local security headquarters. I have the feeling that I am the last detainee still being held in Cape Town, and having me available here in town will save the security men the trouble of travelling out to Wynberg for interrogations. Yet this cell is so tiny and so lacking in facilities that they surely cannot be planning to keep me here for long.

Tomorrow my ninety days will be up. Obviously they will re-detain me, otherwise they would not have bothered to move me at all. Perhaps next week they will bring me to trial. For the first two months of my detention all I wanted was to be brought before a Court. Now I am more ambitious—I want to emerge from detention a completely free man. Yet if they do charge me next week, and it seems likely that that is what they have in mind, I shall at least have a chance to get bail. I shall be able to address the Court, and in making my application for bail I can expose the hell of solitary confinement. I will say that I am emotionally and mentally unfit to stand trial; that my only companions have been the fleas; that the only activity allowed me has been the growing of a moustache; that before being made to face a criminal charge I should be permitted to mingle with people and regain my balance as a member of human society. I will ask for Harry, the leader of the Bar, to defend me. I suppose he is away on holiday now. I wonder if they will shove me into one of those little courtrooms upstairs which they use when they remand prisoners whom they wish to keep out of the eye of the public and away from the Press? I will insist that I be allowed to telephone a lawyer, and also my mother. Being in Court will be one step to liberty. Perhaps, though, they are not planning to bring me to trial at all. Possibly they are hoping that by detaining me for a second spell of ninety days they will break me. I must prepare for an intensive effort on their part in the next few days to induce me to crack. If they feel that I

198

will continue to take whatever they try on me, my prospects for release will improve, but once they think there is a chance of my collapsing they will never let me go.

The more I look at this primitive little cell, the more convinced I am that it has been selected as a mere temporary staging-post. On the walls are the names of others who have been here as political prisoners. Someone has written up slogans in Latin: must be a teacher—who could it be? Yes, of course here is his name, Achmat Osman. He was here for one day only. SIC TRANSIT NOX DOLORIS. Not very spirited that —'Thus passes a night of sorrow.' I think I will add a bit, though it is not easy to write on the wall with a ballpoint. I scratch the words—*Sed sic advinit nova dies*—'But thus arrives a new day.' Or should it be *advenit* and not *advinit*? I am sure Achmat will not mind my making the addition, even if my grammar is weak.

Here he has written another one:

Vae tyrannis and there *Vae tyrannibus*. Obviously he too was not sure which was the right word. Well, no inspector will tick him off for poor work here. Cursed be the tyrants—I think that is what it means.

Vivat libertas. Long live liberty. That is more like it. Trust old Achmat to hurl defiance at them—in Latin. Here near the floor he has written, 'Osman slept here.' Below that are the words, 'April also.' So Jimmy April was here too. The non-White cells must all have been full for the police to have put these two in this cell. I add my name below theirs,

'Sachs too.'

Next to the door I start my new calendar. 'Arrived here— 28th December 1963.' Departed—that remains to be seen.

The only good thing about this cell is the window, which is at eye-level and, although heavily gridded both inside and out, can be seen through when opened. Unfortunately the view is blocked by a red brick wall which is only about a yard away, but if I stand in the corner near the door and look upwards through the window, I can see into a room which is opposite and a bit higher than my cell. Occasionally I see the shoulders and head of a policeman passing by the window of that room.

From that direction comes an incessant din of human voices. At first the noise seemed one harsh blur, but now I separate out individual sounds, from which I infer that that room houses the police who direct the flying squad, or radio patrol as they call themselves. Some of the men take incoming calls from the public.

'Hello, this is 414, radio patrol,' I hear the voices saying again and again. 'Your name please, where are you phoning from? Yes, I know it's from a phone booth, but where, man? Don't be stupid, of course it's in the street, but what's the name of the street?—the main road? What main road, where are you, man? What part of town? Look here, I can't send the van unless you tell me where you are.'

So the questioning goes on. There must be several men receiving calls in different booths at the same time. Their conversations, which take the form largely of shouting, overlap each other like a fugue. In another part of the room a sergeant broadcasts messages to the police radio patrol vans. He transmits complaints to whichever van happens to be cruising nearest to the scene of the incident requiring investigation.

'Calling C2, calling C2, calling C2. Come in C2.' I hear him say. Back comes a reply, crackling with atmospherics and the irritating distortion of shortwave radio.

'This is C2 here. This is C2 here. Sergeant Malan speaking.'

'C2, there is a fight at house number 24 Black Street. The complainant's name is September and he will be waiting for you at the phone booth on the corner of Black Street and Main Road.' C2 repeats the information and is thereupon instructed to proceed. Then the next message is broadcast and the next. The flow is unceasing. Unruly behaviour, a drunk person, theft assault: these seem to be the main complaints requiring attention. My ears are unaccustomed to the constant noise, which makes me tense and edgy. The sound flows in and out of my consciousness, advancing and receding just as the beat of waves is forgotten and then heard again by someone who lives by the sea.

During a moment when my consciousness of the broadcasting

200

has become lulled, I become aware of a new sound emanating from somewhere in my immediate vicinity. Someone is whistling not far from my door. The tune is familiar, a popular piece, but I cannot place it. It is whistled again and again. I stand near the door and take up the melody. My whistling is cautious but clear. I repeat the piece twice and wait.

'That's a nice tune, isn't it?'

A voice has spoken to me. It is Afrikaans-accented, and muffled by the barriers between us.

'Yes, what's it called?' I reply.

'I don't know, but it's very nice. What you in for?' The voice is still addressing me. There is someone out there, and we are speaking to each other.

'Ninety-Days. I've already been in for eighty-nine days. Tomorrow my ninety days will be up, but they can take me in again. What are you doing here?'

'They say it's for theft. It happened two years ago. A motor-bike was stolen and they say someone saw me riding on it. What's it like when you do Ninety-Days?' His voice is friendly and I realise that this is the first normal person-to-person conversation I have had for nearly three months. I shout at the heavy steel door so that he can hear me, conscious that I must be careful not to attract the attention of the police who are near the window in the radio patrol room.

'It's bloody awful,' I answer loudly, 'I've been kept on my own, in solitary confinement all the time. For the first six weeks I had absolutely nothing to do, though now I've got books and pencil and paper. You know, you're the first person I've spoken to other than a policeman for over two months.'

'Gee. It must be lousy. Why'd they take you?'

'Politics, actually they've never given me any reason. There's no charge against me, and I can't have any visitors, not even a lawyer.'

'Hell, that's tough. The police think they can do what they damn well like. What's your name? My name's Bothma, Frank Bothma.'

'Albie Sachs, I'm an advocate, so if you want any advice I'll be glad to help you. What do you do?'

'I used to be a warder, here up in Roeland Street jail. But they kicked me out, and I've had lots of jobs since then.'

'Why did they kick you out?'

'It was all over a gun which I sold. It wasn't a bad life that. They all know me here, I can get anything I want. If you need anything, just ask me and I'll fix it up with the people in charge.'

'Thanks, that's good of you. But I don't think they will be able to do much for me. The security branch are damned strict about Ninety-Day prisoners. But thanks for the offer.'

'Don't you want any smokes, or a cold drink or something like that?'

'No, I gave up smoking two years ago. The best thing you can do for me, though, is just to let me speak to you. For me that's the best thing in the world.'

'What's that you said?'

'Sorry, I'll shout a little louder. I said that's the best thing in the world. Just to speak to somebody. . . . When is your case coming up?'

'I've already been in Court. They're sending me up to Durban and I'm waiting here for the escort. I think I'll be leaving next Sunday.'

'Well, any time you want to discuss your case with me, you can get free legal advice. It's just marvellous for me to be able to talk to you, and I'm dying to do legal work again, even if it is in prison.'

'Okay. I'll speak to you some more later. It helps to pass the time.'

I am no longer alone. I have a thief for a companion. Or should I say, now that I am an advocate again, my companion is allegedly a thief. Thief or not, he has a voice and is a person, and we speak to each other as one human being to another.

Perhaps he is a trap. I must be careful. If he once worked as a warder it is quite possible that they are using him to try to get information from me. Yet he sounded genuine enough, and if he is a trap, why would he tell me that he used to be a warder? Even if my suspicions are correct, he is, nevertheless, someone with whom I can talk; I have broken my isolation. If he and I were to meet outside, we would have nothing to say to each

202

other—he could well be a client of mine, in which event we would discuss his case, but otherwise I doubt if we would share a single interest. Now we are equal. We have a common enemy—the police—and a common goal—to be free. As a result of being moved here, I have lost the sun, but I have gained a friend. Anyhow, the wheels are moving. Whatever fate they have decided on for me, I should not be here for too long. I wonder what they will do with me tomorrow.

23 Release

'WE HAVE COME TO RELEASE YOU.' IT IS SUNDAY MORNING, the 29th December, the ninetieth day of my detention. The captain stands in the doorway of my cell, his large bulk blocking out most of the body of a small man in a neat brown suit whom I half see standing behind him. The captain continues speaking to me:

'Your ninety days are up and you can go now.' I look back at him with suspicion. There is something false in his manner. I say nothing.

The captain moves aside and the short man enters my cell. I recognise him now. He is the colonel, the man in charge of the security forces in Cape Town.

'I am Colonel Macintyre,' he says to me. I notice that he is holding a piece of paper in his right hand. 'This is for you.' He gives me the paper. His lips mash softly together as he speaks and I observe that his gums are bare. The colonel of the security forces is toothless—no doubt awaiting false teeth.

I take the paper and read it. The words are formal and precise:

'... is hereby ordered that Albert Louis Sachs who is at present being detained in terms of Section ... at Caledon Square police station, Cape Town, be released forthwith.'

' I think we have met before,' I tell the colonel. 'Weren't you in charge of the police who dispersed the crowd at the "Remember Sharpeville" meeting? In 1961 I think it was.' He had been a captain in the uniformed police then and I remember that he had acted efficiently and with relative absence of provocation to the crowd. I want now to hear the colonel talk a bit more, for from the tone of his voice I should be able to tell whether or not I am really to be released. I do not believe what is written on the piece of paper in my hand.

'That is correct,' the colonel replies. 'You had better pack your things now.' His tone is cool and the words splash quietly from his pouting lips.

'Am I really free?' I ask.

It is the captain who answers: 'Yes, you are really free.'

'You mean I can go home?'

'Yes, you can go home.'

As I pile up my belongings, I look carefully at the colonel and the captain. Their manner is heavy and formal. Why should the colonel bother to supervise my release when he could have sent a sergeant to do the job? Yet they say I can go home. Little springs of hope start bubbling inside of me. My hands seem unable to co-ordinate properly with each other and I find it difficult to concentrate on getting my things together.

'I can actually go home to my mother?'

'You can go home to your mother and anyone else you like.'

A constable is called to carry my blankets and food. The colonel and the captain push their way out of the cell, which is too small to contain four people, and then we all proceed along the passage outside. The steel gate at the end of the passage is unlocked and the procession passes through to the stairs which lead down from the cells to the charge office. I had almost forgotten that my cell was on a level one floor above the ground. When we reach the charge office my belongings are heaped on the counter, and I am asked to sign the receipt for my property.

'Are you going to arrest me again?' I ask as I sign the property receipt.

'You are now completely free,' the captain replies. I do not trust him. Yet he is very emphatic. The colonel remains silent. We all stand quietly, watching each other. The captain looks at my belongings on the counter, smiles warmly at me and says:

'How are you going to get all that stuff home?'

How are you going to get all that stuff home? The sentence

echoes through my head, and I feel myself tremble. Hope bursts my defences and swamps over me so that I am overtaken by overwhelming dizziness. Those words can mean only one thing. I am really free.

I'M FREE! I'M FREE!

'You mean I really am free?' The words come faintly from my lips. I feel the pressure of tears on my eyeballs. My one hand moves up to my face, and my body begins to rock. The captain smiles genially. I want to hug him, and also to kick him.

'I don't know what to say,' I whisper. 'I don't know whether to say thank you or f . . .' I do not finish the sentence. The occasion is too great to be marred by my using abusive language.

'Can I . . . can I phone my mother?'

The captain is slightly startled by my request, and looks to the colonel. The colonel nods.

'Certainly,' the captain assures me affably. 'The phone is over there. Just wait a minute and we'll get through for you.' I am swooning, I cannot stand. As I seat myself on a bench, I notice the colonel walking out towards the street.

I'M FREE! IT'S ALL OVER! I'M FREE!

The colonel returns accompanied by Warrant Officer Vlok. The warrant officer walks straight towards me and holds out his hand in greeting. He is grinning and I see his brown-stained teeth. I stand up shakily and grasp his hand, ready to mumble something about happiness.

'I am placing you under arrest.'

He speaks pleasantly, as though saying how do you do. I am placing you under arrest . . . under arrest . . . under arrest. It is starting all over again. Why did they have to be so cruel? Why did they go to such pains to let me know I was completely free? I must show no emotion now. They must not feel that I am weak. They are bastards the lot of them. My throat is dry, and I want to lie down and cover my head with a blanket.

'May I have a glass of water, please?' I ask, forcing my voice to be firm.

'Yes, yes,' the colonel says quickly, 'give him some water. He's had quite a shock.' A glass is brought to me, and as I

206

drink I tell myself—keep firm, don't let them see how shaken you are.

I do not want to go back to my cell. For a moment I feel like collapsing and forcing them to carry me. I muster my strength.

'I suppose I will go back to the same cell,' I say. I pick up my bag and walk towards the stairs. An idea occurs to me. Perhaps I can derive some advantage from the situation.

'Oh, Colonel,' I look straight at him, 'now that I can see you, I would like to discuss certain aspects of my conditions with you. It would be convenient if we could do it now.'

'Certainly,' he says, 'you can come to my office. The men here will take your things up to your cell again.'

We proceed to the colonel's office, which is on the first floor, deep in the building. In the centre of the office is a large desk which is surrounded by chairs. The walls are dominated by two giant photographs in thick black frames—the one of the State President, the other of the Minister of Justice. These pictures are placed on either side of a large bookcase. Most of the shelves are empty, but prominently, almost ostentatiously, displayed are two copies of Djilas' *The New Class*. I wonder what Djilas would think of the book which he wrote in prison being used to give ideological support for the imprisonment of anti-apartheid South Africans.

The colonel is the first to be seated. I notice that his two companions appear to be very matey with each other, and that next to them the colonel seems tiny. His manner is brisk, as though he must at all times strive to justify his superior rank. Though English is his first language, he invariably addresses the captain and warrant officer in Afrikaans. They show to him the polite deference due to a senior officer but reserve what warmth they have for each other. The colonel's efforts to assert himself over his large companions are made slightly ludicrous by his lack of teeth. As he speaks to me I am all the time conscious of the two huge stern portraits hanging behind him.

'As Shakespeare said . . .' the colonel begins. I have become unused to sitting like this on a chair or at a desk, or to seeing photographs or bookshelves, so that as the colonel tells me what Shakespeare said—something about when the disease is desperate the remedy must be strong—I find that my mind is wandering. I need a moment to think of my requests for I must now press for what I want while the colonel apparently still feels on the defensive after having deceived me in the way he did.

'We are keeping you for a number of reasons,' the colonel continues, the words plopping out of his lips. 'The main one is that we are satisfied that you have information about certain offences, and we cannot let you go until you answer our questions satisfactorily. Another reason, but this is not the main one, is that we have sent your papers to the Attorney-General for his decision. He is away on leave at the moment and will only be back in his office on the sixth of next month. I must repeat that the main reason for continuing to hold you is your refusal to answer questions. So it is up to you. If you answer questions, I cannot guarantee that you will be released straight away: we will still have to wait for the Attorney-General's decision. But life will be a lot easier for you, that I can promise you. And the prospects of your being released would be very much rosier.'

'Thank you for the explanation, colonel,' I reply as I say to myself—clearly the real reason why they have re-arrested me is to keep me in confinement until the Attorney-General returns from holiday. If I stick it out for another ten days or so, the Attorney-General will give his decision and they will either charge me or release me.

'When I said I would like to speak to you,' I continue, 'I did not intend to discuss the merits of my detention. I have already told the captain that in my view nothing can ever justify prolonged solitary confinement and that it is uncivilised. For the moment, however, I accept that you are carrying out the law which gives you these powers. All I would like to raise now are certain points about the physical conditions of my detention. I'm sure you will agree that certain standards should be maintained for all prisoners, whatever they might be locked up for.'

While I am still speaking, the phone rings. The colonel lifts the receiver.

'Colonel Macintyre speaking. Yes, good morning. No. He is still here.' Hell, he is speaking about me.

It must be my mother, phoning to find out if I have been released—Mommy!—I want to scream—it's me, Albie, I'm here. Yes, they let me go for thirty seconds and then arrested me again. Don't worry, though, I'm all right. I'll see it through.

'No, I'm afraid I can't tell you anything more at the moment. He will be kept here in Cape Town. That's up to him. I can tell you nothing more. Goodbye.'

Goodbye, how hard it must be for you, not knowing what is happening to your son, powerless to do anything to help me except send food and clothing. Please be brave. I have barely enough strength for myself now, so even if I had the means I could send you no support. And please don't worry too much about me. In some ways it is good that they are still keeping me, for it will make many people who otherwise would not care very much, take notice of the Ninety-Day law. I am sure you would want me to hold out.

The colonel and I discuss the conditions of my detention. I realise that I have no hope of altering the main feature of it: the solitary confinement and the complete lack of contact with the outside world. But I can get improvements in respect of some of the details. I write out a list of things which, I tell the colonel, I feel he will agree that I should have: a chamber pot, crossword puzzles from the daily papers, a reduction if possible of noise from the radio patrol office, exercise time when the sun is high, a cell with more space and light, a bed and access to running water. He agrees in principle to all these items and says he will see what he can do to fix things up. I would like the conversation to continue, but I notice that the three security men are getting restless.

'That should be all,' the colonel says briskly, and then he stands up. Obviously they are anxious to get home. My release was well-timed to fit in between Sunday morning church service and Sunday afternoon lunch, and our discussion must have made them late for the latter.

As we walk back in the direction of my cell, Warrant Officer Vlok suddenly takes me aside.

'Look here,' he whispers to me, 'if there's anything I can do for you just let me know. Just ask the men on cell duty and they'll call me right away. Is there anything you'd like me to do for you now?'

I am baffled by this confidence. Ten minutes ago he arrested me in cruel circumstances and now he offers me his help. I tell him no, there is nothing he or anyone else can do for me except to let me out.

'That's up to Pretoria,' he replies, 'but any time you want my help, you must only ask and I will do what I can.'

We rejoin the others and continue walking towards my cell.

As we get to the foot of the stairs it is the captain who now takes me aside. He smiles at me in a friendly way and pulls something out of his pocket. I notice it is a Christmas card. The colours are gay and I see part of a sentence written in a familiar bold handwriting. . . . heaps of love and kisses. It is from Marion! How nice, and how silly of her to send me a card in jail. It's decent of the captain to give it to me. As I reach out for the card, he pulls it back.

'Who is this Marion?' he asks. I stretch out my hand again but once more he withdraws the card from my reach, making me feel like a dog snatching at a biscuit. 'Where does she stay?'

'I'm surprised at you, captain,' I reply, feeling indignant now. 'Imagine interrogating me about a Christmas card.'

'Never mind about that. Where does she stay?' It was in one of the earliest interrogations that Lieutenant Potgieter once referred to Marion. What was it he said? I remember now. Ha! I smile at the captain, delighted because I remember what the lieutenant told me.

'Why ask me?' I say innocently. 'Ask Lieutenant Potgieter. He told me months ago that you people had got hold of Marion. Ask him, don't ask me.' The muscles in the captain's face stiffen.

'I'm not interested in what he told you,' he says petulantly. 'I want you to tell me.'

I can't wait to get back to my cell where I can laugh out loud. I have caught them out, the liars. At the time I suspected that the lieutenant had been lying to me. Now the captain has proved that I was right. They are liars, liars, liars. Oh Marion, if and when I get out, what a laugh we can have over this. I smile pleasantly at the captain. 'I'm not prepared to answer questions,' I tell him. He walks away in anger, and I climb the stairs which lead to my cell.

Back in the cell I feel tired and restless. I have to make an effort to force myself to unpack my things and to place them where they had been before I was released. I go over again and again the events of the morning. Vlok must have been waiting for me outside in the road, I decide. I spoilt their plans a bit by not immediately running out to the street. That was why the colonel went out for a moment—to call the man waiting in ambush. How stupid and how tyrannical law can be. The law says I must be released after ninety days, so they release me for thirty seconds, and then detain me again in terms of the same law for another ninety days. Perhaps they were under instructions to re-detain me, but nothing can justify the manner of their doing so. They could have told me they were going to re-arrest me, or at the very least have said nothing at all. Instead they bluffed me into believing I was really free. Imagine asking me how I was going to get my stuff home when he knew damn well I was going to be re-arrested. I am sure they will go all out to break me before the Attorney-General returns from holiday and decides on whether or not to prosecute me.

The day passes slowly. I have difficulty in eating my food. And at exercise time I feel listless. The noise from the radio patrol seems more jarring than ever. Nighttime comes and after the light is switched off, I find that I cannot sleep. Frequently during the night my stomach swells with nausea. My head feels dizzy and uncomfortable. I turn from side to side, waiting for time to pass. *Sic transit nox doloris. Sed sic advinit nova dies?*

It is Monday 30th December. The district surgeon is brought to my cell. He feels my pulse and takes my temperature. It's just nerves, he tells me.

24 Interrogation

IT IS AS I EXPECTED: THEIR INTERROGATIONS ARE frequent and intense. For the first few days this turned out to be a source of encouragement to me, for I took it to represent a last desperate effort on their part to get me to talk to them before I was charged or released. Now several weeks have passed and I am confused.

Usually they take me to a special room which is not far from the radio patrol offices in the main building, but sometimes they question me in my cell, and sometimes in the little exercise yard. They prepare carefully for every interrogation. Normally they are hard and threatening towards me, but occasionally they are soft and apparently sympathetic.

A big advantage they have over me is that they are in a position constantly to call on new forces. I have no reserves to fall back on: I have only myself. The security branch seems to be swollen with middle-ranking officers. Lieutenants, warrant officers and sergeants are sent in, couple after couple, to try their questioning craft on me. Each new pair arrives eagerly for the interrogation, hopeful that they will be the ones to break me down; usually they are a little less buoyant when they depart. The captain sees me regularly once or twice a week; he is still my main antagonist. My interrogators vary the days of the week and the times of the day during which they come, so as to catch me off guard. I seem to have cracked the pattern of their visits, however, for they are so rigid about altering the times of their interrogations that I am able to determine when they will next come simply by eliminating those times on which they have already been to see me.

212

The interrogations merge into each other. I am subjected to a bombardment of different personalities and different techniques. The main theme, however, remains the same, there is no question of my being released until I have answered all their questions.

They tell me this in a variety of ways. For example, some simply ask if I want to spend the rest of my life like this. Then on New Year's eve the captain wanted to know if I thought I would still be as obstinate when next year's New Year's eve came round. I tell them that I have a mathematical formula that gives me courage: that according to my method of reckoning I am over halfway to the end of a spell of 180 days, and that when they arrest me for the third time, I will already be two thirds of the way through 270 days. A new lieutenant then asks casually how long I will have been in when I am five-sixths of the way through my period. The captain often tells me that he has many years left in the force before he retires. For my part I try to let them feel that I can stick it out for ever. In fact I am not sure how long I can hold out. I do not believe them when they say that they will keep me for ever, and probably they do not believe me when I say I will stay silent for ever. The game of nerves proceeds. Though I feel that they protest too much about how long they will keep me, their visits do take a toll of my strength.

In the early days it was a test of nerve, of ability to withstand the shock. Now it is a question of stamina. I am the only person in Cape Town still being held under the Ninety-Day law, so they can concentrate all their forces on me. The Attorney-General must have decided already on whether or not to prosecute me. The fact that I have not been charged is good in the sense that it means they feel they cannot get a conviction against me. It is bad in the sense that it means that they are determined to hold me for as long as they can. Perhaps they regard it as a matter of principle. If that is so they can keep me for years. Even though any information I might be able to give would by then be stale, they will have made the point that no one who enters prison as a Ninety-Day detainee ever emerges until he has answered all their questions. I, on the other hand, must try to prove that one can stay silent and yet be freed. It will be a case of the whole State versus me.

In a way nothing is easier than to say simply: I will not talk. Yet nothing is more difficult than to live in complete and indefinite loneliness. It may even turn out that they will make me into a hero. That would be ironical: I can barely hold out, I try hard to win the police's approval; I have decided that, if I emerge a free man, I will pack up and quit South Africa. I have never felt more fragile and less heroic in my life; real heroes are surely made of sterner stuff. But if this goes on and on I may find that the days, the weeks and the months have accumulated into a considerable period of time. People outside who are unaware of the tenuousness of my stand and the compromises I have made, may then say—look at that man, how bravely he holds out, there is a real symbol of courage and determination for you.

I wonder what the security men think privately of me. It is incredible how eager I am to get them to regard me as a man of principle. Yet I feel I am not being entirely naïve in this wish. The more they unconsciously respect me, the harder will it be for them to assert their personalities over mine. If secretly they admire my stand, they are partially disarmed before they start interrogating me. On the other hand, there is the danger that they will be doubly determined to break me so as to prove that their principles are stronger than mine, for by grounding myself on principle, I not only impede the progress of their machine, I challenge their very right to hold me. The extreme isolation to which we detainees are subjected can be justified in their terms only on one basis, and that is that it gets results. If it fails to get results then it is exposed for what it is: a refined form of torture. If it gets results then its barbarous aspects are pushed into the background.

Whatever their private thoughts may be, however, they never for a moment concede to me that I have any virtuous qualities whatsoever. They suggest, for example, that I am the biggest fool on earth for sitting here when I could be enjoying myself outside.

One sergeant tells me that all the detainees who face charges have been released on bail, and he mentions a specific sum. The figure is so high, a total of R41,000[1], that I feel he must be lying. I know too that he has a reputation for being reckless with the truth. Furthermore he has over the years frequently been accused by clients of mine of having practised torture on them. He was the man who threatened to kill an African whom I had once had as a client. Three months later this African was detained under the Ninety-Day law, and three weeks after that I was told that he had been found hanged in his cell, the first man to lose his life during Ninety-Days. One of my last acts before I myself was detained was to see to it that the news was published and to arrange for an attorney to press for an inquest. Perhaps the inquest has already been held, and perhaps this sergeant has been cross-examined about his threats to the deceased. At the moment, however, he is in a position of power over me. I am White, and an advocate, and he knows that I will report any physical violence to which I might be subjected. Accordingly I feel safe from being assaulted by him. But nothing stops him from jeering at me for being so stupid. This theme is taken up by his companions, who also mock me for presuming to challenge the patience and endurance of the South African police. All the interrogators say they cannot understand why I refuse to answer questions.

I have noticed that an element of variety has been added to my interrogations. The smooth lieutenant from Wynberg, van Dyk, drops in for a chat one day. He starts telling me that Mrs Cleminshaw, the woman who has been organising my food parcels, must have a soft spot for me. She caused a bit of trouble by parading with a poster calling for my release, he explains. I feel friendly towards him as a result of receiving this information. Then he asks me what I know about the local Ku Klux Klan. Quite a bit, I tell him. I think of the friends of mine who had been shot at, the friend whose car had been blown up, the threatening phone calls which I and so many others had received—all the work of the Cape Town branch of the Ku Klux Klan. 'Oh, by the way,' the lieutenant continues, '——————— (he mentions the name of someone very dear to me) lives on her

[1] South African currency; one Rand is worth ten shillings.

own doesn't she?' He then leaves, without even attempting to question me. The interview ends so suddenly that it takes me a long time to realise that by juxtaposing the Ku Klux Klan with —————— living on her own, he is trying to plant in my mind seeds of fear for her safety. Yet curiously his effort has quite the opposite effect. I feel that everything they say is a reversal of the truth. If they find it necessary to hint to me that people I love dearly are in jeopardy, this proves that in fact those people must be relatively safe. Far from being worried, I am relieved.

The captain surprises me one day by issuing to me what I can only take to be threats of harm. The interrogation on this occasion takes place in the exercise yard, and the captain starts off mildly.

'Ah, come on, man,' he pleads with me, 'you can talk to me now completely off the record.' He opens his jacket and waves its flaps as though he were an amateur magician. 'Look, I've got nothing here, you can say what you like.' I am amused. Without realising it, he has given away to me the fact that they usually record our interview on hidden tapes. For a long time I have suspected that this was the position. Now by implication he has confirmed my suspicions.

'Bring me to Court,' I tell him, 'and I will speak quite openly and for the record.' Suddenly his demeanour changes.

'You realise you have absolutely no rights at all,' he bellows at me. 'We can make your life very hard,' he continues. While he talks he walks menacingly round me and I have to keep moving in order to face him. 'We will interrogate you day in and day out, night in and night out, right through the day and through the night,' he booms.

'If you try that, I will report you to the visiting magistrate,' I reply. This seems to intensify his anger.

'The way we interrogate you,' he storms, 'has got nothing to do with the visiting magistrate.' Then he starts firing questions at me. He reads rapidly from a piece of paper.

'You were born on the 30th January 1935,' he snaps.

'I'm not prepared to answer questions.'

'In September of 1952, you addressed a meeting.'

216

'I'm not prepared to answer questions.' On and on the questions come. As he reaches the end of the page his voice starts slowing down. He has had no support from the warrant officer who is with him, and he finally comes to a halt.

'Okay, let's go to the Carnival,' he says abruptly to the warrant officer, and off they walk. His remark reminds me that it is holiday time.

Should I report to the visiting magistrate the threats made by the captain? Several days elapse before the magistrate arrives and during that period I change my mind frequently. Eventually when the magistrate comes, I decide what I should do. I tell him of the threats, writing out a full report of what the captain said to me. I do so partly to protect myself against possible harm, yet the main reason is that I am so bored that I would like to see what happens if I lodge a complaint. I draft the report carefully so as to exclude any accusation of exaggeration, malice or hysteria on my part. The magistrate, who was once so brusque with me, is now polite and patient, and he promises to pass on the complaint to the authorities.

The next battery of interrogators to fire away at me does not include the captain. I tell them of the report I have made, and ask them to let the captain know, for I am anxious not to appear to be a tell-tale who has sneaked out a complaint about the captain behind his back. A few days later the captain himself comes to my cell. He looks around at my belongings, and sits down on the bunk. The cell is filled by our two bodies. He lights a cigarette, puffs at it a few times, and then speaks to me.

'I see you have made a report about me,' he says.

'Yes, that's right,' I answer.

'You can do that,' he proceeds, 'it doesn't worry me. You had no right though,' he continues angrily, 'to tell my junior officers about it, it's got nothing to do with them. I'm a captain and they are below me in rank.' And so he goes on. I smile inwardly. They must have teased him a lot and given him something of a fright to have provoked this outburst. He looks carefully round my cell once more and stands up. Before he leaves he flings a final sentence at me.

'I'm not worried about what you wrote about me,' he says, 'I
217

know on my conscience that it was all a lot of lies.' As he strides angrily out of the cell I notice worms of ash lying on the floor. What a pig. He sits here depositing ash all over the cell—doesn't he know that I live here?

Later that afternoon the station commander, a quiet kindly man, comes to see me. He has been instructed by security to tell me of certain rulings made by them. I cannot keep food in the cell, nor may I have more than one item of reading matter at a time. I will no longer receive crossword puzzles . . . he runs through a list of minor privileges which are to be taken away from me. The station commander stresses that no other rights or privileges are affected. He is sorry, he says, but he cannot give the reason for the deprivations.

The dossier which the police have on me must be enormous. The summary of my activities, with which they arm themselves during interrogations, itself runs to a dozen pages. In some respects they know more about my past than I do. I was born in their files twelve years ago and since then I have grown slowly month by month. By now my existence as one of their rogues must be firmly established. Speeches I have made, meetings attended, persons visited, places where my car has been parked, snippets of letters intercepted and telephone conversations overheard, titbits from informers—all these have been collected, collated and summarised. They wave the summary in front of me. I see that it is headed *Memorandum on A. L. Sachs*. Sometimes they read from it. On other days they leave it lying in front of me. They try to arouse my curiosity, and also to suggest to me that they know everything I have ever done. Occasionally they read out bits from speeches I made years back. I want to applaud. The language is a bit flowery, perhaps, but it was not bad for a boy of seventeen. They question me about patently innocuous matters. I refuse to answer.

'But this can't possibly get you into trouble,' they say. 'Why don't you answer us?'

'I am not going to answer any questions at all,' I reply.

'We know all these things, anyhow,' they continue.

'Then why bother to ask me,' I want to know. They shake their heads in despair, and look at each other.

'Have you ever seen such a ridiculous person,' they say, 'he won't even say when he was born.'

A favourite stratagem of theirs is to leave near me a page headed: *Addendum on Mamre Sabotage Camp*.

This page will be left half turned towards me on the table in the interrogation room. They deposit it casually, as if without thinking. I know that I should not even glance at it, but my curiosity is too strong for me. As they question me, my eyes drop to that page. Bit by bit I make out its contents: it contains extracts from statements made by three of the persons who had been present at the camp. Each extract purports to reflect the contents of the talk I delivered there. But this is ludicrous. The three reports contradict each other. Their individual contents are meaningless, and taken together they are a hodge-podge of rubbish. No Court would believe that I could talk such drivel. In any event nothing these three people claim I said comes even close to constituting an offence.

Until I saw this addendum I was beginning to doubt my own memory. The months of isolation had tended to wipe my mind clean of past recollection. The constant references by my interrogators to the *Sabotage Camp* was causing me to wonder whether or not I had knowingly taken part in a sabotage camp. By isolating me from the world in which the relevant events had taken place, they had succeeded in destroying my independent recollection of what had happened. Reality is something continuous and integrated. If one is abstracted from normal reality today one has difficulty in remembering aspects of the reality of yesterday. Fortunately for me, however, they have not succeeded in substituting their version of reality for my vanishing recollection. My mind is simply bare of memory, unable to recall the past but still resistant to suggestion. This addendum has helped me to regain mental independence. The sentences which allegedly reflect the gist of my talk are quite false. The idiom, the style, and the concepts themselves are quite foreign to me. Not only did I not say these things at the camp, I could never have said them anywhere, or at any time. If I saw sentiments couched in a manner which I could recognise as being my own, then I would have difficulty in deciding whether or not they were accurate; I could possibly even be persuaded that I gave a talk on a subject far more dangerous than that on which I did speak. By some strange psychological process, however, these extracts with their tiny pieces of truth, remind me that the talk I gave was on economics. They also serve as proof positive that I am not a very good lecturer.

The special room near the radio patrol offices has become the main place where I am questioned. This pleases me, for I enjoy my journeys to and from that interrogation room which I should perhaps call the recording studio. Some trouble has obviously been taken to make the room look as ordinary as possible. It has a table and several chairs and ashtrays are placed in convenient places. But it has no specific character, so that you could say of it this room is habitually used for such and such a purpose. It has no centre of gravity. The focal point of a proper office is the chair behind the desk. A waste-paper basket, a telephone book, files of papers and so on, these would be the normal satellites of that chair, and such features are absent from this room. I notice that, whenever I am taken there, someone goes ahead to prepare for my arrival. I am frequently asked to wait downstairs 'until the room is free'. What makes me sure that my interrogations are being recorded, however, is something of quite a different nature. The demeanour of the questioners undergoes a subtle though definite transformation in that office. Everything takes place at three-quarter speed. There is something decorous, almost ballet-like, in the proceedings there. The interrogators speak clearly and never interrupt each other. They look pained when I speak too familiarly with them, or make some joke at their expense. They make a point of finishing all their sentences, and they identify each other as they talk. Sometimes they repeat performances which have already taken place, presumably unrecorded, in my cell. They lack spontaneity and are over-rehearsed: the knowledge that every word is being taken down seems to inhibit them. I suppose that unconsciously they are mike-shy, or perhaps the colonel is sitting next door listening to all that is being said. I too am affected by it, but I too pretend not to be aware of the eaves-dropping microphone.

It is an elaborate game. We each put on a show of innocence to the other. I stress the portions of my replies about the inhumanity of solitary confinement. I volunteer to be tried on any charge they care to name. I insist that my silence is based on principle and is in no way proof of guilty knowledge. Occasionally I tease them a little: I compare the skill of one interrogator to that of another. I frequently make the point that if I am released I will tell people outside quite honestly what it has been like, the good as well as the bad, without exaggeration.

One day I cannot resist having fun at their expense, even though I do so at the risk of revealing my knowledge of the hidden recorder. The proceedings get under way with the most common series of opening questions. 'How are you feeling?' I shrug my shoulders, as if to indicate not too bad, not too good.

'Are you prepared to answer questions?' I shake my head.

'Tell us, are you prepared to answer questions?' I shake my head again.

'Have you lost your tongue?' I smile and shake my head once more.

'Well, are you prepared to answer questions or aren't you?' I shake my head and grunt a mumbled negative.

'You say, no, you aren't prepared to answer questions, is that right?'

I nod and murmur affirmatively. I keep this up for a few minutes, inwardly overjoyed at the discomfiture I have caused my interrogators. Eventually I break into speech, and they relax. Yet the rest of their interrogation on this occasion lacks zest.

There is one rule to which I still adhere strictly—just as the British colonial official invariably dresses for dinner, or so they say, so I always dress for interrogation. I don my suit and my white shirt, and put on shoes and socks. Interrogation is a serious business, which I must take seriously. The trappings of dignity, which in life outside I tended to scorn, have here become most important. It gives me pleasure to walk in a suit down a corridor. It is the nearest thing I have to an occasion. I comb my hair carefully, and even push my new-grown moustache into its best position. Sometimes I am lucky enough to be asked to wait at the bottom of the stairs, for I then move over a few yards to a position opposite the main portal of the police station, from where I can see the world outside. It is only a framed slice of the world, a few yards of busy road. Yet I see sunlight and cars, and people walking on the pavements; I hear newspaper sellers proclaiming latest editions. Then I am told to go up to the interrogation room, and I am plucked back into the world of total captivity. Later, when I return to my cell, I usually manage a further glance at the street. The world outside seems unreal and dreamlike; I have a strange feeling that I can smell the clothes that the people outside are wearing.

I would say that by now at least fifteen different security men have had a go at interrogating me. In the past I had occasion to cross-examine many of them in Court, but now they are the ones who ask the questions. Others I knew from the days when they were ordinary members of the C.I.D., attending to such relatively unexciting crimes as murder and rape. They have since been drafted into the security branch, the strong right arm of White South Africa. As a general observation on their quality, I would say that their effectiveness as interrogators diminishes in direct proportion to the number of tricks they use.

I am pleased that the colonel has not participated in any of the interrogations. Possibly a month or two ago the captain and the others were prepared to recommend my release; now I feel that I have become a challenge to them. Just as a gambler carries on with the hope that his luck will change suddenly, so they seem to feel it worth their while to persevere with me, and as with a gambler, the longer I hold out the greater the prize when I finally do break. The colonel is to some extent above the battle. Presumably he is more sensitive to outside public opinion, and questions of policy. He could easily realise, too, that whether or not one prisoner more or less is broken down will not be of great significance in the total pattern of 'security' in South Africa. I depend to some extent on his retaining an objective perspective on my case, and am pleased that he keeps away from the interrogations.

One day the colonel does come to me. He is alone as he enters my cell, and I notice that he wears an elegant brown check suit, and that in his hand he carries an elegant hat. His false teeth have been fitted, and his voice now sounds crisp and comfortable.

'Would you like a seat?' I ask.

'Thank you,' he says briskly. I wonder why he has come.

'My men tell me that you refuse to answer any of their questions,' he informs me, 'I came to check up from you personally whether this is so.'

'Yes, that is the position,' I reply. He stands up, holding his hat lightly in his hand, and as he leaves, says quietly:

'I'm afraid then the outlook for you is very bleak.' This one softly delivered sentence frightens me. It has more impact than the whole barrage of words that have been fired at me in the four months that I have now been in detention.

25 Reflections

TWO CONCEPTS HAVE BECOME ALL IMPORTANT TO ME: honour and dignity. It is through these ideas, which previously I would have rejected as being vague and meaningless, that I am able to achieve the necessary fusion between my objective ideas and my subjective strength. Has my world view, for so many years the spring of my actions, been right or wrong? Probably right, I feel, but that is not the essential enquiry. Right or wrong, it is not for me to abandon any views just because my captors tell me to do so, or because to continue to hold them means further persecution. To betray others, even if we were all wrong, is dishonourable, and a dishonourable life is not worth living. Dishonour is without hope, whereas suffering can always end.

I cling tenaciously, lovingly, to the idea that I must be honourable and never dishonourable. The word dignity takes on a new meaning for me. It is not essentially a question of physical bearing, or of what people think of me. To have dignity means to face life honestly, without panic, without vanity and without self-pity. Self-pity is the main threat to my dignity. I have no right to feel sorry for myself. I feel strangely hurt that other human beings can treat me in the way they do; a certain innocence I have always possessed has been violated. This feeling is in order I am sure. But nothing can justify my feeling sorry for myself. I even go so far at times as to regard my imprisonment as a sort of penance for all the hurts I have brought upon others in my life. I reason that it will do me no harm to suffer a little. I have always been so adroit at escaping situations in which I might feel pain, and there are so many people I have made unhappy over the years. I have lived a comfortable life while so many have had a whole lifetime of deprivation and sorrow. It follows that there is no reason for me to complain at receiving some punishment myself. My life is being evened out, I am being equalised with the majority of humanity. The debt I feel towards certain individuals is eased, and the sense of responsibility which has for so long gripped me and almost oppressed me is relaxed. I am able to review many episodes in my life without a load of guilt obscuring my vision.

In some ways this sense of responsibility has in the past spurred on my will, and a feeling of guilt at never doing enough, never being brave enough, has been an important factor motivating me to good action. Thus my 'penance' clears my mind in a number of respects and frees certain emotions from the clasp of guilt, but it also contributes to a weakening of my will.

Self-pity, on the other hand, threatens to lead to extreme demoralisation, and the total collapse of dignity. It is so easy to feel sorry for myself when all my attention is concentrated, whether I wish it or no, on myself and when my life is so wretched. Yet to give way to that feeling is to invite moral disaster. There are people worse off than I, and have been all through the history of mankind: I think of the monstrous cages in which prisoners were entombed in the late Middle Ages, where men could neither stand nor lie nor sit stretched out, where they crouched in perpetual darkness and received food through a trap-door. I think of the victims of the Nazis in Europe, the men thrown into furnaces by Chiang Kai Shek, the resistance fighters caught by the Portuguese secret police. I think too of the Algerian freedom fighters in the French torture centres, I think of the Africans in the Kenya detention camps, I think of all who the world over have suffered these things, and most of all, I think of those of my own countrymen detained as I am but who are without the protection of a white skin.

That some of them have not been gently treated I have little doubt, though I am relieved at the absence of signs of physical brutality where I am at present being held. In many cases in which I have appeared in the past strong evidence has been given of the application by the police of smothering, electric

225

shocks and beatings as a means of extracting information. I have never known any of the victims other than through my work, though some personal friends of mine have been man-handled to some extent. At the best of times the thought of torture is revolting, but to visualise individuals whom one knows and loves being assaulted and crushed is almost unbearable. Compared to them, I am lucky, and clearly have no right to complain.

In trying to keep my dignity and to convince myself that resistance is worthwhile, I think of all the people throughout the world who faced with determination and nobility death at the hands of a cruel and superior enemy. I think often of the Russian civilians who had resisted until death Nazi armoured assaults. They did not have to fight, they could have fled, or surrendered, or tried to hide, but they chose to live out what remained of their lives in honourable fashion. I think too of the men and women of the Resistance in occupied Europe, who began with such small numbers and such high casualties, and I think of the lone agents who were dropped by the Allies and captured by the Gestapo. I also think of the peasants of Vietnam who fought first the Japanese and then the French, and who are now still fighting in the swamplands of their country. I am just one of a hundred thousand men and women who refuse to collapse in the face of an overwhelming fate. I am weaker than many, braver than some. To some extent we are all volunteers. This makes our responsibility higher, not only to the groups to which we belong but to ourselves. It is important to resist. Human action does matter. Even if changing the world takes a little longer than once I had thought, even if 'our side' is not as guiltless as once I believed, the effort to bring about the change matters for those engaged in the task. To give up is to harm not only the things which I have felt ought to be pro-moted, but also to harm myself. Having thought this out, weak though I have become, I am better able to face my captors.

26 Robbers

A YOUNG AFRIKANER BOY IS SNIVELLING IN THE CELL
opposite to mine. While I was doing my exercise he was brought
in, and I took note of him as a tall thin boy wearing a white
shirt and grey short pants, and heard him sob as the detectives
pushed him into the cell. That was a quarter of an hour ago.
Now he is still sobbing. Stop moaning—I want to shout at him
—it won't help. The whimpering continues, and I become
agitated.

Police cells are a place of woe, and anyone who stays here for
more than a few days must learn to live with repeated howling.
Women prisoners do the most screaming. Their shrill cries of
anger and hysteria pierce the station. Occasionally men can be
heard yelling. They bellow out in animal rage at being enclosed,
and bang furiously with their fists against the cell doors.

The sound I hear today is different. It is a child crying. I
would say he is about fourteen years old and the detectives were
rough with him. Not that they assaulted him, but they terrorised him with their bullying and shouting. Still, there is no
reason for him to moan so much. Shut up, can't you—I feel
prompted to yell at him. Pull yourself together; you won't
get anywhere by crying; the police are not much moved by
tears, they see them every day; all you do with your crying is
to upset me. After all, who the hell is he—a young White boy
with every opportunity open to him. Why should I worry
about him? He probably hates all non-Whites and one day will
gladly carry a gun to kill them. Right now he couldn't give a
damn about anyone else. All he thinks about is his own misery.

Stop crying, you baby, you will be out of here in a few hours probably, while I have been in for nearly four months, all on my own, and there is no end in sight. If you knew what I was in for, to the extent that you understand these things, you would probably be glad that I have been locked up. You might even say shoot the bastard, that's all he deserves. Now you are crying away in the cell opposite mine, looking for sympathy. Why should I concern myself with you? You belong to the master race. It is your people who rule this country. It will do you good to taste a bit of the wretchedness to which so many millions are subjected by your people. Stop crying, dammit.

Oh, all right, all right, for the time being you are my neighbour and I cannot turn my back on you. I suppose children have no race or class.

'Listen,' I call out in Afrikaans, 'listen to me. It doesn't help to cry. Why have they locked you up?'

The crying stops for a moment, and then starts up again. I repeat my call. This time an answer comes. The boy's voice has not broken fully, so that the sounds which reach me are a mixture of soprano and baritone. His sentences are left incomplete, and what he does say is interrupted by snivelling. It is difficult to follow his story, but it appears that he and a friend were found in possession of an electric razor which had been stolen from a shop. He tells me now that the friend gave him the razor to keep, and he himself knew nothing about its having been stolen. I ask him if his parents know that he has been locked up and this produces another bout of crying. Obviously he cannot expect much support from them. I tell him that the sergeant will be round in another hour and that he must ask the sergeant to phone his father to come and get him out on bail. For a few minutes I manage to engage him in conversation and keep him from sobbing, but bit by bit the crying starts up again. I realise that he would rather cry than be comforted. In his present state of upset only one thing can console him and that is to be released. Still, he knows he has a friend nearby and I know that I tried. You can bring water to your neighbour, but you can't make him drink.

228

I have become a sort of hidden Father Christmas to the prisoners who are brought in here. During most of the day the cells are untenanted. Suspects and arrestees are usually locked up at night and released or charged next morning. Once they are charged they will be either released on bail or else sent to the central remand prison. The only prisoners I get to know are those who are kept here in the cells while they await transportation to face trial in some other centre. Occasionally an awaiting-trial prisoner is brought here from the remand prison so that he will be prevented from interfering with witnesses who are lodged in that prison. If a prisoner is kept here for more than a day I usually manage to see his face once or twice while I do my exercise, and to have a shouted conversation with him through the doors when the guards are gone. At meal times I send fruit and magazines to the other prisoners. I also give them legal advice. They seem to enjoy having an advocate as a neighbour, and presumably I lend a touch of class to the neighbourhood. My advice is almost invariably the same: get an attorney to look after your interests. They take my fruit but not my advice. Never mind, once or twice a week I have someone to talk to for a few moments. That is all that matters.

Frank Bothma left a fortnight ago, so now I have become the wise old man of these cells. I tell the prisoners when to ask for exercise time, what time food comes round, which sergeant to approach for a cigarette. I am not as expert as Frank was in this respect. He used to tell other prisoners how to engineer an escape, and how he could get them anything they needed. He also would provide them with detailed defences for their respective trials. One day he called a guard over to his cell and bet the guard a Pepsi cola that he—Frank—could unlock the cell door. The guard called him a bloody windbag, whereupon he produced a spoon he had previously hidden in the lavatory, and twisting its stem a few times, inserted it into the lock and opened the door. Sometime later, another prisoner in Frank's cell told me how stupid the police were, that they were half-asleep most of the time. Whenever he went downstairs to receive a visitor, he said, the police in the charge office did not even keep their eyes open; he could have run away easily without anyone noticing. On hearing this, there arose in me once more suspicion of a trap. Were these two prisoners encouraging me to try to escape?

This cell-mate of Frank's proved to be the prototype of many other prisoners who were later to be locked in here. Well-built, of handsome boyish appearance, his demeanour was friendly and impressive. The charge which he faced was fraud. It was all a mistake, he assured us. He had already been charged and found not guilty. The police had made a mistake. He would sue the Minister of Justice for a thousand pounds, and the longer they kept him in, the bigger the damages he would get. The rivalry between himself and Frank was intense. Each called the other a liar with equal justification. They vied with each other to win my esteem, and each did what he could to belittle his companion. Yet after Frank had gone his cell-mate spoke fondly of him and was more than delighted when he heard the story of Frank's escapade en route for Durban. Apparently Frank had persuaded his escorts to get off the train with him at Kimberley station in order to have a beer at a pub nearby. The three of them had gone to the pub where Frank had managed to get the escorts so drunk that he was able to handcuff them together and, so the story went as told by the guards, march them off to the local police station. The cell-mate now began to boast of his great friendship with Frank.

I am surprised at the number of personable young men who are arrested for fraud. One of the things they all have in common is that they are never so overcome by their misfortune as to be unable to tell anyone within earshot all about themselves. One chap even bragged to the police about his exploits. Now that he was caught there was no point in denying his guilt he said. He had driven off from work one day in a Government car and treated himself to a grand holiday tour of the country during which he represented himself as an important Government official. In one hotel he had had a narrow escape, he explained. Had to drop his suitcase out through a window three storeys up. His wife gave him away eventually, she sent the police to a nightclub where he was with another girl. Only after boasting about his adventures round the country did he learn that the sole charge being investigated against him was one of unlawful use of the car.

The more tales I hear from these young criminals, the more amazed I am at the lives they have chosen for themselves. They come from homes that are not poor; they have every chance of getting employment and they have before them the prospects of ease and comfort that go with being a White in South Africa. Instead of taking advantage of all this, they live at odds with society, preferring to work harder at crime than they would have to do in an ordinary job. They do so for less financial reward, and with the ultimate certainty of detection and imprisonment. Perhaps the theorists are right when they claim that these men, who apparently have no consciences and do not feel the difference between right and wrong, unconsciously seek out punishment for themselves as a compensation and a penalty for their wrongdoings.

Sometimes, especially over weekends, a number of prisoners are collected together in the larger cells. These cells have steel gates through which I look as I pass on the way to the exercise yard. I notice male bodies sprawled on the mattresses, all higgledy-piggledy like so many Cézanne bathers. Summer-wear for the experienced awaiting-trial prisoner is quite informal, it consists of a pair of bathing trunks. These men loll around displaying their flesh as though they are on holiday. For them the awaiting-trial period is a time of relaxation and preparation. They reminisce about prisons they have been to, much as travellers discuss countries they have visited, and their heroes are a few well-known criminals who have distinguished themselves in battle with the authorities.

One day I overheard them talking of a one-time client of mine, who has now apparently reached great heights in his campaign to outwit the law. He no longer employs counsel or attorneys to defend him. Formerly his main accomplishments were daring frauds and bold escapes. Today his fame rests on the way he defends himself in court. He was one of my first clients and at the time of his case it had come as a shock to me to find such an engaging person pursuing a career that necessarily entailed lengthy imprisonment. I remember remarking to myself that he and I were of similar age and appearance, yet his fate was to be behind bars, and mine to be a respectable lawyer. Now I am behind bars, and he is playing the lawyer. Apparently he has had considerable success in defending himself; his speciality, no doubt, being an ability to influence witnesses behind the scenes. As a result of these forensic achievements his fame has soared so that he has become legendary. Generations of prisoners will revere him. He has established a new fashion, and it is his achievements which explain the presence, in between the piles of comics, photo stories and trash newspapers that lie in the main cell, of weighty and boring legal text-books. One of his admirers and would-be imitators occasionally asks me to explain passages in a book on the law of evidence. Apparently the man's case is due to be concluded soon. He is defending himself and is quite confident of success. Someone else has confessed to the crime, he tells me, and he has no doubt that the magistrate will disbelieve the policeman who claims to have seen him emerging through the broken plate-glass frontage of the shop. A few days later, while I am doing my exercise, I overhear one of the guards complaining to his companion about a case in which he gave evidence. The magistrate said he believed me, the constable grumbles, yet he says he cannot find beyond reasonable doubt that the accused was the one I saw coming out of the shop window, so he got off completely free. Right now, I imagine, the shopbreaker will also be telling the story of the trial. But he will do so in triumph, regaling his listeners with a vivid and probably exaggerated description of how he made a monkey out of the cops. No doubt he will be sufficiently encouraged by his success to start planning a new venture in his game with the law. So it will go on. For three months, six months, a year maybe, he will be at liberty. Yet eventually he will lose a round, and he will find himself back in prison. He must know that the career he has chosen will inevitably involve him in spending a large portion of his life behind bars. Yet he carries on with it.

I should not be too surprised, I suppose, at youngsters like him. After all, I must be an even more puzzling phenomenon to them than they are to me. As they must see it, I am a chap who could be coining good money as a lawyer, yet instead I allow myself to land up in jail. Not for money, not for kicks, not for a girl, not for liquor, simply for an idea, a dream. Must be completely crazy. Wonder what those psychiatrist blokes would have to say about that?

27 Cops

Policemen are all pigs because their mothers are sows. THESE words were written on my cell wall in Afrikaans by one of my predecessors. *The only good policeman is a dead policeman,* someone else scratched nearby. I almost envy the simplicity of the hate expressed. Why is it that such hatred as I have is always for abstract things and never for people, not even for people who are cruel and wicked? I should hate the police, particularly the special branch: instead I hate apartheid.

I remember what one African said at a meeting. At the time it had seemed like heresy: 'People say we should hate White domination but not the White man,' he declared, 'but what is the point, in hating the whip and not the man who wields the whip.'

There are three policemen with regard to whom I have special opportunity for feeling antagonism. A policeman's day is divided into three shifts: morning, afternoon and night. These three men alternate as cell warders shift by shift and I see more of them than of anyone else. Of the three I would class one as a good man by any yardstick, though I judge him mainly by the way he deals with the convicts who clean out the cells in the morning. The second warder is lazy and mediocre in every respect. The third is a harsh bully.

Only once have I heard the good warder raise his voice. That was when he ducked into the cell next to mine and, pretending he was drunk and had just been locked up, yelled through the window to one of his colleagues in the nearby radio patrol office. 'Mathee,' he screamed, catching perfectly the raucous intonation of a drunkie, 'you're drunk. Pay my bail, please man, Mathee, it's only two pounds.'

Normally he speaks quietly both to the awaiting-trial prisoners and to the convicts. He gets through his work quickly, and whenever he is on duty things run smoothly. His main interest is not how to boss men but how to fix motor cars. It seems that his spare time is spent on repairing cars.

The second warder is concerned about only two things— his back and his house. He has been put on inside duty because of a slipped disc which causes him great discomfort and which he uses as an excuse for falling asleep whenever he is supposed to be watching me at exercise time. Before and after his doze he chats about the house he recently acquired to whoever is on guard with him. There is always something to be done to this house—a garden wall to be fixed, a room to be painted, a cement floor to be laid. One day he asks me if I know the advocate who defended him when he was in trouble. It was five years ago when a prisoner laid a charge against him of assault down here in the charge office. The advocate was very good and got him off. 'Of course I was guilty as hell,' he laughs. Today he no longer seems to have the energy to assault anyone. Occasionally he yells at the convicts, but for the most part he is too absorbed in thinking about his house to be able to expend any emotion on his work.

The worst of the three cell warders is a young man with a florid face on which appear the beginnings of a moustache. He shouts so much that it comes as a surprise when he does occasionally use a normal speaking voice. He seems to be under a compulsion to test his authority at all times, as though having power over men makes him uncomfortable. Given the choice of being rude or pleasant he will be rude. He attends to none of the prisoners' requests, making it plain that he regards them as so much trash. His greatest harshness, however, is reserved for the Coloured convicts who come to clean the lock-up each morning. These convicts are long-term prisoners who are too old to do ordinary hard labour. They arrive with mops, brushes and slop buckets, and wash out the cells and sweep the yard. Most of them are bent, grizzled old men with thin shaky legs and trembling arms. They flurry around the cells, anxious to give the appearance that they are hard at work. When they are under the supervision of this particular policeman they dart around frantically. The more he yells at them the wilder their movements, so that their bare feet do a continuous furious dance on the concrete floor. Only one of them wears a pair of shoes, which are several sizes too big for him, so that their clip-clopping causes the warder special amusement. He chases the convicts as though they were a flock of geese. When they work methodically he abuses them for being such lazy bastards. If they then work more quickly he accuses them of not doing a simple job properly.

'Do you call this clean?' he screams. 'Do it again, you rubbish.'

The convicts have some consolation for their menial work. Part of their duties consists of stacking the plates which are left in the cells by the White prisoners. There is always food left over on the plates, and as they pile the plates one on the other, the old men stuff cold rice, stew, sausage, egg and pieces of bread and pumpkin into their mouths. Their hands move quickly. A few chews, and each mouthful is gulped down, for since they cannot handle the plates for long they eat voraciously. Food is not the only treasure they find in the cells. Buttons, combs, cigarette stubs, pieces of cotton, magazine covers, all things of possible value found lying on the floor are tucked away in their trousers. They are adept at hiding large quantities of things on their person; at times they seem like conjurers acting in reverse. Each time the bully is on duty I gasp at his cruelty. These old men are so frail and defenceless and he so vigorous and powerful that his yelling is pointless. There is nothing I can do to protect them, but I make a point of piling extra delicacies on my plate, such as sweets and peanuts, before handing it over for cleaning, I also try to engage the bully's attention and every now and then deliberately speak of the 'old men'. Yet all this does little to mitigate his brutality.

These three constables are the men charged with the responsibility of watching over the cells. They lock up and release prisoners, bring food, come on occasional inspections, see that the cells are cleaned out, and supervise exercise. Each of these warders is subject to the control of a duty sergeant who also makes periodic inspections. The duty sergeant in addition must allocate a second constable to assist each cell warder. Over the weeks I have got to know more than a score of policemen. At first they tend to be cold towards me, but after repeated contact they become less hostile. They realise that I will not try to escape and that I have not got any plans to convert them to the legion of the Anti-Christ. I turn my cheek to insults, but insist on being accorded what small rights still remain to me. Perhaps, too, the ease with which I deal with high-ranking officers enhances my status in the eyes of these constables and sergeants.

I try to cause as little inconvenience as possible, spacing my requests carefully and waiting for the least unsympathetic policeman to be on duty before asking for anything. When exercise time comes I see to it that a pile of Afrikaans magazines is on hand for my guards to peruse. Very few of the police say more than a few words to me, but they chat volubly to each other, and to me a conversation overheard is almost as good as a conversation participated in.

Looking back over the weeks a few incidents stand out with special clarity, not because they have any particular intrinsic interest, but because of the impact they made on me at the time of their occurrence.

I will never forget, for example, the sight of one sergeant leafing through *Punch*. At the beginning of my exercise time he asked if he could look through copies of 'that magazine which comes from England.' He is a burly, slow-moving man, who thinks slowly and speaks slowly. His manner is grave, and he seems unmoved by the turmoil of the world. Methodically and ponderously, as in all his activities, he placed the copies of *Punch* in a pile at his side, and leafed his way through them one by one. By the time my exercise period was over he had worked through the whole pile. His progress was absolutely steady, except for his lingering a little over those pages which carried tobacco advertisements, which seemed to have a special attraction for him. For the whole half-hour that I ran round the small yard, his face was set in a baffled frown. Six editions of British humour in concentrate failed to stir him to a single smile.

One day a rather wild young constable newly arrived in Cape Town from an outpost in the country bragged about his athletic prowess. He had done particularly well with the javelin, he declared. In fact with his second throw he nearly beat a record. He had never thrown the javelin before, and his arm and shoulder got so stiff that the next day when he tried to hit a kaffir he kept missing the bastard.

Another young policeman told me that he once spent two weeks in jail and did not like it one bit. It was while he was stationed at Kimberley. They arrested someone for diamond smuggling and could not find the diamonds anywhere. They were sure that the suspect had swallowed the diamonds, so they locked up this policeman with him to keep a twenty-four hour watch on him. The policeman's main job was to collect and examine the stools of the suspect every time he had a . . . , well the policeman had a simple word for it.

This story gave me the chance to make another of the jokes for which I have become famous amongst the policemen. 'Hell,' I tell him, 'your job must have been up to . . .' and I repeat the word he used. Loud roars of laughter assure me that my standing as a wit has been further consolidated.

One afternoon when I ask to be supplied with a fresh roll of toilet paper I remark to the guards that I wonder how many yards of toilet paper I have used since I was first detained. Instead of measuring the length of my stay in months and days I could measure it in miles and yards, I tell them. Our estimates of the length of a roll of toilet paper vary from five yards to fifty, and this prompts one of the guards to recount to us the first case in which he gave evidence. A policeman was being charged with the theft of a few hundred rolls of toilet paper from the barracks. Apparently the case turned on how many yards of toilet paper twenty men could use in a week. The court examined the matter with all judicial ceremony, and in the absence of conclusive evidence on the yardage-consumption of toilet paper at the station, gave the accused the benefit of the doubt and acquitted him.

The policemen in the radio patrol office are a spirited crowd, so that being tied to telephone and microphone for hours on end produces a restlessness in them that manifests itself in a variety of ways. One plays a guitar, another croons sad melodies over the air to the policemen cruising around in vans. A number cluster around a gramophone from which a sound emerges which corresponds with the description I have read of the music made by a new group called the Beatles. I get to know the songs quite well. Another favourite of the police is a record they play which contains the 'Hammer' song. Not many years ago that was a song associated with left-wing causes. Now, because they like the beat of the song, the South African police gaily sing about the hammer of justice, the bell of freedom and the song of a love between all my brothers and my sisters, all over this land.

One evening the sergeant on broadcast duty asks the African sergeant who is in charge of a patrol van to sing something. I hear a deep voice, crackling with atmospherics, sing in reply the first verse of the anthem of all Africans in Southern Africa— *Nkosi Sikilele Afrika.*[1]

'Afrika,' the White sergeant says. 'You mustn't sing about Afrika or you'll get Ninety-Days.'

Another group of policemen seem fond of what they would call 'chaffing girls'. Their conversations are my only regular source of humour. Sometimes the girls phone them, sometimes they phone the girls. I stand next to my window eagerly eavesdropping on the conversations.

'How old do you say you are?'

'You can't be only twelve. You sound like at least fifteen.'

'Tell me, hey, what are your measurements?'

'22-38-22! How can that be?'

'Oh, you're pregnant! You got to be more careful, man. You need someone with experience. Where do you live?'

'Why do I want to know? Well, perhaps, I can come and take you out when I'm off duty—at 10 o'clock.'

'You say it's too cold to go out. I know something that's very good for the cold. . . .'

[1] 'God Save Africa,' the national anthem of the Africans in South Africa.

Only three times in six weeks has anyone from the radio patrol office ever taken any notice of me. Every evening after supper when I have my sing-song I make a point of directing a number of songs out through my window towards the radio patrol room. The first recognition I received was from a policeman who stood at his window and screamed at me in Afrikaans:

'Mr Sachs, *jou moer!*' (you scum). The abuse was unpleasant but I was amused that he called me 'Mister'. A few weeks later another policeman saw me singing and shouted in a sympathetic voice:

'You must be lonely there, what you in for?'

'Ninety-Days,' I called back.

'Oh,' he said and walked away.

Then just the other day something happened which delighted me. Four young policemen crowded to the window nearest mine. 'Mr Sachs,' one of them shouted, 'sing that song "Always".' They were friendly, not mocking, so I sang with all the tenderness and irony I could muster. As I finished they clapped enthusiastically, and after they had shouted: 'Encore. Encore!' I sang the song again.

Thus I fraternise with the enemy. I know that they and I form parts of separate and antagonistic formations. Yet I have now been thrust down next to them. We live side by side through the hours of the day and a web of human contact is woven between us. I remain a captive, and I fight them by refusing to answer questions, yet human beings are naturally curious about each other. One day, perhaps, those policemen in the room opposite my cell will be trying to kill me and I will be trying to kill them. But now they are my neighbours, just as the prisoners in the cells nearby are my neighbours. I enjoy peeping at them and listening in on their songs and horseplay, just as I am hurt by their frequent boorishness over the telephone.

Sometimes I worry over my lack of hostility towards the police, especially where they manifest cruelty to others. A sergeant comes round on inspection one evening, as he opens my cell door I notice that he is trembling. This is the first time we have seen each other, yet I realise that he loathes me. His whole body shakes with aggression. I ask if I may empty my pot. He gestures to me to do so, and as I walk to the lavatory I am aware of his stalking me.

'Hurry up! Hurry up! Hurry up!' he yells. He keeps within striking distance of me, and I notice that his fists are clenched. All the time that I am out of my cell he growls at me, and for once I feel relieved to be locked in my cell again. The next morning I ask the quiet warder why the sergeant was so aggressive.

'Oh, he's all right,' the warder tells me. 'He was inside for two years himself. They said it was murder,' he adds.

'What was it all about?' I ask.

'He filled up a prisoner with water,' the warder replies, 'and jumped on his stomach until he died.'

This brute is once more in charge of prisoners. He barely restrained himself from assaulting me. Yet I see him as a sick and emotionally distorted man who urgently requires medical assistance. The men I hate are those who took him back into the police force knowing that they give him scope to practise further violence on defenceless people. Who are the men who took him back into the force? I do not see them. They are abstractions and, such being the case, my hatred for them is intense.

28 Activities

All I am faced with is wall.

That is not a bad first line. I cannot make up my mind about this poem. When first I wrote it I thought it was very good. Then I re-read it a few days later and it seemed terrible. Now after another week I look at it again and think that, well I am not sure what I think. I read the rest of the first verse.

> *Placed high, higher than I,*
> *Who am tall, if stretching*
> *Stood could reach, is the*
> *One breach, a grate,*
> *Small and straight, but*
> *In from which height*
> *Through bars streams air*
> *And light and sound of*
> *Distant cars and out*
> *Through which insistent*
> *Swirling dreams*
> *Can flood.*

It must be read aloud, slowly and sonorously so that the echo words can be heard but not be noticed as rhymes. A monotone must be sustained, broken only by the constantly shifting rhythms of the lines. Perhaps it is rubbish and I am rationalising what is really my inability to rhyme and scan. I read the last two verses.

Clangs the steel gate
Unlocked the iron door
Stone the hard floor
Tin the cold plate
Of food

I, like the cat, sit on the mat
And feel my whole being brood
Seeing, I with my own eyes,
What they would and can
Do to such a man
Who tries, as I know I had,
Not to be bad
But good.

It was fun writing this poem, whatever its merits. The impulse came suddenly, after I already had had pencil and paper for more than two months. A few days later the urge came again and I rapidly scribbled more lines. I could call the second piece

DOGGEREL FOR SUNDAY

Ding dong dell, ding dong dell,
I have a song to sing, I have a tale to tell,
Ding dong, to tell, ding dong.

Ding dong dell, ding dong dell,
Sing a song of Sunday, loud rings the bell,
Ding dong, the bell, ding dong.

Ding dong dell, ding dong dell,
The Christians with their keys, have locked me in my cell,
Ding dong, my cell, ding dong.

Ding dong dell, ding dong dell,
All bad people go to church, all good people stay in hell,
Ding dong, in hell, ding dong.
Ding dong dell, ding dong, ding dong dell,
Ding dong, ding dong, dell.

I speak it aloud and it is as satisfying as a long curse. Lastly I wrote:

See-saw, minority law
Sachs will have a new master
He will get but many a day
Because he won't work in with Vorster.

Perhaps this is more my mark. I should stick to parody.

My writing progress has been very slow. I am not short of time of course, and in terms of the Court order I am entitled to receive a reasonable supply of writing materials. Yet I have produced very little. It has taken me over two months to start on something other than word games.

For the first few days, after the Supreme Court order came through, all I could do with pencil and paper was to jot down requests to the station commander. Then I started thinking out word games and only now have begun anything that approaches creative writing. I will not get very far with my writing. Apart from my inherent inadequacies, I am held back both by lack of incentive and by fear that what I write will be seized.

It is difficult to write without directing my thoughts to someone who will read the script. Yet now I must write for no one. It is writing in the air, mere exercise not unlike my physical jerks. I do it because I know it is good for me; it helps keep my mind in trim. Thus, apart from the poems, everything I put on paper is neutral. Abstract drawings, word games, crossword puzzles—I have a folder full of pieces of that kind. There are no deep thoughts, no descriptions of my new world, no commentaries on life as a prisoner. I have thought out nothing new, nor reformulated anything old. My special thoughts, the insights I have gained, the new emotional depths I have sounded within myself, all these must remain secret until I come out. The police must never be allowed to see into my mind. They must never be allowed to get hold of and to crush my thoughts, for the police are book-burners, destroyers of things delicate. There is only one safe place for my thoughts: in myself. Also, being alone all the time, day in and day out, has had a disintegrative effect on my thinking, and I find it difficult to organise ideas and to sustain interest in them. My present world is stale and largely depopulated. I suck from it what materials

244

I can to feed my mind, but I am always starved of stimulation. The mind is not a free-floating entity that can activate itself and function independently of its physical habitat. My mind lives in my body, and my body is caged here in a tiny world which is like a zoo without visitors. My thoughts prey on themselves. It is true that the books which I read unite me with the world outside and that through them I see the people, the places and the events of mankind. But in books all is frozen for the actual experience has already been processed by the author.

What I need is direct stimulation, so that my senses have immediate contact with the world of movement and emotion. In order to write I must live. It is not enough merely to stay alive. Every now and then a new thought germinates in my consciousness, but it swells quickly and then drifts away for ever, like a balloon lost in the sky.

When I look at the folder of scrap paper, I see that I have collected three pages of word ladders. From jail to free in the fewest number of steps, changing one letter at a time. Jail – fail – fall – fell – feel – feet – fret – free. Seven links in the chain. Every few weeks I think of a new batch of words. Finding the word-pairs is more difficult than working out the chains. Lock to door—let me see—four steps. Busy to lazy—nine, dog to cat—three, sick to well—four. Sometimes three-letter words prove more difficult than four-letter words. From one to two takes no less than fourteen steps. One day perhaps I will submit my word chains to a newspaper. Let me see, I have one hundred and twenty-six of them. I should write out a neater list.

I also have many pages devoted to what I call the Quick Brown Fox game. For weeks I have tried to write a sentence which contains all the letters of the alphabet but which is shorter than the famous: quick brown fox jumped over the lazy dog. That sentence has thirty-three letters. My best effort, I feel is: Quick brazen fights vex jumpy world, which has only thirty letters. Even shorter, but with less sense, is: Wild brazen fights vex jumpy quack, which has only twenty-nine letters, a new world record I am sure. Equalling the record is: Why just quiz and vex grim black fop, but alas it must be rejected on the grounds of poor political content. Lazy frogs vex quack with bad jumping, in thirty-one letters is not bad, while: Beg crazy cops fix with vim quick end jail is all of thirty-four letters, but very topical, and accordingly worthy of a consolation prize. If I am released, perhaps a newspaper will be interested in this game too.

A game in solitary confinement is worth something only if it carries its own built-in scoring system. I must know what the challenge is that I have to meet and beat. I tried playing three dimensional noughts and crosses, for example, but it was not much fun, because I was challenging myself.

Similarly, trying to remember lists of things seems pointless unless I have some record against which to check my memory. An advertisement page in an American magazine, which listed stores in each of the several states of the United States, gave me the incentive for an enjoyable exercise of mind. I tried to write down the names of all the States. I managed to spend most of a day on this, for I tackled the matter first geographically, then historically, and finally phonetically by running through the alphabet and repeating sounds to see if they revived any names by association. I surprised myself by being able ultimately to remember all the States but three. There are so many things which I have forgotten. For example, I can no longer remember the licence number of my car, and I cannot remember court cases in which I appeared shortly before my arrest. Yet it would seem that things learnt at school are more firmly established in my mind than the experiences of my life immediately prior to my detention.

I wonder if *Justitia*, the police magazine, will print my recent crossword puzzle? The station commander promised that he would send it to the editors. What is the good of constructing a crossword puzzle if there is no one to work it out? I made up my first crossword puzzle soon after getting pencil and paper. Looking back it seems an obvious thing to work on, yet in fact the idea came slowly. My first action after receiving pencil and paper was to draw little blobs. Later the blobs opened into cubes. Like growing cells, the cubes expanded across the page. It was these shapes which I had unconsciously drawn that made me think of a crossword puzzle. Only then did I set about working out clues, and so my Ninety-Day crossword puzzles were born. I have made up three of these puzzles. The first is dominated by words relating to prison life, the second has words common in an average vocabulary, and the third is a combination of the first two. It was this last puzzle which I sent in to the police magazine. I made especially easy some of the clues so that there would be a better chance of the puzzle being accepted. One thing I have not lost is the capacity to admire my own humour, so I frequently re-read some of the clues: One across—'See you later, plainclothesman (twelve letters).' Seventeen—'To begin with for keeping people in but altogether for keeping wine (6).' Ah, here is my favourite. Twenty-one—'Hath April, June and November and certain types of prisoners! (6, 4).' Twenty-three—'The printer spoke out of turn and so was locked up (4, 8).' Nine down—'Prisoners in flight? (4, 5).' Appropriate clues for policemen to follow up. On another page I have written the answers—'Investigator,' 'cellar,' 'Ninety Days,' 'kept prisoner,' 'jail birds.' I think the station commander said that before it could be published the puzzle would have to be approved of by the Commissioner-General of the police. Perhaps the general thinks a crossword puzzle is simply a code for sending messages. I rather fancy the idea of the head of the security branch conferring with the general on my crossword puzzle.

I turn over the pages in my folder. During one week I was taken up with a quiz and puzzle book which I had bought. Here I still have the answers. Every fortnight a local magazine carries I.Q. tests. My reasoning power seems to be good, though I do not know how I would have fared if I had done the tests in the period immediately after I had received books or pencil and paper. On a separate batch of pages I have recorded my answers to the tests. I must be one of the first prisoners in history to administer to himself intelligence tests while undergoing solitary confinement.

Finally, I have a dozen pages of my nearly completed short story. The idea of writing the story came fairly suddenly, as did the idea of writing the poems. I was excited as I mapped the outline of what I would write. It would be a magazine-type story that would give away nothing of my deeper thoughts. The hero, I decided, would be a young advocate, who meets his match in the shape of a pretty young lady whom he cross-examines. I wrote the first few pages with enthusiasm but thereafter my energy waned, and it has been a struggle to continue. I have thought of two more plots for stories about the young advocate; in one of them he wakes up in jail the morning after a Bar dinner and finds that he has to face a charge of drunken driving. Yet I cannot finish the first story. There is no one to read it, no magazine to publish it. It will lie in my folder, nearly finished but not quite, a relic of an enthusiasm that could not be sustained, the spirit of which has blown away.

I find that I have at no time had difficulty in concentrating on reading. I read greedily and relentlessly and, unfortunately, at a great pace. If I receive a magazine I read literally every single word in it. I read advertisements, cooking hints, all about Elvis and about Cliff, who the magazine is published by, love stories, comic strips, and even the astrology column. The latter provides me with a regular chuckle as I read of impending journeys, strange meetings, financial advances and reverses, turns in romances and unexpected happenings which I must expect. I think frequently of destiny and fate, and the pressure towards irrationality is strong, so that I find it philosophically reassuring to be able to laugh out loud at the absurdity of the horoscopes.

The security men never lose a chance to remind me how precarious my supply of reading matter is. They tell me that the Court order will be taken on appeal, and that pending appeal they are not obliged to give me anything to read. A few weeks ago I was informed by one of the sergeants on cell duty that his new instructions were that I was not to be supplied with any magazines. Fortunately the other sergeants do not seem to have been told of these instructions, so I delay my requests for magazines until these other sergeants are on duty. I have to be careful with my timing, for any request made towards the end of a shift is invariably held over for fulfilment by the next shift. When I do receive magazines I make a point of not leaving them in positions where they can be seen by visitors.

Thus, hidden away as though it were a pamphlet on guerrilla warfare, will be a copy of *Punch*, or of *Time Magazine* (my only source of news). Another new instruction is that I may have only one book at a time for reading, and that after finishing each book I must wait a clear day before getting another one. If I finish reading a book in the morning then I have to wait for two more mornings before I can order another book. I time my reading therefore so as to come to the end of whatever I am reading in the evening just before lights-out. It is apparent that they are slowly cutting down on the amount of reading matter they give me. The promise to get books from the library has never been fulfilled. I no longer receive crossword puzzles. They refuse to get me certain books, for example *Resurrection* by Tolstoy, on the grounds that they do not know enough about the books to be sure that they are suitable. At the same time the speed of my reading has increased. Once my eyes fall on a page, I cannot restrain them from galloping along the lines. The only remedy is to reduce the number of hours per day during which I read. I now try not to read anything at all before eleven each morning. Occasionally I force myself not to touch my reading matter until late in the afternoon. This keeps me emotionally prepared for a sudden deprivation of books and magazines. I have also stockpiled a certain amount of unread reading matter which is hidden in various parts of my cell like so many ammunition dumps, to be unearthed should an emergency arise. A ball-point pen is lodged deep in my mattress, while some sheets of paper are stuck away behind a pipe. The hidden reading and writing materials should, if rationed to a few minutes a day, last me for a couple of months. They will soften the impact of a withdrawal of reading matter.

As the weeks pass by the pile of books which I have read grows higher. These books are locked away in an unused cell nearby, for I am not allowed to send them to anyone outside. One wonderful feature of books is that they do not carry any advertisements, except sometimes for other books. I receive a pure pleasure from reading books. My preference is still for novels, but I am running out of authors. It is increasingly difficult to think of the name of books which I have not read but would like to read. I do not know what new titles have been released and many of the books I request are no longer obtainable. I try to buy only paperbacks so as not to spend too many pounds per month on books, and this further restricts my choice.

Yet I have managed to read some excellent books. Anything less than five hundred pages is like a short story, so I judge a book as much by quantity as by quality. By both tests *Don Quixote* has been splendid. Poor old knight of the sad countenance—each time I read of him raising himself winded and bruised from the dusty ground, I cannot help thinking of myself emerging from interrogations. Then I have read *Buddenbrooks* by Thomas Mann, *The Agony and the Ecstasy* by Irving Stone and *Hawaii* by Michener, all thousand-pagers and each with its special quality. A thick book to me is like a thick steak to a gourmet. Shorter novels which I have enjoyed include *The Scarlet Letter* by Hawthorne and *Claudine at School* by Colette, the two books presenting a fine contrast in sensibility. I have also read some non-fiction, the most notable work being *The Rise and Fall of the Third Reich* by Shirer. This is the most daring item for which I have asked and certainly the only political work. The sergeant who brought it to me flung it on my bed with feeling and muttered something about lies and only one side of the story. I was not surprised to discover that he was pro-Nazi, and neither was I surprised to learn that one of the other sergeants was an ex-serviceman who had fought against Hitler. In their dealings with me both sergeants follow the regulations strictly but, within that framework, the former is dour and antagonistic, while the latter is human and tolerant. One of the books which I have hidden away is the *Greek Myths* by Robert Graves. It is slow reading and will be ideal for iron rations. Another book which is out of sight is *Honest to God* by the Bishop of Woolwich. A pamphlet given me by the station commander at Wynberg attacked this book with such venom that I determined to get it as soon as possible. I could not, of course, ask for it while I was at Wynberg, but it was one of the first books I asked for when I arrived here in town. I am pleased I did so, for at last I have found a book which makes intelligible to me the philosophy of a number of Christians I have known whose belief in a supernatural order I found hard to credit. Christianity without religion, Christianity as a doctrine of love, is an exciting and attractive concept. Yet I wonder how it differs from say, Buddhism or communism in its essential ethics. The language of each creed may vary, but love-thy-neighbour and worship-not-thyself is common to all. I have hidden the book away so that should my reading supply be cut off, I will have a perceptive and provocative guide to aid my Bible study. At the moment I am unconvinced that the text of the Bible permits of the interpretation put forward by the revisionist bishop, though modern knowledge and experience would hardly seem to permit of any other interpretation. Twenty years ago the theologian Bonhoeffer wrote his anti-theistic pro-Christian testament in a Nazi prison. His ideas as taken up and propagated by the Bishop of Woolwich have now come back to jail, and lie wedged on my outside window-sill; waiting for the day when I am driven back to thoughts of life and death and of why the world is.

29 Body and Soul

THE WORST IS THE DIZZINESS. SOMETIMES WHEN I LEAVE my cell to go to the exercise yard a strange lightheadedness overcomes me. My head feels like a balloon. There is no pain, but rather a sensation of being in an expanding void which is dimly aureoled by the presence of unhappiness. Emotionally I feel faint. Only the momentum of habit and the strictures emanating from the rational centre of my brain keep me upright and running. Yet, though I move sluggishly, the exercise provides relief.

If this were the only distressing symptom I would not have the need to call for the doctor. But there are other weird sensations which, when taken in conjunction, present a picture of incipient mental disintegration. Often when I lie on my bed I feel as though my soul is separating from my body. I know, of course, that the sensation is illusory. It is nonetheless distinct and disturbing. My limbs, my trunk and my head lie in an inert vegetable mass on the mattress, while my soul floats gently to the ceiling, where it coalesces and embodies itself into a shape which lodges in the corner and looks down at my body. Usually the shape is that of an owl that stares at me, calmly, patiently, and without emotion. It is my own owl, my own I. It is I staring at myself. What is more, I am aware of the whole process as though there is yet another self which watches the I staring at myself. I am a mirror bent in on itself, a unity and yet an infinite multiplicity of internal reflections.

As if to get a revenge, my body reminds me of itself by means of periodic spasms of shock. It happens when I am off guard,

252

when my mind is at rest. Without warning my limbs contract and kick out, and my whole body is shaken by a twitch, as if an electric current were passing through me. A myriad of suppressed tensions are suddenly released at one moment and when it is over, I feel stunned and trembly. My heart beats rapidly and the pores of my skin seem to dilate. Slowly the terror subsides. My body relaxes and my pulse becomes steady again.

Less disturbing than the shock is the pain I occasionally get above my heart. It hits me sometimes when I straighten up suddenly from a hunched position. The muscle feels pinched. If I keep still and inhale deeply, the muscle relaxes, and the pain disappears.

Sometimes when I am sleepy and my body is stretched out, relaxed on the bed, I imagine I hear my name being called. It is a warm, golden sound that speaks to me, just once, and just my name. At first when I heard it I would jump off the bed and listen avidly at the door or window, with the hope of hearing the voice call me again. I would whistle, and sing out 'hullo'. Now I realise that there is no one calling me. One of the radio patrol policemen might be attracting the attention of a colleague whose name is similar to mine, and in a trance-like state of near sleep I might imagine that it is I who am being called. Possibly there is no sound at all, and I am suffering from what the medical people would call auditory hallucination.

When I have a shower after exercise time I am overtaken by another odd feeling. I had been here a month before someone discovered that the shower worked. Now every day after running round the yard I soap myself under the shower and let the sunwarmed water run over me. At present it is with a feeling of dread that I enter the corner where the shower pipe juts out of the wall. As I stand on the cement, naked and slippery with soap, I feel myself become tense with an urge to tumble down and crack my skull open. Terror and wish mingle as I imagine my cranium splitting wide apart, with my brains and thoughts bursting out like pomegranate pips.

The worst symptom of all I will not mention to the doctor when he comes; I am losing the will to resist. Nothing seems to matter any more. I feel flat and lonely, and I do not seem to care about anything. 'So what' sums up my attitude. Life is purposeless. To continue to live like this is purposeless. What am I trying to prove by holding out? If the others want to carry on fighting, well and good, that is their business, but it has nothing to do with me. I want some peace. That is not an unreasonable wish. All this human heaving and straining, where does it get anybody? Is the world any less cruel than it ever was? I have spent years of my life panting and pushing after slogans. Is anyone the happier for it, is anyone the freer?

Once again I realise that my lack of drive is a consequence of being confined, and that my thoughts are a product of their environment. In the depths of my rational being I still believe in the value of man and the need to struggle for the further progress of mankind. Yet I feel powerless to achieve anything. Time and isolation have dissipated my emotional energy. I need medical observation.

Footsteps and a key-ring are approaching. The gate at the top of the steps is unlocked, swung open, swung to and locked again. Voices sound outside my door. The padlock is unfastened and a key turns in the doorlock. My door swings open and I see that standing next to the cell warder there is a long burly man whom I take to be one of the local district surgeons. He stares at me and then looks around the cell.

'You've got a bed, I see,' he says. His speech is harsh and marked by a Jewish accent.

'Well, what's your complaint?' Before I can answer, he walks into the cell and peers again at my bed. I move back to give him room to look around.

'I know what you are going to say when I walk out of here,' he continues, 'you are going to say that we doctors are all useless, we don't do a thing to help. The fact is that there is nothing we can do to help you. You got yourself into this mess, and only you can get yourself out again.'

'I am sorry, doctor, but I don't think I know your name,' I say politely. I want him to see me as a human being, an equal, and not as just another 'malingering prisoner'.

'Dr ————,' he tells me. 'You know, you are lucky about your conditions here. Prison conditions have improved enor-

254

mously. You should read the life of Elizabeth Fry before you complain. Prisoners have an easy time of it today.'

'Doctor, I've asked to see you because I'm worried about certain symptoms I have been having. I am in a very difficult and vulnerable position here and would like to be assured that there is nothing physically wrong with me. There's probably nothing serious the matter, and if I were outside I might not worry at all. But being alone all the time I feel I can't take any chances with my health.' I ask him if he would care to sit down, and then I tell him about my mental and emotional sensations. I speak quickly for he gives me the impression of being impatient to get away. If I do crack up, they cannot say that I did not warn them, and the responsibility will be entirely theirs. The doctor is so strange and perfunctory that I almost feel that he is not real but merely another of my symptoms.

When I finish speaking, he shrugs his shoulders, and prods at the mattress with his fist.

'I don't know what you are complaining about,' he says gruffly. 'You've got a bed and blankets and you get three meals a day. If you don't like it here, it's quite easy. All you have to do is to co-operate with the Government and you will get out. You can't fight the Government you know. The Government is for the whole country, whether you like it or not, and you have no right to oppose it.'

I am too amazed and hurt to say anything. It is not his function to act the policeman. He should examine my body, and watch me and listen to me to see if my mind is all right. Instead, he does most of the talking and spends more time examining my bed than examining me. I remember now where I came across his name. It was in a newspaper report a few years ago. He was found guilty by the Medical Council of negligently administering an anaesthetic. As he stands up to go, I say to myself:

You are damned useless as a doctor—and then realise that he had predicted that precisely this would be my reaction. After passing through the doorway he looks back and, as the policeman prepares to lock the door, says to me:

'You don't know how lucky you are in this country. If you had been living in Queen Elizabeth's time, you know what would have happened to you?' He turns to the policeman. 'Tell him what would have happened to him.'

The policeman draws his finger across his throat and makes a croaking sound.

'That's what would have happened to you,' the doctor carries on, 'your head would have been chopped off.'

The door is slammed and locked, and the footsteps disappear through the gate and down the stairs. I am near to crying. I feel angry and humiliated. But above all I feel hurt. The district surgeon has betrayed my belief in the medical profession. A doctor's job is to heal the sick. He knows that I have been more than four months in solitary confinement. Yet instead of examining me he gave me a lecture on politics. I am not a malingerer. This is the first time in nearly four and a half months that I have asked to be seen by a doctor. In Wynberg the district surgeon saw me once a week, as a matter of course, not at my request. When on the day after my re-detention I felt nauseous it was a policeman and not I who sent for a doctor. This man who has now come to see me is nothing but a clumsy oaf. If my arm were broken, or blood poured out of my mouth, he might do something. But he probably does not believe there is such a thing as mental illness. At present I have insight into my mental disturbance. Later it may be too late. Must I tell him that I am Napoleon before he investigates the effects which isolation is having on my mind? How dare he call himself a doctor. And how dare the Government employ a man like this to watch over the health of prisoners.

How powerless I feel. If I complain about the doctor he will say I am malingering, and my chances of medical treatment in the future will be diminished. If I say nothing, he will report that I am quite healthy, which is not true.

I pace backwards and forwards along the narrow space between the bed and the bunk. Then I decide I had better try to take my mind off the subject. In a few weeks time I can ask again for a doctor. For the present I must do my best to keep my mind functioning in a balanced manner. I sit on the bed and

256

pick up the novel I have been reading. It is difficult to concentrate on the words. Damn that doctor! I force myself to read. I finish a page, and realise that I have let my eyes run through the paragraphs without absorbing any of the sense. I read the page again and lay the book flat on my lap.

A few minutes pass and I still sit disconsolately on the bed with the book lying spine upward on my thighs. Voices and a key-ring approach. They are coming early for exercise time today, I muse. The door opens. As I place my book on the bunk and reach for my sand-shoes, I notice that a short elderly man carrying a square black bag is standing in the doorway.

'I'm Dr Samols,' he says, 'I believe you are worried about your health.'

'Yes,' I reply. I am puzzled. 'Dr ———— was here just now to see me . . .'

'I know that. He reported to me and I decided that I had better come myself. We can go out into the yard in a moment where the light is brighter. But first just tell me what's worrying you.' He speaks with the briskness and efficiency of a man used to dealing with many patients and confident of his ability to diagnose their illnesses. He places his bag on the bunk and sits facing me on my bed. I tell him of the dizziness, the shocks and muscle spasms, the separation of body and spirit, about hearing my name called, and of the urge to crack my skull open on the cement. He listens carefully, but without apparent reaction. I speak dully, for I am repeating what I have already explained in full only a short while ago. When I give my theory of why I have the urge to split my head and why I think of my skull as a pomegranate he smiles. The strain of refusing to answer questions is beginning to tell on me, I explain. If I fall and my head breaks open, I cannot be blamed for letting the police see what is on my mind. The image of a pomegranate comes from the myth of Persephone in the Underworld which I have recently finished reading.

I wish he would comment on what I say. I tell him that there is probably nothing seriously the matter with me, but that in my present position I cannot take any chances. I am particularly worried that there might be something physically

257

wrong with me. I would be glad if he would give me a check up to make sure that I am all right.

At the doctor's request two chairs are brought up from the charge office and placed in the yard. As we walk to take our seats there, he remarks that my hands are very pale. 'They always have been,' I reply. In the yard we sit facing one another. I tell him that I am not used to sitting on a chair and talking to a human being who is not a policeman. 'Is that why you called for me?' he asks.

'Oh no,' I answer, 'I would not do that, my health is far too serious a matter to be used simply to get company.'

He records my blood pressure and tests my lungs and heart with a stethoscope. As his hands potter around my body, I feel mildly happy. Someone is showing humanitarian concern for me. I have some worth. The world is not entirely alien. I lift my arms and he prods in my armpits. 'Lean back,' he says. Two chairs are placed together and I lie on them. 'Now, kick off your slippers,' he tells me. I do as I am told, and watch him fiddling in his black bag. He cannot find what he wants, so he puts his hand in his trouser pocket and pulls out a bunch of keys. They are small and domestic—car keys, house keys, office keys—unlike the hefty pieces of metal the warders carry around with them. He grabs one of my feet by the heel, and runs a saw-edged Yale key along the sole.

'Ha ha ha!' I burst out laughing. He grins back at me. My foot tingles from the tickling, and I grin at the doctor.

'That's the first time I've laughed in nearly four and a half months,' I say, 'thank you very much.' I feel gay and start chatting to the doctor. I ask him if there is anything he can do for the rash below my eyes and the tiny pimples in the corner of my mouth. I then tell him that I was a little surprised at the attitude of the other doctor who had given me a lecture on politics and not examined me at all.

'Was it your son I knew at University?' I ask. There was a chap named Samols at Medical School who graduated at about the same time as I did, I explain. While I chatter on, he writes a series of items in a prescription book.

'There is nothing wrong with you physically,' he says.

258

'Mentally you are also all right. You are showing some signs of the effects which should be expected in the circumstances, but there is nothing to worry about. I've prescribed some pills for you to take and they should help.'

I frown. The thought of taking pills worries me. Drugs might undermine me and I may not be able to control their effects.

'Do they have side effects?' I ask.

'No. They are very mild and should take away the dizziness and other things you describe. They can't harm you at all.'

'I'll see how it goes, then,' I reply. 'If the symptoms don't go away in the next few days then I will try the pills.' Will they affect my will-power—that is what I really want to know—if I take these pills, will I still be able to resist their interrogations? I feel I dare not ask these questions.

'I've also prescribed some ointment for your skin troubles, and a shampoo for your hair. The rash probably comes from dandruff. Is there anything more I can do for you?'

'Perhaps you could speak to the station commander about letting me have more exercise time. I am out of my cell for only half an hour in the morning and half an hour in the afternoon. This means that I get hardly any fresh air and very little sun.'

'All right, I'll speak to him. And anytime you want me, don't hesitate to ask. I'm not far away.'

'I'll try not to trouble you. I find it best to save up my requests for something serious.'

The doctor packs his bag and gives the prescription to the policeman who earlier had unlocked my cell door.

'It was my son you knew,' he says to me. 'He used to speak about you. He is in Canada now working in one of the big hospitals there. Is it true that you refuse to answer any questions?'

'Yes, it's true.'

He gives me a grave look, slightly quizzical, slightly amused.

'Well, I won't give you any lectures.' His face is expressionless as he says these words. But—am I imagining it—I think I detect a note of respect in his voice.

I am locked in my cell and the voices and key-ring disappear in the direction of the charge office. I feel elated. Thank you

259

doctor, for being a doctor. You have reasserted for me the norms of civilised society, where a doctor is a man who tries to heal, and not someone who condones torture. I suspect that part of me secretly wanted to be ill, for that would have provided me with a way out without dishonour. Yet now I am glad that I am well. If my health gives way there is no telling how I might react. My mind and my body must not be divided against themselves. I need all my health and all my strength to hold out, for the truth is that my will to resist has reached its lowest point so far.

30 Sufficient Unto the Day

THE NEXT TIME THEY COME I WILL ANSWER THEIR questions. It no longer matters what I do. I will not say anything about anyone other than myself so I cannot cause any harm. One hundred and thirty days have passed since I was taken, which means that all political trials pending at the time of my arrest must have long since been concluded. The police will not be able to use what I say to put me on trial, nor will they be able to use it against anyone else. They are keeping me now purely as a matter of principle, for they want to demonstrate that no one is released from Ninety-Day detention until he has answered questions. I would like to prove that the opposite is possible but I do not seem to have the necessary stamina. Ultimately I will have to break down. Why should I suffer for another year or two years, when the end result will be the same? I can answer their questions without endangering myself or others. According to my calculations, the interrogators will come again on Friday. I will speak to them then.

It is Friday and the captain is in my cell. Accompanying him is a warrant officer whom I knew some years back when he was a sergeant in the murder squad. The captain looks sternly at me and booms:

'Are you still persisting in your stubborn attitude?' The bully! Who is he to tell me I am stubborn?

'Nothing has changed for me,' I reply. Why should I change my mind—I'm damned if I'm going to give him the satisfaction of seeing me give way.

261

'Well, I won't waste your time and I won't waste mine.'

'I've told you before, captain, that I'm only too glad to have my time wasted.'

'Hmm. We can't let you go until you answer our questions. Don't make any mistake about that.'

'It's not for me to comment on how the police carry out their work. But still, I can't see how you can continue to keep a human being locked up all on his own, day after day.' I speak bitterly and provoke him to reply.

'You people have no right to complain. If you got your way you wouldn't worry about how you treated others.' He repeats the words easily, as though he has learnt them off by heart. 'What's more, if it wasn't for this Ninety-Day law, we would have had a revolution on our hands. Not a big revolution, mind you, just a small one; but it would have caused a lot of harm to innocent people.' He is answering me, but not arguing with me. I have the feeling that he and all the other interrogators go through a special toughening-up course before being let loose on us. This is not the first time that I have noticed how pat their answers are to suggestions that they are inhuman or uncivilised. It seems that they undergo ideological training so that they believe what they are doing is right. To have doubts or to feel pity would deprive them of the ruthlessness which they require for maximum efficiency.

'But you can't justify a policy purely by results,' I answer. 'After all, torture gets results, and surely you wouldn't justify torture.' He is startled by my mention of the word torture. After a pause he says:

'Allegations of torture have been made. They are being investigated and I hope they prove to be unfounded. As far as I am concerned I am not aware of any of the men working under me having engaged in torture. I myself do not approve of torture.' He pauses again, and looks around my cell. 'Of physical torture, that is. I suppose this,' and he waves his arm around the cell, 'is a form of torture. But this is mental torture, not physical torture. This is legal torture and I believe in it. I don't approve of the other kind of torture. But I do approve

262

of lawful torture.' I am amazed at these words. The captain has been speaking with a sincerity that is rare for him. Usually he is emotionless, as calculating and hard as a machine. Now, being in the cell, perhaps he speaks more freely than he would in the 'recording studio'. I wish I had a tape of what he has just said.

'In my opinion torture can never be lawful,' I say. I desire to remind him of the Nuremberg Trials.

'We are not getting anywhere,' he complains. 'So I won't waste . . . Ach, let's go.' He and the warrant officer leave.

How could I ever have thought of answering their questions? Just seeing them in the flesh provides me with sufficient emotional charge to withstand the pressure to give in. Their presence, their manner, their ideology remind me of what my imprisonment is about. I have held out all this time. There is no reason why I should not continue to hold out at least until the end of my second ninety days. The mere fact that they will have to detain me for a third term will be a defeat for them. Set against the span of a lifetime the extra weeks and months that I spend in confinement are not long. At the end of a hundred and eighty days I will review the position again. Until then I must fight on, day by day, week by week. That is the only way to survive.

A further week has passed. I am going to try the pills. After the news I received today, I will need them. I was trying to sleep after lunch when the door was unlocked and a security man told me that my mother was waiting to see me. I dressed quickly and combed my hair. I last saw my mother at Maitland. As we stood in the yard while a cold wind blew, it had been infuriating to have to speak only about unimportant matters, such as my flat and my car. I could tell her nothing about my conditions, while she was not permitted to tell me anything of what was happening in the world or what my prospects were. That one brief visit, the only one allowed, had been a strain, both for her and for me. Since then more than three months have passed and not a soul from outside has been able to see me.

Today I was taken to the 'recording studio' and there I saw my mother again. She was very good. Her hair had been done specially, I could see, and she wore a bright new dress. We were allowed to embrace, and then she told me why she had been granted the visit. My brother Johnny has entered Guy's Hospital where he is to have a hole-in-the-heart operation sometime in the coming few weeks. The exact date has not been fixed. I told her that I would rather not know the date of the operation but, when the outcome became known, would like to be informed. While we talked we studied each other carefully. I noticed that she had a wrinkle in the heart of each of her cheeks, and there were more grey hairs on her head than I had seen before. Yet she was spirited and strong, as though the crises affecting each of her sons had summoned in her all the hidden courage which she had accumulated in a long, hard, and full life. She told me of the bright letter Johnny had written to her. I remarked that each of the three of us was trying to cheer up the other two. It was at this stage that the security man who had been supervising the conversation got up and left the room. My mother mouthed at me 'Be careful'. I nodded back. Her lips shaped the words 'tape recorder'. I nodded again, and soundlessly my lips replied 'I know'. Then, speaking aloud, I asked her how she was and she said fine, and she asked me how I was and I said fine.

'It's not easy,' I added, 'but I'll stick it out for as long as necessary.' That last bit I stressed more for the ears of the security men than for my mother. Let them think I have the spirit to last out for ever. My mother told me where my car was being stored. Then she said that she had been asked to tell me that I must not worry about my practice because it would be waiting for me when I came out. Implicit in this statement was the expectation of my being freed. It was the most cheering piece of information which could have been conveyed to me. The security man then returned and told us to finish what we had to say to each other. I was proud of my mother. She had remained calm and dignified, and had given me the support that I needed. We embraced in farewell and she left. She carried herself bravely as she walked down the corridor. I felt glad that I might possibly have given her some additional strength to face the ordeal of Johnny's operation.

There are six ways in which I can get out of this hell. I have rationalised and distilled my experience, so that if I were set an examination question on the subject I should get full marks.

The first way out is suicide. That has the advantage of denying them access to any knowledge I might have. It will further demonstrate to the world how horrid the Ninety-Day law is, and will accordingly embarrass the police. For me the pain would be over and I would not have lost my honour. I have never before in my life been morbid. Yet on three distinct occasions in the early weeks of my confinement I thought seriously about hanging myself. I no longer have those death urges. I realise that for me to take my life would cause anguish to many people and lessen their courage to struggle on. Yet I am still frequently beset by a profound philosophical pessimism. The world seems to be a pitiless place which is made bearable purely by the palliative of illusion. I sometimes think of my family being wiped out. My brother might die on the operating table, while I might linger on for ever in prison. Our two parents will be left ageing and grief-stricken.

The second way out is serious illness. I have worked hard, almost fanatically so, at keeping fit. At times, however, I have wished on myself terrible diseases. If I became grievously ill they would have to send me to a hospital. Even in a prison hospital I would probably have company. Possibly if I developed cancer or something equally grave they would let me out altogether. In the early days thoughts such as these often pushed themselves into my consciousness. This was, I suppose, the product of the conflict between the dictates of conscience and the pressures to escape from solitary confinement. More recently I have considered the possibility of simulating madness. I know very little about the symptoms of insanity, but I could exaggerate the bizarre feelings which I have already had. In particular I could concentrate on hearing voices. Pretending madness would give me something interesting and challenging to do. Yet it would be a dangerous activity that could bring

265

about permanent and irreversible damage to my mind. Furthermore, if they discovered that I was malingering, they would realise how weak I was and they would be even more determined to hold on to me. No, even contemplating illness has a demoralising effect on me. Whatever decision I make will be the better for my being physically strong and buoyant.

Another possible way out which I must discard is escape. At the time when I felt most desperate and shocked I would occasionally have escape fantasies. I would dream of being rescued, or of tricking guards and climbing walls. Then I would have nightmare visions of myself fleeing into the city, frantically seeking a hideout, while police vans drove up and down searching for me. I can understand why some prisoners spend all their hours planning means of escape. By the time of my arrest a total of five Ninety-Day prisoners had escaped. Four of them got out of their cells by bribing a guard. All four managed to slip out of the country. As a result extremely strict security measures have been enforced which make it virtually impossible for Ninety-Day prisoners to be alone with one guard at a time. The guards are told never to talk to us and, as a further safeguard, the keys to our cells are locked away in a safe which is under the supervision of the duty sergeant. The fifth escapee went 'over the wall' but was caught half an hour later. As a result of his escape the doors of all the Ninety-Day cells now have padlocks on them as well as ordinary locks. Viewed from the outside, the cells look more like sheds for storing things than places of human habitation. Tunnelling is out of the question, and there has never been any means of getting out through the ceiling. On only two occasions has even the possibility of effecting an escape arisen. The first would have involved knocking unconscious the Wynberg station commander and the second thrusting myself through a window during exercise time. In each case I had only a moment to decide, and in both cases I chose not to involve myself in any risky undertaking. Unless I had someone to assist me, from both inside and out, any attempt on my part to escape would be doomed to failure.

Another possible way for me to get out of my present predicament would be for me to ask for a permit to leave the country. The authorities might prefer to exile me rather than to continue to hold me. It would be a great humiliation for me to leave on an exit permit. Worse, however, would be the way in which the police would capitalize on my departure. They would say that I had been released to go abroad as a reward for betraying political associates and I would have no means of combatting such a falsehood.

Fifthly, I could answer their questions. I could try to limit my answers to questions which could not possibly incriminate anyone other than myself. Possibly they would be satisfied with a page or two of unimportant information merely to establish the principle that no one is released until he has answered questions. Yet, on principle, I should say nothing to them. In this instance, at any rate, principle is based on the realities of experience. One break in my resistance could precipitate total collapse. Once they see that they can make me answer questions they will never let me go until they have drained me completely. Perhaps, too, they have prepared traps which will assist them in bringing me to trial and by making a statement I might jeopardize my own position.

Finally, I can continue to refuse to answer questions. They may keep me for months more, even for years. Yet they surely cannot keep me for ever. The scandal would be too great. I would become a symbol of one who has been victimised by tyranny. The longer they keep me the more my detention could be used as a stick with which they could be beaten. It is important for me to hold out; I can help set standards of resistance. Without hope it is difficult to survive. Yet I should be able to last out until the end of my second Ninety-Day period. There is only one month to go, but it looks as if they will then re-detain me again. Perhaps they anticipate that the shock of a third detention will break my will to hold out. Their expectation might turn out to be correct, but I will worry about that problem when the time comes. For the present I must continue to organise my day so as to keep my morale as high as possible. This is the only real way out, to fight them day by day. I will see today through. Tomorrow, and each day thereafter, will present new challenges to me which I will meet as they arise.

267

Therefore, do not worry yourself over the morrow, for sufficient unto the day is the evil thereof. That must continue to be my motto.

Last night I had an unpleasant dream. I dreamt that I was being arrested by the special branch for breaking my ban. A year ago I was ordered by the Minister not to leave Cape Town. In the dream I was nearly a thousand miles away, and as the vivid police figures closed in on me, my anguish was intense.

'Oh no,' I moaned, 'after resisting for so long, am I to be tried and convicted just for this.' At the climatic moment of the nightmare I awoke. As I came to consciousness in my cell relief and joy swept through me. I am safe, I am safe, I told myself. I have been in this cell all the time, so I could not have broken the order imposed on my by the Minister, thank heavens I am safe in this cell.

Beautiful nervous whistling comes from the cell across the passage. A jazz theme is being whistled in endless fluttery cascades. Every now and then the whistler stops and yells in an anguished voice: 'You f . . . bastards, I've escaped twice and I'll escape a third time. You can't hold me. I want to be free.'

After hearing this a few times, I whistle to him, and shout: 'What are you in for?'

'It's a long story,' he shouts back. 'But they won't keep me here long. I've escaped twice from the bastards, and I'll escape again. If I'm convicted I'll get five to eight years. Just for riding about in a stolen car.'

'Why's that?' I ask.

'Six months ago I finished a sentence of two to four years corrective training. Now, if I'm found guilty of anything, I will get a compulsory sentence of five to eight. But they won't keep me, the bastards. They talk about justice. They used to give us lectures about trying to do the right thing by ourselves. When I was released I said I was going to go straight. I tried, like they told me. Thirty-seven letters I wrote. I've got copies of them all if you don't believe me. I wrote letters of application for thirty-seven jobs. I told the truth. I could have lied about my past, but I told the truth. And what happened? Nobody would take me on. I walked round this town until I was sick of walking. I was starving. You know what I had to do? I had

268

to go and live with a queer. Yes, to get some bread for myself, I had to live with a bloody queer. Then I fell in love. You know what real love is? Until I met this girl, I never knew what love was. I never knew my mother and my father and until I met her I never knew what love was. It changed my life, I went to Johannesburg to see if I couldn't get a job there. Then I was going to send for her. You see she was pregnant and as soon as I found something we were going to get married. I tried to get a job there, you can ask my friends. I tried. I walked up and down from place to place until I couldn't walk any more. Then some friends of mine said, "Come for a ride in a car." I didn't know the car was stolen. How was I supposed to know? Well the police caught us, and I knew it would be five to eight years compulsory for me. So I escaped from the police station and came down here again. They caught me, but I escaped again. It was in the cells below Court. They called out my name and another bloke went forward. I wasn't listening properly, and they took him away instead of me. Then they called me by his name and told me to pay a fine. Well, I had a few pounds on me and so I paid the fine and they let me go. I was out for ten days before they caught me again. But they won't keep me for long. You'll see. I've escaped twice and I'll escape a third time.'

I advise him that before he does anything further he should get a lawyer to help him. He might be able to get off the charge of car theft, and it is possible that escaping from custody is not one of the crimes which would make it compulsory for the magistrate to give him five to eight years. He thanks me for the advice and says that I have given him new hope. He then takes up whistling again, enthralling me with his restless but melodious trilling.

I wonder what it is like to go to jail for eight years. Jack Tarshish got ten years for transporting dynamite. The Rivonia people might by now have received the death sentence and the least they could have got was imprisonment for between twenty and thirty years. I wonder how they are all being treated. The number of political prisoners serving sentences in South Africa must run into thousands. I do not want to give up hope of being free soon, yet I must brace myself against the possibility that I will spend the middle portion of my life in prison. Perhaps they will allow me to study; I would like to do a thesis on prison literature. There could be a section in my thesis on books written in prison and another on books about prison. It might even turn out to be worth publishing. On the other hand they might force me to do hard labour all the time. A chap who was in here a month ago gave me a terrifying picture of what prison life could be like. 'It all depends on where they send you,' he said. 'In some prisons you work like a dog twelve hours a day, and feel starved all the time because the food is so poor. In other prisons the work is more interesting and the guards are decent.'

If the prison board were to ask me whether I repented of my political activities, I wonder what I would tell them. From their point of view it would be a legitimate enquiry. It would be out of the question for me to repudiate my beliefs, yet it would be unwise for me to appear defiant. Perhaps I would say something to the effect of:

Gentlemen, there are certain things that one grows up with that are deep in one and do not change overnight; I need time to think them over; but for the present all I am interested in is furthering my studies and finding some peace and quiet for myself.

How does one cope with a sentence of many years imprisonment? The answer is, I suppose, that the world of jail becomes one's new world. Just as one spends so many years at school, and then so many at university or at work, so does one spend a certain portion of one's life in prison. The prison walls are one's horizon. One adapts to life in this special world and finds new sources of stimulation and satisfaction to replace the old. When it comes to voluntarily enduring privation human beings may be feeble, but when necessity governs, they have extraordinary powers of survival and adaptation. Just as I have endured five months of isolation, so could I endure five years or fifteen years or twenty-five years of imprisonment if I had to.

In the early days at Maitland I often found myself composing mental letters which I would in imagination send to a variety of

270

recipients. There was always a formal element in whatever fantasy communications I indulged. I could never, for example, conjure up a natural conversation with anyone. What speaking fantasies I did have took the form of speeches being made to a crowd—from the stage, on the beach, or in Court. One of my imaginary letters was addressed to the Bar Council thanking them for intervening on my behalf. As the days went by I polished and rubbed away at the opening sentences until there was nothing left. Another letter was addressed to the curator of a nearby church thanking him on behalf of Ninety-Day detainees for the bell-ringing I heard every Sunday and asking him if it were not possible to have a little more variety in the peal.

Now I have pencil and paper and the possibility of writing real letters that will be sent to real recipients. The police have been clever in this regard. They have allowed me to receive two letters from England, both of which, though not so intended, are in fact calculated to undermine my morale. The first was from my brother, wishing me as happy a birthday as I could have in the circumstances and telling me that he was confident about the outcome of his operation. The second was from someone in Sheffield who said that there were a number of people in his town who remembered my stay there ten years ago and who would be happy to pay my fare to England should I be able to leave South Africa.

The police were not so clever, however, in allowing me to see birthday greetings which had been cabled to me from London. Someone had slipped up, for shortly after I had received the cable, an embarrassed sergeant came to my cell to take it away again. The signatories to the cable included Barbara Castle, Niall McDermott, Jeremy Thorpe, and a number of other prominent British legal men and parliamentarians. No doubt my dad had been busy campaigning on my behalf in London. A bold, vigorous man with a thrust and energy that carries him into regions where others would fear to tread, my father can be relied on to evoke some sort of rumble in London against my detention. Though his life has been beset by political and personal storms, and though perpetual controversy eddies around

271

him, his strength and dedication remain undiminished. Since my arrest I have felt confident that he would wield a weighty lance on my behalf. I wish I could speak to the senders of the cable. How often must they be called upon to protest against this and appeal for that. Perhaps at times they tire of pleading for distant peoples and faraway causes. If only I could tell them how important their petitions are. They do not effect any radical changes, but they do give us courage. Our captors wish to obliterate us, if not physically, then spiritually, as personalities. When we hear our names being called out by people in far-off lands we are revived. A prisoner is so helpless in so many ways that he needs people outside to speak and act for him. It is not gratitude that I feel for those men and women abroad who do something on my behalf, but affection and respect. If they were in South Africa, the Gerald Gardiners, the Barbara Castles and the Jeremy Thorpes would be behind bars. They and I and all the other political prisoners are involved in the same quest for human advance, though we find ourselves working on different frontiers under different conditions. Their efforts and ours are essentially indivisible. Our bodies suffer for them in South African prisons, while their voices speak for us in the halls and on the screens of Britain. We must never forget each other.

I will write to my benefactor in Sheffield, thanking him for the offer and pointing out the difficulties in the way of my arriving at a decision. I will stress that I expect to be detained for a long time (the more confident I sound of being able to last out, the sooner I will be released). I will also mention the feeling I have for my country and my reluctance to desert it. I will not write to my brother until after his operation. The matter is between him and the doctors. What could I say to help?

There is another letter, however, which I may very well write and which should reach its destination. For several days now I have considered sending a letter to the Minister of Justice. If he had even the slightest sense of humour I would not hesitate to do so, for the idea which I have in mind appeals to me as being rich in irony. It will be something along the following lines:
Dear Minister;

You are the author of my dilemma so I write to you. I am being held, under your authority, because I refuse to answer questions. During the Second World War you were held in solitary confinement by the South African police because you refused to answer questions. Recently in Parliament you scolded former comrades of yours who had 'ratted' during the war. Thus your personal example inspires me to continue to refuse to answer questions, while officially you demand that I do answer questions. Vorster, the man, says 'Don't answer,' while Vorster, the Minister, says 'You must answer.' In three weeks' time, namely on Good Friday, my second spell of Ninety Days will be up. This gives you the chance to emulate the great Greek god, Zeus who, after learning that Persephone had tasted the red pips of a pomegranate while in captivity in the Underworld, decreed by way of compromise that she spend six months of the year in the Underworld and six months on Earth. My six months in the Underworld (not underground!) will shortly be up. I respectfully ask you to exercise your power then, to let me go back to ordinary human society.

It would not be tactful, I suppose, to remind the Honourable Minister that the reason for his detention was that he was associated with a pro-Nazi sabotage group in South Africa at a time when South Africa was at war with Germany. As the punner would have it, one man's meat is another man's prison. I wonder what my attitude would be if, say in twenty years time, I were to find myself in a position of authority and I received a letter such as the one I propose sending the Minister now?

I have seen the doctor again. The policemen respect him for his medical ability and so do I. I asked him if I could be sedated on the day of my brother's operation, but stressed that I did not want to know about it in advance. He wanted to know how, in view of my own position, I could be so concerned about my brother. I asked him how he could possibly compare the two situations: I might be suffering, but my life was not at stake.

A special branch man summons me to dress quickly.

'What's up?' I ask.

'You'll see,' he replies. I put on my clean shirt and my suit, and follow him to the 'recording studio'. He opens the door and

278

there I see my mother. With glasses perched low on her nose, she is engrossed in a crossword puzzle and does not notice me immediately on my arrival. Then she looks up and bursting into a smile, says, 'It's all right. Wonderful news. Johnny's all right. The operation was a success. Your father phoned last night and said to me: "Your son has been reborn." '

We greet each other joyfully. Our conversation is broken and uncontrolled. I ask again and again exactly what my father said and what the prognosis is. My mother is too relieved, too happy for her younger son and too sad for her elder, to answer coherently. Eventually the captain comes in and asks my mother if she has anything more to say to me. She says, no, she's told me the main thing, and then she leaves.

The captain sits down in the chair which she had occupied, and I thank him for allowing my mother to see me.

'You see,' he answers, 'we of the South African police are not as inhuman as some people always say we are.' He then proceeds to interrogate me. I am too distracted to pay much attention to his questions. The sun rises high in the sky and I feel annoyed that he begrudges me even a few moments of quiet to enjoy my happiness. Only when I get back to my cell does it occur to me that probably the captain allowed my mother to give me the news because he hoped that I would be so overcome as to be unable to resist his interrogation.

The captain is interrogating me again. The questions he asks are more formal than usual and I detect a peevish note in his voice.

'The arm of the law is long,' he says, after there have been repeated refusals on my part to answer questions. 'If I get tired of questioning you, there are many other police officers to take my place.'

I say nothing. My silence seems to disconcert him far more than my arguments.

'So you are quite adamant in your refusal to answer questions?' he continues.

'Yes,' I answer.

'Well, you know what the position is then?'

'Yes.'

274

'We won't be soft on you.'

'I know.'

'You can't complain that we didn't explain your position to you.'

'No, I can't.'

'Any time you want me, whether it's during the day or the night, just ask, and I'll come straight away.'

'Thank you. I don't think it will be necessary.'

'If there's someone else you prefer to me . . .'

'No, I've nothing personal against you. You've been tough, but those are your instructions.'

'Good.'

He drops his cigarette end on the floor of my cell, and prods at it with the toe of his shoe. The cell smells of crushed burning tobacco. Then, putting a stylish green hat on his head, the captain walks away down the passage. There was something particularly childish and cross about him today, I muse. A wisp of smoke drifts up from the cigarette end. I extinguish the last glowing strands with my slipper and flick the pulverized butt under the door and out of my cell.

31 To the Sea

I AM FREE. It is a quarter to five, the sun is low, and I am running to the sea. I am free! With every three steps I take I repeat the words to myself. 'I'm free!' I yell as I pass the entrance to the Magistrate's Court. I fling my arms into the air and clasp my hands in a victory salute. 'I am free.'

People stare at me as I jog past them. If only you knew, if only you knew, I say inwardly. If only you knew. The phrase bumps through my mind keeping time with my jerking arms and knees. You people going about your afternoon business, you think I am one of those cranky runners trying to keep fit. Well you are wrong. I am a Ninety-Day detainee who has just been released. I have had five and a half months in solitary confinement, and now I am free.

> *I am off to the sea*
> *I am free. I am free.*
> *I am off to the sea.*

I want to feel the city with my feet, and to feel my body move past cars, buses and buildings. I want to see men and women and children walking, talking and laughing, for my jailers have let me out of my cage and I am on my most thrilling journey ever. I stare wonder-filled at the open world through which I am running. To think that I ever wondered what real joy was, and that I doubted if I should ever know happiness again.

Exactly half an hour ago the colonel came on a surprise visit to my cell. His new false teeth smiled and he handed me a piece of paper and said:

'I've got good news for you.'

276

Ha, ha, ha, ha, ha. Now I can laugh, but when he spoke those words I was so wary that I cringed. I had become used to dealing with bad news, but no longer knew how to take good news. Then I read the paper he handed me.

'. . . order the liberation of Albert Louis Sachs . . .' Liberation! Freedom! Real freedom this time.

'Of course your banning notice still applies,' the colonel warned me, 'but if you toe the line there shouldn't be any further trouble.'

I am free. I have won and they have lost. In fact it took a full ten minutes for the knowledge to penetrate the elaborate defences which lay between my brain and my heart. But now I am running with my whole body through the city on my way to the beach, where I will throw myself into the water and let the waves roll over me.

To think that in days gone by we used to argue about what was meant by freedom! Freedom is simple. This is freedom—to run along the street and feel cool fresh air brush past your cheeks, to hear human voices speaking in the rhythms and accents of the street—to pass by men and women and children who walk without having guards to shout at them and walls to block their way, to see the throng and commerce of humanity, and the buildings, the goods, and entertainments of mankind, to be able to run as far as I like for as long as I like in whatever direction I like—this is freedom.

I suppose I look funny as I run. But a man should look funny when he becomes free. It is not every day that a man becomes free. So it does not matter if my hair is long and wild and if my moustache is black and unkempt, and if my shirt sleeves are too short and my trousers too long and my sand-shoes dirty and torn.

It is six miles to the sea and I am going to run there and fling my body into the waves. This is my freedom run, my celebration of liberty. I will not stop until I feel the water flowing over me. This is the day of all my days. This is my day. Let the people stare.

My body is moving well. I must be careful when I cross the roads, though. It would be terrible to be knocked down by a car on this my freedom day. The cars move so quickly. I must concentrate as I cross the street. I hope my mother will be at the beach. She has waited for me for so long and yet when I was released she was not at home. Jack, my colleague, said he would find her wherever she was. What a good friend he is. He came over from Chambers straight away. I will never forget the warmth and the strength of his handshake. Oh it is good to have friends, to know people who love you and let you feel that they are proud of you.

He thought I was mad when I told him I was going to run to the sea. He asked me if I knew what day it was, for he was testing my sanity, and I said it did not matter. I'm quite all right, only a little excited at being released, and I have been dreaming for months about running to the sea. Then he tried to humour me, said he would drive me to the beach after taking me home, and I laughed and said:

'Now that I'm free, can't I even decide the first thing I want to do for myself?'

We packed my things in his car which was parked across the road and I was nearly run over because I was so unused to traffic. Then he said to me, 'How can you swim if you haven't got a costume?'

I am still laughing at that question. 'Costume,' I said, 'after five and a half months inside I won't worry much about a costume.' Imagine worrying about a costume! When I get to the beach I will run across the sand and throw myself, clothes and all, into the water. Those hundreds of miles that I have covered during exercise time are standing me in good stead now. I have never before run six miles. But then I have never before become free. Freedom is the finest, the most exhilarating fuel of all to propel a runner on his journey.

On and on I run, driving my pent-up feelings into the ground. With each step I take, hatred and fury drain out of me. I am flexing myself, breathing deeply of the world, surrounded by people but alone and unchallenged. This is the way I wanted it to be—a long lonely journey through the city to the freedom of the sea. Soon I will be ready to speak to people, to find out what has happened, to tell them how I am. But first I want to

278

revisit the world, to see the universe which I am re-entering, to feel its dimensions and movement.

I run past a sports stadium. It is empty: I am the only athlete here. I have already won my race and the running that I do now is the lap of triumph of a victor. Today is no day for me to be modest. For one hundred and sixty-eight days I have been crushed and humiliated. They have mocked me and punished me and jeered at my determination to hold out. But I have won. I refused to answer questions, yet I am free. They could not break me. My stand was justified, my judgment has been vindicated, I did the right thing, and I have won. I have won. I am free.

I cross a patch of lawn and feel green and gentle grass under my feet. I am approaching the sea front. On my left is a police station. You cannot touch me now, you policemen. I have survived your captivity, and now I am immune to your tyranny. What will happen in the future I do not know. For the present all I will do is celebrate my release. Later I will worry about the others and later I will decide on my own future. But now I am utterly happy, without thought or care and without the slightest sense of guilt or constraint.

Slowly I move past the giant multi-coloured luxury flats that line the sea-front boulevard. I am two-thirds of the way to the beach. Cool sea air tickles my sweating skin. My legs pound on the pavement with the regularity of a machine, my breathing is heavy, and I feel runnels of sweat coursing down my body. I wish some friends of mine would drive by and encourage me on my way. Jack said he would catch up with me, and also that he would get hold of a camera to take a picture of me.

Now the road turns uphill and away from the sea. Every step requires a conscious effort, and I am tempted to walk the rest of the way. I will run as far as the next lamp-post and then to the one after that. Even to enjoy my freedom, I must discipline myself and keep myself going by a series of short incentives. At last the road bends round again and I am once more running on flat ground parallel to the sea. My progress is slow, but I am confident that I will reach my objective.

What will I do with my watch when I plunge into the water? I hope I don't drown; that would be a joke. There is only one more mile to run. The mountain rises steeply on my left and far down below, on my right I can hear waves breaking against the rocks. I round a bend in the road, and there lying ahead of me is a break in the rocks, and a long white strip of beach, which will be my gateway to the sea. In a few minutes I reach the top of the steps which lead down to the sand. Halfway to the steps I see a man kneeling with his back towards me. He is taking a photograph of the beach and mountain. I am nearly upon him now. I will ask him to take a picture of me.

'Excuse me,' I say as I run round and round him (I must not stop) 'please don't think I'm mad. I want you to do me a very special favour. I've just been released from prison where I've been held as a Ninety-Day prisoner and I've run here straight from town, and I'd like someone to take my picture. My friends were supposed to have come but they don't seem to have turned up yet.' I keep running round him and he stares at me in the way all those people in town stared at me. I am panting and jerking my arms like engine pistons, and I realise that my appearance must seem as strange to him as my request.

'My name is Albie Sachs,' I continue. 'I know it must sound crazy to you, but it's all true what I've said and I'd be terribly grateful if you could do me the favour I ask, I'll pay for the whole spool. This is a wonderful day for me, and I want a record that I can keep of my having run here.' I seem to have convinced him.

'All right,' he says, 'but you'll have to run the other way because of the sun.' I run as he directs me and then he takes the picture. I ask him how I can get in touch with him because I'm off for a swim now, and he tells me his name and the name of the hotel where he is holidaying. I thank him effusively and breathlessly, and then continue my run towards the top of the steps. I hear a car hooting. It stops and out of it jumps my colleague, Hirshel.

'Hullo, you bugger,' he yells at me. He looks smart in a grey office suit. 'We didn't realise you'd get so far,' he continues. 'Hell, what a moustache you've got. Are you okay?'

280

'Here, take my watch,' I answer, 'it's terrific seeing you. I'm going in for a swim first and then I'll talk to you properly. You'd better come down there to see that I don't drown.'

I run until I come to the steps and then jog down towards the beach. My legs jolt against the cement steps, the rhythm of my running is broken, and my excitement and tiredness are so great that I feel an urge to fling my body down and let gravity pull me to the sand. I have reached the beach. The sand is soft and white, and I struggle to cross it. A girl is leaning against a rock and on a hard strip of sand near the water's edge two tanned men are playing with a beach ball. I run past them, urging myself on as though I were a tired racehorse. The surge of the waves echoes through my ears. My sand-shoes tread in the wet sand. Cold water laps around my ankles and splashes against my calves. I am running into the water. A wave comes towards me. I fall forward and the cool oozing sea sweeps over me and rolls around my weary body. My head is covered and I am carried towards the beach in a gentle surge. The water retreats and I lie sodden on the wet sand. I stand up, invigorated by the chill water, yet exhausted in limb and trunk after having stopped my running. I look across the beach towards the steps. Coming down towards me I see Himie and Dot and there's my mother and there's Michael and. . . . They all look so funny coming on to the beach in their smart city wear, especially my oollonguon with their dark sober suits. I walk towards them, heaving for breath, my arms and legs shaking, my body in a tremble. My hair lies long and wet on my head, my moustache droops down the sides of my mouth, my clothing clings clumsily to my body and water splashes inside my sand-shoes. I can barely force myself across the sand. The people who have come to greet me now wait in a group for me. I wave to them.

'I'm coming in a moment,' I yell. Then I turn round and face the sea again. Slowly I push myself towards the water. Soon I will say hello to everybody. But first I must throw myself into the waves again. I cross the firm sand at the water's edge, and splash into the sea. A wave comes towards me and I lean forward waiting for the cool, cleansing water to wash over me.

Postscript

RECENTLY I WENT AS DEFENCE COUNSEL TO SEE TWO young prisoners at present being held at the Cape Town remand jail. I came away from the consultation inspired by their spirit, yet nauseated by what I had learned of their experience as Ninety-Day prisoners, and with full realisation of how lucky I had been during my detention. My two clients were both held in solitary confinement before being charged with political offences which carry a minimum sentence of five years and a maximum sentence of death. Alan, British-born and twenty-four years old, has only one source of recrimination, and that is that he failed to withstand the treatment to which he was subjected. He was punched and kicked and his leg was twisted until his ankle broke, he told me, and then he made a statement. Stephanie, of an old South African family and twenty-three years old, was also beaten and had her hair pulled out and her face battered, she said. Then she too made a statement.

Police torture is nothing new in South Africa. What is new is its barbarity and its being applied to Whites. Alan is a University lecturer, the son of a doctor and a British subject. Stephanie is a physiotherapist, beautiful, girlish and vulnerable, the very image of White South African womanhood, whose protection is claimed to be at the heart of official policy. If such *respectable* people can be assaulted then no one is safe in the hands of the South African police. It was some measure of comfort for me to learn that 'the pompous words' (that was the phrase she used) which I had written on the wall of my cell in Wynberg, had given Stephanie courage at the time when she was subjected

282

to her greatest trial. She told me too of grimmer words scratched by someone who had followed me in the Maitland cell: *Four days, no eat, no sleep, no sit.* From revelations made in Courts throughout the country, the police seem to have devised one major weapon to break down prisoners. They keep the detainees standing on one spot for days on end, interrogating and jeering at them in relays. When the prisoners faint they are revived with cold water and made to stand again. The process continues until there is complete moral and physical collapse on the part of the prisoners. Little wonder that last month a young Indian detainee broke from his captors and flung himself to his death from a seventh floor window. Two other detainees hanged themselves, while at least five have suffered severe mental breakdowns. I was told that, on being released, a distinguished teacher who had preceded me in my Caledon Square cell and who had written the Latin slogans on the wall, had to receive psychiatric treatment. Apparently two experts from Pretoria had broken him down by stripping him naked, throwing cold water over him and interfering with his private parts. Zollie Malindi, my hidden companion in the Maitland cells, had an even worse time of it. He informed lawyers that he was flown to Pretoria where, amongst other indignities, he suffered electric-shock treatment. Other prisoners in Pretoria were shown the body of a suicide and told that they too would be killed. Ultimately Zollie was brought to trial and, after having spent more than a year in prison, was found not guilty and set free.

The manner in which the electric treatment is said to be given was referred to in Parliament by the lone Progressive Party member who quoted from the experience of one of the detainees:

I was told to undress except for my trousers. One African policeman was called and handcuffed me with my hands behind my back and a sack was put over my head. On my small fingers electric wires were connected to a current. I cried and fell down. I was knocked with fists and sticks. I then promised to talk. When I complained I was being killed, wires were once more connected. When I fell down a policeman stood on my head with his feet. My face was swollen and my jaws were stiff. I was unable to eat for a week.

Dorothy Adams—the third detainee of the days when I stayed at Maitland (it was she after all who whistled to me)—was tricked into making a statement and agreed to be a prosecution witness. When she went into the witness box, however, she said 'No, I can't do it,' and was herself arrested and charged. Eventually the case against her was withdrawn, so that it has turned out that the three of us who were at Maitland have all emerged free.

Of those who have been less fortunate nearly a thousand are doing hard labour on Robben Island, a prison settlement seven miles off shore from Cape Town. Leaders of the African people, Nelson Mandela, Walter Sisulu, Govan Mbeki and others, cultured, dignified men, are breaking stones as they serve out their life sentences. Robert Sobukwe is in indefinite exile on the island, although the sentence imposed on him by Court has long expired. More trials throughout the country are pending, most of the accused being young White liberals and socialists. In their ranks are journalists, lecturers and students, bright people who in other countries would be in the Government, or writing plays or speaking out against the Bomb, but who in South Africa face the death sentence. Men and women of all races and a great variety of political persuasions, labourers, peasants, lawyers, doctors, pregnant women, schoolchildren, wives, fathers and sons, are held, in wave after wave of arrests, under the Ninety-Day law. At least eight detainees, all of them African, including three women, have done spells of continuous solitary confinement for more than six months. The separate racial statistics which are kept even in relation to Ninety-Day detainees, show that at present my one hundred and sixty-eight days represents the longest period for which a White has been kept under Ninety-Day detention. It is not out of vanity that I hope this record is never broken. I have become something of a tourist attraction as visitors from various parts of the country and abroad from time to time drop into my chambers to have a look at me. I feel a bit of a fraud when I speak to them. There were many factors in my favour, in particular I was never subjected to physical torture, so that my story is a pale one compared to that of many other detainees. Captain Rossouw claims that he would have broken me down if I had not received books in terms of a Supreme Court Order (this was in fact reversed on appeal in a judgment handed down about a week after my release, in which the Appeal Court held that detainees were not entitled to reading and writing material). Perhaps he is right. I saw him in the street about a fortnight after my release. He was striding buoyantly towards the Supreme Court to hear sentence being passed on a group of young Coloured intellectuals. I nodded to him, whereupon he rushed up to me, grabbed my hand and told me how glad he was to see that I was prepared to greet him. I have since seen him at a distance from time to time. South Africa is a wonderful country for a policeman, if he likes exercising power, and the captain's buoyancy seems to increase with each new wave of detentions. Clearly he regards the growing prison population as a tribute to the prowess of the security branch. I would like to ask him if he still disapproves of physical torture and if so, why he did not stop the assaults upon Alan and Stephanie. Perhaps I will put these questions to him during cross-examination in Court one day. Perhaps he will answer them by deed as well as word by detaining me again. In the meantime, I have not left the country. I write and I write, just as once I sat and I sat. I must record my story as accurately and honestly as I can. Then should they take me in again I will know that there is something of me outside which will continue to exist whatever they do to me.